Routledge Revivals

Adventures in Philosophy

First published in 1925, *Adventures in Philosophy* presents a series of essays dealing with some of the chief problems of metaphysics and beginning with a defence of that somewhat unpopular pursuit. The first part of the book is mainly constructive in character, and not only attempts to put as clearly as possible the metaphysical views of the author but indicates their consequences from an ethical standpoint. The later chapters discuss two of the most important developments in philosophy associated with the names of Einstein and Bergson. Finally, the author considers how far religion, especially the Christian religion, is affected by the conclusions reached earlier in the book. This is an important historical reference for students and scholars of philosophy.

Adventures in Philosophy

J. C. Wordsworth

First published in 1925
by George Allen & Unwin Ltd.

This edition first published in 2024 by Routledge
4 Park Square, Milton Park, Abingdon, Oxon, OX14 4RN

and by Routledge
605 Third Avenue, New York, NY 10017

Routledge is an imprint of the Taylor & Francis Group, an informa business

© George Allen & Unwin Ltd, 1925

All rights reserved. No part of this book may be reprinted or reproduced or utilised in any form or by any electronic, mechanical, or other means, now known or hereafter invented, including photocopying and recording, or in any information storage or retrieval system, without permission in writing from the publishers.

Publisher's Note
The publisher has gone to great lengths to ensure the quality of this reprint but points out that some imperfections in the original copies may be apparent.

Disclaimer
The publisher has made every effort to trace copyright holders and welcomes correspondence from those they have been unable to contact.

A Library of Congress record exists under LCCN: 26012518

ISBN: 978-1-032-82376-8 (hbk)
ISBN: 978-1-003-50418-4 (ebk)
ISBN: 978-1-032-82378-2 (pbk)

Book DOI 10.4324/9781003504184

ADVENTURES IN PHILOSOPHY

BY

J. C. WORDSWORTH

LONDON: GEORGE ALLEN & UNWIN, LTD.
RUSKIN HOUSE   40 MUSEUM STREET, W.C.1

First published in 1925

Printed in Great Britain by
NEILL AND CO., LTD., EDINBURGH
All Rights Reserved

CONTENTS

CHAP.		PAGE
I.	INTRODUCTION	7
II.	THE POSSIBILITY OF KNOWLEDGE	24
III.	THE NATURE AND FORMS OF CONSCIOUSNESS	69
IV.	SUBSTANCE AND PERSONALITY	93
V.	THE UNITY OF THE WORLD	119
VI.	TIME AND SUCCESSION	140
VII.	RELATIVITY	163
VIII.	MECHANISM v. VITALISM	203
IX.	THE PHILOSOPHY OF BERGSON	215
X.	RELIGION	308

ADVENTURES IN PHILOSOPHY

CHAPTER I

INTRODUCTION

METAPHYSICS is nothing but common sense carried farther than is common, and perhaps that is the main reason of its unpopularity. Advanced mathematics and science, which are closely akin to metaphysics, do not trouble the man in the street; they even inspire him with a certain respect, for they use terms and speak of things of which he has no conception whatever. But the metaphysician talks of familiar things in an unfamiliar way; he takes in vain the names we have used from childhood, and shows either that they have no meaning, or that they ought to have a very different meaning from that which we have always attributed to them. Metaphysics might also be termed the self-criticism of common sense, and the man in the street, as Socrates found, does not enjoy the process of turning himself mentally inside out. It is the habit of most men to make a moral duty of any form of slackness to which they happen to be prone, and the criticism and correction of our ideas of the world demand such an effort that neglect of it has become the most popular of our virtues.

The reasons usually given for condemning metaphysics are that it deals with entities remote from real life, that instead of correcting our ideas it confuses them, and that it has no practical value. The first accusation seems inconsistent with what I have said, that the metaphysician talks of familiar things. Certainly he is always discussing the meaning of words in everyday use, such harmless, necessary monosyllables as " space," " time," " cause," " I," " self," " mind," and "thought." But the complaint is that in doing so he not only introduces such abominable words as no Christian ear can endure to hear, for instance, "synthetic unity of apperception" and "psycho-physical parallelism," but employs the monosyllables as names for certain creatures of his own brain. As to the second objection, those who seek to correct our ideas are said to correct them in so many different ways that we are worse off than before; they were simple enough at first, but every new philosophy makes them more complicated, especially as it contradicts all the others. In practical life metaphysics is not credited with any marketable value, for the general belief is that it has never invented anything but words and phrases.

There is one sufficient answer to all three charges, or to any others that can be made; metaphysics is implied in all our thought and therefore inevitable. This may seem inconsistent with the definition of it given in the first paragraph, but I was speaking there of that advanced metaphysics which is conscious of itself as such. But in a wider and more correct sense it is common to all men. The man who warns you against theories is saturated with theories himself, and when he talks of facts he means nothing but the theories he happens to accept. You cannot choose whether you will be a metaphysician, but only whether your metaphysics is to be elementary or advanced. Every child adopts a certain system of philosophy as soon as he learns to speak; he has some notion of "substance" and "cause" as soon as he uses a noun or a transitive verb. Grammar is closely akin to logic, and that again to metaphysics, which can no more be avoided than the use of speech and thought. Whatever subjects we study, that is to say, whatever regions of our thought we try to clear up, it comes more and more clearly to light, though we do not always recognize it for what it is. Anyone who has devoted himself for long to theology, mathematics, natural or political science, art, or literature, is continually coming near to the province of the avowed metaphysician; centripetal force often carries him beyond the border, though he may not be aware of the name of the territory on which he is trespassing and usually becomes lost.

But this is only the territory of the avowed, the more

advanced metaphysician. We all talk and think metaphysics of some kind all our lives, as we talk prose, though most of us are unconscious of the fact and might be less pleased to find it out than M. Jourdain was on discovering that he was a man of letters. But it is a fact, of course; the man in the street has a whole system of philosophy as he has a system of grammar, but may console himself with the reflection that both are inadequate. This is quite apart from any religious opinions he may have. His religion, it may be remarked, is on the same level of thought as the rest of his metaphysics, but helps to make the whole system work and prevents him from falling into the mental and moral confusion which would otherwise be inevitable. It imposes some kind of unity upon the haphazard notions he has formed of the world. It would be interesting to point out in detail how his Sunday ideas act as a check on his week-day superstitions. But all that is necessary here is to point out a few of those superstitions, enough to prove that he has a metaphysical creed in spite of his professed rejection of metaphysics.

The first article of his faith is the belief in personality. He regards himself as a being essentially distinct and separate from the rest of the world and remaining one and the same throughout his life. He would find it difficult to say what he meant by the word " I "; from his use of it one would infer that he meant something which " has " a certain body, " has " certain thoughts and feelings, and has many other properties more or less closely attached to him. The owner of this large and miscellaneous estate remains in obscurity. But the use of these expressions implies that the " self " is taken to be a simple entity distinct from its body, thoughts, feelings, and the rest. All these change, but the self remains the same. The " unmetaphysical " man in fact belongs to that eighteenth-century school of metaphysics which held that every human soul was an absolutely distinct entity, without parts in itself, though capable of entertaining many thoughts and sensations. He might protest that he meant nothing of the kind: if so, every other sentence that he speaks is meaningless. As for the essential distinctness and individuality of the selves, the problem how such beings can act upon one another, that is to say, how events in one can affect events in another, never troubles or even enters his head. In fact it would take some time to prove to him that it was a problem at all, for it is one of those things which men take for granted without noticing the difficulties which it involves. The still harder questions how they come to have duties towards one another, why selves are expected to be unselfish, is either ignored or met with a vague reference to religion, which, as I said, is usually called in to make good the defects of popular metaphysics.

The idea of distinct personality is one of those that dominate our lives. It cannot be regarded as unimportant that ninety-nine men out of a hundred are unable to give it any clear meaning, while their words logically imply a meaning of which they are unconscious. The preachers of Individualism have seldom carried out the elementary duty of explaining what an individual is, and why they give that name to a man and not to a nation, nor to the whole of mankind.

Another deeply rooted notion of the human mind is that the world is just a miscellaneous collection of separate elements which somehow happen to be there. On this theory, if it can be dignified with the name of a theory, it must be merely a lucky coincidence that any two things are in the least alike. Evolution may account for the likeness of the living species, but there are more fundamental things than these, the identity of which cannot be so explained. For instance, there seems no reason why the number of colours should be limited: it seems just as possible that each thing should be of a colour, or during its existence pass through a set of colours, completely different from those of the rest. The fact that millions of them are alike in this quality could only be regarded as a stroke of good fortune. If you have advanced so far in metaphysics as to believe that colours do not exist in the things but are produced by their action on the mind, it must appear equally strange that this action produces on all minds the same set of colours. This argument may be applied not only to the other qualities but to the quantitative properties of things. Most men have a vague belief in the atomistic theory, but do not ask themselves why the atoms, or electrons, or whatever the ultimate elements of matter may be called, are so much alike in size, and why we should not come across atoms as large as a cathedral. The very suggestion seems an absurdity, but the usual theory of the world gives us no reason why the atoms should not be of all sorts and sizes. Most men, again, are aware that the influence of gravitation is everywhere in the same proportion to the size of the bodies and the distance between them, but this too, if they ever think about it, must appear as a remarkable but fortunate coincidence. The uniformity of the world is as little noticed as other universal things; it is the differences that strike our attention, as it is the unusual events that appear most conspicuously in the newspapers. The chaotic view of the universe prevails, but in so far as the "unmetaphysical" man is conscious of the uniformity everywhere apparent I suppose that he explains it by the religious doctrine of the Creation. Clerk Maxwell compared the atoms to "manufactured articles," and though the atom may now be resolved into still smaller elements the comparison has only to be carried one step farther; whatever the ultimate constituents of the world may be they must be very much alike, as though they had all come out of the same factory. If they were self-existent beings this would be unintelligible. It is strange that the theologians have generally neglected the argument from uniformity for the more vulnerable argument from design. But no more need be said upon this point to show that the "unmetaphysical" man has a metaphysical theory of the universe, a theory so absurd that he has to invoke the aid of Providence in order to correct it.

To turn to another dogma of popular metaphysics, it is generally supposed that the objects of sight and touch, and perhaps of the other senses, are "outside the mind." The colour just seen and the warmth and hardness just felt continue to exist when no one is conscious of them, and the colour seen by one man exists in the same place as that seen by another man who is looking in the same direction. About the size of the object perceived there is a confusion of thought which with most men passes unnoticed. The size of a house as seen from a great distance is smaller than that of a pebble as it looks when held just in front of the eyes; one cannot believe, then, that the size actually seen belongs to the distant house and exists over there. Yet it is not believed to exist in the mind, for evidently it would be absurd to say that the size exists here and the colour over there, a hundred yards away. But this rudimentary metaphysics is not consistent even in assigning a position to the colour seen; " real " colours are supposed to exist in the object, while those seen by a man distant from the object, or suffering from the jaundice or other abnormal conditions, appear to have no such fixed abode but are vaguely attributed to the mind. To summarize the popular *Empfindungstheorie*, pink rats exist in the mind, grey rats outside it. At the same time it is true that many men who would not call themselves metaphysicians have glimpses of a more consistent theory, according to which the objects of sight are images or representations of the " real things," the actual house or tree standing over there. How far these latter resemble the images they impress upon our eyes is left in doubt, but generally they are thought to possess the same colours and to have a definite size which is almost the same as that of the image seen when we are standing nearest. The belief that they have any colours, however, is abandoned by those who have heard the scientific account of light.

The most evidently metaphysical of all elementary ideas is the idea of time; in considering this subject even the man who prides himself on his adherence to hard facts begins to have a dim suspicion that after all it is impossible to escape from metaphysics. Popular philosophy divides time into past, present, and future, and holds that neither past nor future exists. Yet they are supposed to be non-existent in different ways, for otherwise they could not be distinguished, and evidently that is a very obscure supposition. The precise meaning of the present is hard to fix; some would define it as a moment of time, *i.e.*, a time of no length—*i.e.*, no time at all,—others use the word for a period covered by a certain thought or act, or series of acts, or by a whole lifetime, or a stage of civilization. It is supposed that we observe a certain order of succession in time, though we cannot see either past or future if neither exists, and without such perception it may well be asked how we can know which events are past and which are yet to come. Besides, there seems to be nothing in the laws of nature to prevent us from believing that the whole course of the world moves in the opposite direction to that which we suppose it to follow. What we take for cause might equally well be taken for effect, and *vice versâ*. To come to another point, most men hold that there is only one time series, *i.e.*, that each event in everything throughout the world is simultaneous with some event in every other. Anything that has happened in the farthest star we can see must have come before or after or at the same moment as any incident in the history of the earth we like to choose. We take this to be self-evident, and do not even understand what alternative there could be. But if many separate beings A B C . . . pass through a series of states, it by no means follows that every state of A must stand in a temporal relation to every state of the others. An event in A can only be simultaneous with an event in B if they are both states of one wider reality which includes both A and B; if these were separate and self-existent entities each would be a separate world and have a time of its own.

This is perhaps carrying the subject rather too far for an introductory chapter, where a more detailed explanation is impossible. But we have all nowadays read something about relativity, and Einstein's criticism of the idea of "simultaneous" events must have forced many men to realize for the first time how metaphysical that idea is. Now that they have been "awakened out of their dogmatic slumbers" by Einstein's examination of this subject they may perhaps be led to consider other metaphysical notions which, though unnoticed, pervade all their thought. We are sometimes told, by the way, that Einstein's theory is not metaphysical but helps us to rid ourselves of metaphysics. That is precisely what Berkeley, Hume, and others have said of their own philosophical systems. If it is true of relativity it is true of every other philosophy propounded by man. But one must not be frightened by the unpopularity of a name. If the relativist is not a metaphysician, then M. Jourdain's father was not a tailor.

I have mentioned a few articles in the creed of the man in the street, and they are enough to prove my point. In one sense I am quite willing to believe anyone who declares himself no metaphysician. The man who spends all his days on the links without reducing his handicap below eighteen is sometimes heard to admit, in the truth-inspiring atmosphere of the nineteenth hole, that he is no golfer. He does not mean that evil is not real but intends the word " golfer " to be taken *sensu eminenti*, as the schoolmen would have said. It is only in this sense that any man can pretend to be no metaphysician. But those who are only at the elementary stage of metaphysics might argue that however bad their philosophy may be, it is good enough for practical life ; it works, as the Pragmatist would say, and that is enough for them. This would only be a satisfactory argument if practical life were the only form of life, and if it were perfect. But false or confused thought would be an evil, even if it could produce good results, and in any case the results of that elementary metaphysics which governs the average mind have been very far from ideal. It is obvious that if some of the fundamental notions of that mind are wrong or inadequate, as some of them certainly are, the effect on human action can only be disastrous. Error or ignorance in particular sciences does not distort our moral philosophy, but a mistaken idea of personality must do so. It is as dangerous as the exaggerated idea of nationality.

The study of metaphysics may indeed be justified as an end in itself, apart from its effect on our ethical ideas. The desire to learn the fundamental facts of the universe is itself a virtue, like the desire to have news of one's own family. It is true that some members of the *bella d'erbe famiglia e d'animali* are very distant connections ; still more so are some of the branches of that universal family which includes inanimate as well as animate beings. But the whole world is more or less akin, and the chief merit of the search for truth consists in this impulse to know about the whole of which we are insignificant parts, not in any desire to form in our minds a correct model of an alien world. We must admit that the impulse to know is not attended by the power to help, for when we have discovered the essential facts of reality we cannot change them. In that metaphysics is unlike some of the sciences, which enable us to change the objects with which they deal. Yet even if we could not help our kindred it would be unnatural not to wish for news of them, and no one could condemn the wish as idle curiosity. There are some who profess themselves content with having no religion or metaphysical system, and usually inflict verses from the *Rubáiyát* upon anyone who is misguided or unfortunate enough to hear or read them. It is strange that any man should expect applause for saying in effect that he does not care to know whether the world as a whole is a good thing or a bad. One may be convinced that knowledge of the truth is impossible and try to resign oneself to this ; it is an ill-grounded conviction, for no one could prove the impossibility, but it is reasonable enough compared with indifference. However, both the self-complacent and the resigned sceptic have all the time a complete metaphysical system which they express in every sentence they speak and on which they act every day of their lives. They suppose themselves to know nothing about the real nature of the world and act as though they knew everything. In this they are as inconsistent as the pessimists who doubt whether the continuance of life is a good thing but take the preservation of it to be a duty. Every man's actions are prompted by a philosophy, either one which he has worked out for himself or one which he has inherited and obeys mechanically, without any clear consciousness of its existence.

Metaphysical knowledge is an end in itself, but it can also be justified on what the narrow-minded call " practical " grounds. Our actions are determined by our ideas, especially by those general ideas which form the basis of human language and permeate all our thoughts, those which are so general, in fact, that we rarely single them out and become aware of their presence and of their influence upon our conduct. The correction and improvement of these is supremely practical. I have already mentioned the harm that has been done by a false idea of personality. If you believe that every man is a separate centre of existence and action, not a part of something greater which lives and acts in him and all others, you cannot fairly expect him to extend his interests beyond himself and work for the good of a world altogether alien from his own being. You cannot demand of an atom that it shall think and act as God. On the other hand, it is natural that men should so think and act if they are not essentially distinct entities, if " the human mind is a part of the infinite intellect of God."

It appears still more natural when we rid ourselves of the notion that the world is a haphazard collection of things that happen to be there, and recognize not only its unity but uniformity. That recognition brings us into closer sympathy with the rest of Nature.

My next argument is perhaps more open to dispute, but seems to me not only valid but important. It is usually supposed that the objects each man sees directly are " outside the mind," visible to all, and that he creates nothing by seeing them. All that he contributes to sensation is the bare consciousness; the colours, shapes, and sizes would exist just as much if they were not present to his sight. But if the objects of his sensations are not the external things themselves, the " real " trees or houses, but images of these, images which could not exist without him, then every new mind that enters the world creates a new miniature of it. And though the external things must have some qualities, not merely sizes and shapes, it is not probable that their qualities are the same as those we have in sensation—for instance, colour; these, for all we know, only come into being wherever a living body is formed. The eye, then, is an artist that not only reproduces in miniature the shapes of the outer world, but creates for that world colours and other qualities of which it is devoid. However worthless a man's thoughts may be, his sensations, the other half of his life, are of infinite value, for all the finest things in heaven and earth gain in them a new existence. Imagine that the most contemptible man who ever lived had been the only man who ever lived, and you can realize that his life would have been of the highest importance to the world, which his sensations created anew. But the fact that there have been countless millions of other men cannot lessen the value of that one, for the worth of a thing is not reduced because it is common. The knowledge how much each man adds to the world in this way is our best reason for attaching so much importance to all human lives indiscriminately, without regard to their other qualities.

To come to the fourth point I mentioned in describing the metaphysics of the average mind, most men assume that there is a succession of events in time and that neither past nor future exists. Now and then some lover of paradox may hint

INTRODUCTION

at the possibility of taking events the other way round, but this is not put forward as a serious suggestion. Yet it is true, in so far as it implies that there is no succession in time. The proof of that must be left till a later chapter, but it is worth while to point out here how inconsistent men are in the other assumption, in believing that the past does not exist except through its consequences in the present. Any man who repents of a crime—if one may use such old-fashioned language nowadays—regards it as a disgrace to himself even though it is past and according to the popular theory of time should therefore be regarded as wiped out of existence. He is still troubled by it, apart from its consequences now, and even if it has no consequences now, or has proved in the end really beneficial to the person against whom it was committed. One may repent even of an intention which could not be carried out. You may say that what troubles him is the knowledge of the evil in his character revealed by that intention, and the consequent suspicion that the evil is still there. But this seems to me too far-fetched. Men have surrendered themselves for crimes of which no consequences now remain, and that although the very will to surrender themselves proves their reformation. They do not suspect that the taint is still in them, but think solely of the act committed years before. The slightest self-examination will convince any man that he is affected with pleasure or pain by his past actions, quite regardless of the present. Yet he should not be so, if the past had been really annihilated.

Besides, even though men say that the past does not exist it is evident from the distinction they make between it and the future that they think of it as still existing in a sense. They picture it as time filled up, while the future appears as a void. Several expressions in common use imply this; so does the word "past" itself, for what we have passed is still there behind us. But to confine ourselves to the moral effects of that elementary metaphysics which governs the average mind, it is clear that only a strange inconsistency saves men from the conclusion that the past does not really matter. Morally they view events *sub specie æternitatis*, intellectually they regard them as being continually wiped out.

But it is in the idea of personality that the greatest difference appears between their moral and the intellectual outlook. For elementary metaphysics the belief in an absolutely separate self is fundamental, whereas in ethics it is regarded as our first duty to forget it. If every man were such a self the demand that he should be unselfish would be unnatural and absurd. Nor can one avoid the difficulty by saying that unselfish action is really the best for the self, for though that may be so that is not the ground of the obligation. Every man is expected to do his best for others without considering that such action will save his own soul or give him an easy conscience. But though the self is usually considered to be the fundamental, the only unit in the conscious world, as the atom or electron is in the material, phrases are often used which contradict that opinion. Even the use of such words as " nation," " humanity," or " Man," and " world " in the singular would be meaningless if such words did not signify a unit. In their more exalted moods men altogether disregard the self, the individual ; or rather it is the nation or the whole of humanity that becomes for them the individual. Such sayings as " Who dies if England live " and " Nous sommes un moment de la France éternelle " blow away our everyday metaphysics like smoke. In religion, too, especially in its more emotional or mystical forms, the ordinary idea of personality dwindles almost to nothing. It is this inconsistency between our Sunday and week-day thoughts that leads, with others like it, to the farther stages of metaphysics. That is to say, it leads some of us, while others are content to leave as they are those untidy collections of miscellaneous and ill-matched ideas which usually pass for minds.

The objection that metaphysicians have always disagreed, that they have no universally accepted conclusions to show, like those of the scientists, has probably more weight with men than any other. Yet there is not, after all, such a variety of opinions in philosophy as is supposed. Throughout its history there have been two great schools of thought opposed to one another, though each has passed under several names. The one insists on the unity of the world, the other on its multiplicity ; the one points to the general and the universal, the other to the particular and the individual. The first is represented by Parmenides, Plato, the Realists, and Spinoza,

INTRODUCTION

the second by the Atomists, Aristotle, the Nominalists, and Leibnitz. Later examples of both might be given, but in none is the distinction so clearly marked. This seems to me the fundamental difference in philosophy; the controversies on the method and possibility of gaining metaphysical knowledge are less important. The sceptical and critical philosophers have to assume so much at start that their negative conclusions must always appear inconsistent; besides, they affect not only the more advanced metaphysics but all knowledge whatsoever, even the beliefs which the average mind regards as safe. No one could prove from Hume's philosophy or from Kant's that any external world existed at all, or any other mind than his own. But to return to the fundamental difference in metaphysics, it is not a fatal objection, for it proves no more than this, that there are two sides to reality, and that each school of thought tends to emphasize one and forget the other. Each is right in what it affirms and wrong in so far as it denies. The first school comes nearer to giving us the whole truth, for most of its members, while insisting on the oneness of the world, have also admitted its multiplicity, whereas the other appears to accept the individualistic notions of the man in the street and does not concede any real unity.

Few men are kept back from voting or from a political career by the consideration that there are two or three parties in the State. The conflict between the opposed factions has often been so bitter as to make unpopular the name of "politician," but I suppose that no one but the Anarchist would dispute the necessity of politics. It is generally recognised now that both parties, the conservatives and the reformers, are necessary elements in the State; every voter chooses between them according to his own character, and in choosing he is wiser than those who stand aloof and take no interest in the government of their country. He is a better citizen than the man who thinks his duty to the State is ended when he has paid his taxes. There is a good deal to be said for the sweeping methods of the Athenians, who literally roped in their "moderate and impartial men" whenever they held a political assembly. The suggestion that metaphysics, *i.e.* the study of that subject, should also be made compulsory is perhaps Utopian. But certainly the philosopher who attaches himself to one of the two schools of thought is wiser than the opponent of philosophy. He at least holds part of the truth, whereas the other does not even hold a respectable error.

If you deny any truth to metaphysics on the ground that metaphysicians have disagreed, you must also deny that there is any beauty in architecture, music, or poetry because different styles of these have been thought beautiful by some and worthless or inferior by others. The Greeks would have been horrified by the sight of a Gothic cathedral, and the mediæval architect would not have admired the Parthenon. The Classical school of poetry has always looked down upon the Romantic, and the Romantic has been equally contemptuous of the Classical. But for all that it is now generally admitted in both cases that each side was right in its admiration and was wrong, or would have been wrong, in slighting the other. In the same way we should accept all the great philosophies as giving us a part of the truth. Perhaps it may be thought that this is a dangerous analogy for metaphysics, which many consider to have only a subjective value, like that which they attribute to poetry. They admire it only for the thoughts it contains, without troubling their heads about its truth, just as they admire a poem for the fine images it calls up in their minds. But it is not the business of metaphysics to give us pretty pictures of an imaginary world. It proceeds by argument and avoids any appeal to the emotions. Besides, as metaphysics is inherent in all our thoughts it would be just as reasonable to say that all these had only a poetical and subjective value, and had nothing corresponding to them in reality. On the contrary, it is doubtful whether one is right in saying " poetical *and* subjective," for most of us believe poetry to be an expression of reality. It is expected to be true to life and, if it creates, to make its creations conform to the laws of the actual world, as far as these are known by the average man, or at least to consistent laws of their own, so that their existence seems possible. Not everyone would admit this, but certainly the poetry which is remotest from the actual world has the least effect on the mass of mankind.

If the avowed metaphysicians contradict one another it is only because the metaphysics of most men contradicts itself. It contains in an undeveloped state all the doctrines held by the opposed schools of thought, and the history of philosophy is nothing but the disentangling of our confused and inconsistent ideas. For instance, every man speaks of " the world " or " the universe " in the singular, from which we might infer that he accepts the doctrine of Spinoza. Anyone who protests that he means nothing of the kind may well be asked what he does mean by his use of the singular substantive, if he does not believe the world to be a single substance. Again, we say that many things have the same quality, but not many of us suspect that in saying so we become disciples of Plato and the scholastic Realists. For this same quality existing in many things is just the " Idea " of Plato and the " Universal " of the Realistic school. There is no difference between the unconscious and the conscious metaphysician, except that the latter happens to think what he means. In clearing up those notions of the world with which all men begin he becomes aware of their inconsistencies, and that is a necessary step towards bringing them into harmony. Even if he can go no farther he is in a better state than the man who bears about with him a mass of self-contradictory ideas and prides himself on his common sense.

It is often said that metaphysics makes no progress, but it is seldom said by those who have troubled to make any serious study of the subject. The great philosophers have not simply repeated one another or cancelled one another out; even where they have not revealed new facts they have discovered new problems, and that too is progress, or at least necessary for progress. The form in which they have presented their new ideas may not be accepted by all men, but we can be sure that the ideas in some form will be found in the ultimate and complete system of philosophy, whenever we reach it. This is equally true of the most important discoveries of science. The theory of evolution may not be accepted in its entirety as it was presented by Darwin, but I suppose very few nowadays would deny that there is any truth in it, and that it marked a step forward in our knowledge of the world. The Newtonian doctrine of gravitation is being transformed at the present time, but who would say that it was altogether false? The most important revelations do not spring in a moment from the head of one man, but are brought to light by the labours of many men carried on for several years or generations. It is no objection to metaphysics that it needs thousand of years for the discovery of the complete truth; we have time enough. Until then we may not be able to see any part of the truth in the form in which it will be finally presented, for the ultimate solution of every single problem may require a knowledge of the whole. But we may at least discern the "shadowy prefaces of their truth." This defence of metaphysics is confirmed by the fact that throughout its history we continually find the same doctrines reappearing in new shapes, an evident indication that they are not mere fancies but are each inspired by some reality.

A century ago ninety-nine men out of every hundred in Europe had a clear and coherent picture of the world, for they accepted the Christian religion in its traditional form. Intellectually, then, they were above the average man to-day, whose philosophy is chaotic and unconscious of itself. However inadequate a metaphysical system may be, it is better than the absence of any system, for that means the absence of any life in our knowledge. Most of us still have those elementary metaphysical notions I mentioned before, but the religious doctrines which in some measure made up for their deficiencies are losing their hold on the man in the street, and nothing else has yet succeeded to their authority over his mind. He is left with a vague idea that the world began in a mist and will end in a frost, and without any basis for his moral code but the instincts inherited from God-fearing ancestors, or the fear of the policeman. He has learned a number of hard scientific facts, but these either give him no general view of the world, or one that is hopelessly distorted and does not in any way correct his elementary metaphysics. Nor has he gained much from literature, for a great part of literature is intimately connected with religion, or at least with views of life quite alien from his individualistic creed. What can he be expected to make of the *Adonais*, or of the *Lines composed a few miles above Tintern Abbey*? Like Hassan, though he may admire poetry, he suspects that all poets are liars.

The decline of the traditional religion should bring about a greater interest in metaphysics, which, like religion, presents or seeks to present a clear and coherent picture of the world.

Not that it could ever wholly take the place of religion in Europe, for that is based on historical facts, on the personality of Christ, and on an institution, the Church. But it will provide the emotional elements in life, religion, morality, and art, with an intellectual basis. Some modern thinkers—for instance, Lange, the author of the *History of Materialism*—have suggested that no such intellectual basis is needed, that we can live on fine imaginations unsupported by any belief about reality, or even contradicted by our beliefs. But the union of a prosaic husband and a wife who possesses the artistic temperament is seldom a success, and if the ideal element in the mind is continually faced with a materialistic or agnostic theory one or the other is bound to give way. Lange might have been reminded of that passage in the *Phædrus* where Plato describes the two horses that draw the chariot of the soul. High ideals must be dragged down by low ideas, and the intellect in turn must be puzzled to account for the existence of its more exalted companion in such a world as its philosophy describes.

Even if it could reveal no positive truth metaphysics would have several great merits. It unloosens our fixed ideas when they are wrong or inadequate, compels us to examine our meanings, makes us critical of journalism and political rhetoric, and gives us a better sense of proportion. Perhaps the last is not in all respects an advantage; the man who acts even in small matters as though the fate of the universe depended on his efforts is often unpopular but successful. And yet it is well that the mind should have its Sundays, and look at things *sub specie æternitatis*, in order that we may not exaggerate the importance of our own achievements or failures. All this, however, is subsidiary to the main purpose of metaphysics, which is, like life, an end in itself. It has all the attractions of a voyage of exploration. It is unfortunately true that the explorer in one way separates himself from the majority of mankind as much as though he were wandering among those stars whose distance from the earth is measured by light-years. But at the same time he comes closer to the heart of things and discovers how artificial is the barrier which a popular superstition has set between each man and the rest of the world.

CHAPTER II

THE POSSIBILITY OF KNOWLEDGE

IF the "unmetaphysical" man were asked what reasons he had for believing in the existence of things outside and independent of his own mind, he might reply, if he troubled to reply at all, that he had five, of which the most important were the senses of sight and touch. He would maintain at first that he saw directly the things before him, the tree ten yards away from him or the hill two or three miles distant, and that these things continued to exist just as he saw them, with the same colours and other qualities, when he was no longer looking in their direction. It was this "naïve realism" which was destroyed by Berkeley's criticism in the *Three Dialogues between Hylas and Philonous*, perhaps as good an introduction to the study of metaphysics as any other. The gist of his argument is that all the qualities, shapes, and sizes we attribute to a material thing, such as the tree or the hill, only exist in our sensations : that the green and brown, for instance, which existed when we looked in a certain direction— at the tree, as we should say—are no longer anywhere when no one is looking that way. He concludes that since the qualities do not exist outside our minds, there can be no "external" or "material" things, for a thing stripped of all its qualities is a nonentity. This argument will perhaps be more easily understood if one remembers what a colourless thing modern science has made of the material world, leaving it nothing but a series of mathematical problems instantaneously solved by beings without a quality they can call their own.

It will be readily admitted that some at least of the things men see exist "in the mind" only and have no reality or permanence apart from the sensations in which they appear. We call these hallucinations, but the name does not solve the problem, for men see these in just the same way as they see the things which are supposed to exist outside the mind. One cannot, then, appeal to the mere fact of seeing any object as a proof that it has any existence apart from our sensations.

Besides, we have to be very careful in saying what we actually do see. When you are standing at some distance from a house you say that you " see " a building thirty feet high, with four sides. But what you actually see is a patch of colour smaller than the patch of colour which appears when you hold up your hand in front of your eyes. The first patch increases in size as you approach the house, and yet you do not suppose that there is any alteration in the size of the building. It is obvious, then, that what you actually see is not the building itself. You cannot escape from the difficulty by suggesting that you see part of the house at first and then see more and more of it as you approach. You may see every part of it, every window, every brick from the beginning; you see the whole at once, but the whole on a small and then on a larger and larger scale. But since the house itself does not exist on a number of different scales it must be something else that you see, something like a series of photographs of the same object. What you really see, then, does not exist after the sensation is over; you do not believe that all those patches of colour you saw as you walked towards the house, different in size and in clearness too, continued to exist after you left the point at which you saw each.

The immediate object of sight, then, is not the house itself but a continually changing picture which you will suppose to be produced in your mind by the unchanging house. The existence of the latter is only inferred, not directly perceived. This becomes still clearer when you consider the differences in quality you have before you at different times when, as you believe, you are seeing the same thing. A tree looks green when you are near it, black when you are far off; the sun looks white at one time but red or of a golden or copper colour at another. It may have all these appearances at once, but each of them to a different set of people. Again, what is red to a man in a normal state is yellow to a man with the jaundice or black to another who is colour-blind. In these cases which is the " real " colour of the thing? What reason can you give for preferring this rather than that? They all look as though they existed outside the mind, in the tree or the sun itself. Even the man suffering from the jaundice sees the yellow in just the same way as another man sees the red, and if he did not accept the opinion of the majority would suppose it to exist outside his sensations. But in these matters we cannot decide the question by the vote of the majority. On another planet jaundice might be the natural condition of the inhabitants, and they would with equal right insist that theirs was the normal state, and that they saw the real colour of things. Since we have to admit that some at least of the colours seen do not exist outside the mind, it is clear that the mere fact of our seeing a colour does not prove it to belong to a thing outside us, independent of our sensations. You admit that the colours seen when your eyes have been dazzled by the sun only exist as long as you see them; might not that be true of all the colours you see?

Again, the same water may be warm to a man with a cold hand, cold to another who has just been holding his hand in front of the fire. Yet obviously it cannot possess both temperatures. We usually judge the temperature by the feeling it gives to a hand in the normal state, but if the human blood were warmer than it is we should attribute quite a different quality to the water. The fish probably do, and if they had voices might argue that the cold we felt was not really there at all. Here too we must conclude that even if the water has a temperature of its own, the temperature attributed to it by men and other living beings exist merely in the feelings, and not in the thing said to be felt.

Some of those who maintain that we see directly the " real " thing, the distant house, for example, hold that it possesses all the shapes, sizes, and colours we see when we look at it from various directions and distances. But they do not mean that all these exist in the space we suppose the house to occupy. Really they are extending the meaning of the word " house " to include all the waves of light proceeding from that space, and the impressions they make upon the retina of any observer. If they like to define the " real " house so we need not object. The direct object of sight is then " a part of the house," but in a different sense from that in which we apply the term to a brick or window. This is the theory to which most of those who believe in a direct perception of the "real" thing are logically reduced, for they do not suppose that the small, blurred object of sensation is a part of the house, if by house is meant the body occupying a certain extent of space a hundred yards away. But in speaking thus they are departing from the view generally attributed to common sense, for by the "real" house common sense certainly means that distant body. Nor are they helping to prove that any object exists outside us unperceived. From the part actually perceived, the image in the brain, one cannot conclude anything about the existence of any other.[1]

It has been held that in sight we have a feeling of "outness" or distance, which assures us of the existence of things outside the mind. Unfortunately for this argument we have just the same feeling about the blackness of a wood far off, a blackness which we no longer believe to be there when we come nearer; then we suppose ourselves to see there another colour, green. But as both colours cannot exist there we must be wrong in one case at least, so that the sense of outness is no proof. We have it in all the other cases previously mentioned, where we admit that men see colours which certainly do not exist in that particular place; we have it in dreams, which are generally admitted to exist only in the mind. If everything which men saw and felt as outside them were really there the number of fauna on the earth would be considerably larger than is usually believed. Besides, we often mistake distances, which would be impossible if we perceived distance directly. The feeling exists here, where we are, and not all along the space from us to the object, so that in sight we do not come into actual contact, so to speak, with the distance; it can only be inferred.

Even if we assumed the existence of a material world outside us one would naturally suppose that our senses do not present this world to us directly, but only give us representations of it, produced *viâ* light-waves, sound-waves, and the

---

[1] This argument is valid against such a doctrine of perception as that outlined by Professor Varisco in *I massimi problemi*, ch. i., but not against that of Professor Alexander in his Gifford Lectures. I have dealt with the latter theory in an appendix to this chapter.

nerves. It might be suggested that these only produce in the brain an instrument for the direct perception of the external object. But as this instrument must correspond to every detail supposed to be directly seen, the most obvious conclusion is that it is this instrument itself that we see. That idea explains much better the variations in size and colour already mentioned, when we look at the same thing from different distances. There is no more evidence, then, that colour exists in a tree, or hardness in a stone, than that sound exists in a bell. The colour is produced in the mind by light-waves of various lengths as the sound is produced by vibrations in the air. The qualities we see, feel, or hear at one moment cease to exist when others take their place in the brain.

The realists who suppose that the brain is only an instrument for the direct perception of external things must admit that it has forms and qualities of its own. Is every man, then, blind to those of his own brain, which one would think the most obvious to sense, and yet capable of perceiving distant things? If the object of sight is the external thing, then the brain must be just what appears to the anatomist. But one would expect its owner to have a much clearer and more direct perception of it than any other man. Yet we are asked to believe that for him it is only the invisible means by which he sees other things, including the brains of other men. It is generally admitted that, as I said, there are forms and events in his brain corresponding to every detail seen of the object before him, but of these he is supposed to be ignorant, though another man might conceivably see them. His knowledge begins anywhere rather than at home. The theory of the realists is thus reduced to an evident absurdity.

But it is too early yet to talk of light-waves, of nerves, or even of the " brain " of any man, if by that is meant the brain as it appears to others. All that any man has before him in sensation is a number of colours variously shaped, of sounds, feelings, etc. And the question is how he comes to believe in the existence of something beyond these, and what justification he can give himself for this belief. Why should he not believe that his own sensations are the only realities? Even if he supposes that there is some object outside of, and distinct from, the mind, and perceived by it directly, might

THE POSSIBILITY OF KNOWLEDGE 29

not this object be always one and the same, though continually changing the quality and shape of its parts, like a kaleidoscope? In sight each man has always before him the same extent with a filling of various colours and forms; it might seem, therefore, that he had no ground for belief in the existence of anything outside that extent. It might seem so even if the visual area became larger and smaller; what is the reason for believing in anything outside that area at any particular time? As for the objects of the other senses, might they not begin and cease to exist with the sensations themselves? Even supposing that they are permanent, need there be more than one object for each of the five senses, or one for all, a thing essentially the same though often changing its qualities?

The theory that we see many " real things " outside the mind gives us no proof that these things continue to exist when no longer seen, for the reason why they cease to be seen might be that they no longer exist. We have no conception what their existence can be like apart from consciousness, and no ground for believing that consciousness is something that can be switched on them and off again. It might be necessary for their existence; at least we have no proof yet that it is not so. Each man, therefore, in proving the existence of the outer world must prove it from the existence of those parts of which he is immediately aware, without assuming at once that those exist any longer than he is aware of them. This is equally true whether these immediate objects of sense are in the brain or in the external thing. It must be noted that he can at first rely only on his own sensations, for he has not yet proved the existence of other minds; that must come later.

If his sensations were altogether chaotic, or if they formed a regular and self-consistent whole he would have no reason for believing in the existence of anything beyond them. In the first case they would need no explanation, and in the second they would explain themselves. From a mere jumble of colours and shapes succeeding one another at random one could not infer the existence of anything else; and if the same combinations of colours and shapes came up continually in a regular order, like a number of patterns turned over and over again, each pattern having a certain degree of resemblance in all its parts to the one before it, it might be supposed that each called its successor into being; there would be just that "invariable sequence of phenomena" which is all that science offers us, and there would be no necessity to go farther. But the sensations of each man are in fact neither a chaos nor a cosmos. They resemble stray parts of a jig-saw puzzle, from which we infer the existence of other parts completing the picture. When I look at certain objects, turn away, and then look in the same direction again, I have before me, first, a certain assemblage of coloured shapes, then a completely different set, and then the original set once more. If I assumed that my sensations were the only realities I should be unable to account for the exact resemblance of the third sensation to the first. It could not be a mere coincidence, for the number of possible sensations is unlimited, and there are too many such recurrences to be explained in this way. Yet the repetition of the same shapes and colours cannot be caused by the first sensation, for that ceased to exist when the second sensation, completely different from it, came into being. There is no regular order of shapes and colours appearing to the sight, but every now and then, at irregular intervals, precisely the same design as before comes up. We must suppose that our sensations are called up by some comparatively permanent cause, for if they simply came into existence from the void there would be no reason why the same ones should recur. But we cannot find the cause in the sensations themselves, since one of them often has no relation or proportion to its predecessor, and the same set of shapes and colours when repeated may be preceded and followed by sets quite different from those which preceded and followed it before. We are therefore obliged to place the cause outside our sensations, and so to assume the existence of something else besides these.

That a number of different colours and shapes all reappear together at the same time and in the same position relatively to one another is the fact which gives its main strength to this argument, for it would be unintelligible on the assumption that they passed out of existence when the first sensation came to an end. They might recur separately in such a case, but that they should all come into existence again together cannot be explained as merely a coincidence. They must have continued to exist together all the time between the two sensations, or else they must be produced by one and the same cause which has continued to exist. We conclude this for just the same reason as we should conclude that a picture exactly similar to one we had seen before was the same picture—*i.e.*, that it had had a continuous existence between then and now—or that it had been derived by a continuous process from the other, the shapes and colours passing from one canvas to another *viâ* the painter's mind, or else that they were both copies of one original. We must suppose that there was some kind of continuity between the picture we see now and the picture we saw then. Applying this to the case of sensations, when the same set of colours and sensations recurs we naturally infer that there must be some continuity between its present and its former occurrence, and since this is not to be found in the chain of sensations themselves it must be found outside them.

It might perhaps be objected that past sensations may cause the occurrence of others like them, in spite of the fact that they are past. For of any two successive events A and B the first is said to be the cause of the second, in spite of the fact that when B occurs A no longer exists. Might not an event A^1, then, call into existence a similar event A^2, although many others intervene between the two ? Might not action from a distance be possible in time as well as in space ? And might not this account for the self-consistency of a man's experience, without the assumption of an outer world ? If his sensations always recurred in the same order, at the same interval of time, that assumption, it is true, might not be needed ; though I doubt whether the idea of action at a distance in time is tenable. But in fact they do not so recur. We have, then, to explain why it is that A^2, B^2, C^2, sensations similar to A^1, B^1, C^1, are not followed by D^2, similar to D^1, but by an entirely different sensation X. As soon as we find that the repetition of events in the mind may be interrupted by one quite different from that which occupied its place in the former series, the repetition, unless explained and shown to be really universal by reference to an external world, becomes a mere string of coincidences ; for if the repetition can be interrupted at one moment it might equally well be interrupted at any. That is to say, there is no reason why A^2 should be followed by B^2, or B^2 by C^2, rather than by X, something wholly different. It is this principle which prevents us from being satisfied with a fairly regular sequence of events and makes us look beneath it for one that is invariable. It prevents us from believing in any form of indeterminism. For if we could be satisfied with a fairly regular sequence of events we should not need to look beyond our sensations, which form such a series, and so to believe in the existence of an outer world.

To put the argument briefly, the existence of things apart from our sensations is proved by the very fact that we are able by filling up the gaps in our sensations to form a coherent picture of a whole world, a picture which is continually confirmed by the appearance to our senses of fresh parts of it inferred but not perceived before. One could not suppose that our sensations were in a conspiracy to deceive us into believing in such a world. If they simply arose out of nothingness or were produced by our memories they could not, as they do, confirm our calculations, based on the assumption of a real world of which they only present fragments to us. If you suppose, with Berkeley, that our sensations are created by God and not by an external world you must at least admit that every detail of such a world exists as an idea in the divine Mind, which otherwise could not work consistently. But it is hard to see how such a world of ideas would be different from a real world. A similar answer might have been made by Descartes to his own scepticism, when he imagined it possible that he had been deceived by a malicious demon into the belief in an external world. For the demon who had the bad taste to perpetrate such a practical joke must have had a very complete working model of the world in his mind, a model so complete, in fact, as to be indistinguishable from the real thing.

The fact that at different times the same shapes and colours occur in the same position relatively to one another makes us believe that these shapes and colours existed continuously so even when they were not present in sensation. At first, therefore, we divide the sensation into two elements: these shapes and colours, which are the objects, and something that perceives them, the subject. The subject, in sensation, is not thought to have any qualities of its own, or any activity except perception. All the qualities belong to the object, and can therefore exist even when the subject does not perceive them. The green of that tree or the tone of that sound remain though there is no one to see or hear. This, as I said at the beginning of the chapter, is the metaphysical system which first occurred to men and satisfies most men even now. They do not stop to inquire what green or any other colour or any sound is like when it is by itself, unperceived; how the colour, for instance, exists for the tree itself, or warmth or cold for the water.

At a later stage in metaphysics these ideas are abandoned owing to the objections against them already described. The theory next accepted is that the permanent objects which account for the identity of our sensations at different times are not the shapes and colours themselves but certain things which produce these in our minds. The things themselves are not perceived immediately but affect our senses through a medium, variations in which explain the various ways in which the same thing may appear to us at different times. This theory has several forms. Sometimes the cause of the sensation is supposed to be altogether unlike the sensation itself and unknowable, sometimes it is supposed to be like sensation in quantity, *i.e.*, in the " primary " qualities of extension, shape, solidity, and motion, but to have nothing like the " secondary " qualities, *e.g.* colour, sound, or taste. There are, besides, different views of the relation between the sensations and the brain, upon which the things themselves act. Sometimes the brain is believed to produce the sensations in a separate being, the soul, sometimes it is believed to produce the sensations as entities, by themselves, and sometimes these latter are regarded as occurring parallel to the movements in the brain, but not as produced by these.

The problem of the connection between sensations and the brain may be left aside for the time, for the difference in the theories on this subject will not affect the question how far we can gain any knowledge of the outer world, of the things which cause our sensations. One answer to this question is, as I have said, that the things themselves in no way resemble their effects in our minds; that they have no position in space, no extension, no colour, no hardness or softness, and no taste. Those who answer thus assert as a general principle that a cause need not in any way be like its effect. But this is to abandon the sole ground for believing in the existence of these things as permanent causes of our sensations. If one of these things has itself no position in space relatively to others, no size and no shape, why should it produce in our minds at many different times an image of the same size and shape, and surrounded by the same images at the same relative distances? If it has no nature of its own and is just a cause of sensations, nothing else, it cannot exist when it is not causing these, and therefore cannot be the permanent thing we want to account for the identity of the images present in our minds at different times. And if it has a nature of its own, in no way corresponding to these images, it is impossible to explain why it always produces an image with the same number of parts and of the same size proportionately to the images produced by others and occupying the same position relatively to those produced by others. It could not be said to account for the reappearance of the same image in the same position; there is no reason for saying that it has anything to do with the image at all, and if it were a fact that it produced the same image on many occasions this would be just as much a coincidence requiring explanation as would the reappearance of this image out of the void, uncaused. Such entities as Kant's " things in themselves," bearing no resemblance to our sensations but supposed to produce them, are quite unnecessary and useless for explaining anything; one might just as well suppose that the sensations caused themselves.

We are forced to believe that there are in the things themselves and their relations to one another as many varieties of form as there are in the images they produce in our sensations. Otherwise several things which were identical in nature would have to produce different sensations in us, and in that case there would be no reason why one and the same thing should not on different occasions present completely different images to our minds; no reason why it should on any two occasions present the same. The identity of our sensations at different times would then be left unexplained. We must also suppose that two things which are very like one another produce images which are very much alike, for otherwise a slight change in one and the same thing might make it produce very different sensations on different occasions, and then too it would not account for the resemblance of our sensations at widely separate times. There must, therefore, be the same gradations of form in the things themselves as in the images which they produce in our minds, so that there will be a correspondence between cause and effect. Take any figure one sees, the shape of a chair, for instance. There must be in the real thing that produces the image in our minds four parts corresponding to the legs in the sense-image, a relation between those parts corresponding to the distance between the legs, a fifth part corresponding to the back, and so on. The whole real world must have an order corresponding to the spatial order apparent in our sensations, and if it is to account for that spatial order it must have properties corresponding to all the properties of the spatial world presented to our minds, to all the dimensions, distances, and shapes we see. If it were not so there would be nothing to make the same set of things produce their images all together, and at the same distances from one another as before. We are forced, therefore, to attribute to the external world something identical with space in all its characteristics, so that it would be futile to call it anything else but spatial. This argument is fatal to Kant's doctrine that the spatial "form" is impressed by the mind on the "matter" given in sensation by the "things in themselves."

There are many, chiefly among the scientists, who differ from Kant and agree with Descartes and Locke in attributing to the causes of our sensations what are called the "primary" qualities, extension, shape, resistance, and motion, but denying to them the "secondary" qualities, such as colour and taste. They only allow to the external world what should not properly be called qualities at all but quantities. This colourless picture of the world is much older than the philosophies of Descartes and Locke, for two thousand years before them Democritus had declared that such qualities as bitter and sweet were appearances, and only the atoms and the void were real. But it was from Descartes that the modern physicists learned to regard reality as a problem in mathematics, and from Locke that the division of qualities into primary and secondary was derived. The main reasons for this purely quantitative philosophy are that changes in quantity are much easier to understand and calculate than those in quality, and that the qualities present in our sensations depend upon some quantitative element in the causes of those sensations. When the mingling of two colours produces a third it seems impossible to trace any connection between this last and the former two; at least, that is often so when two chemicals are mixed together. But the addition of two quantities to form one seems intelligible enough. The two quantities are still visible in their total, but it is not always possible to see the two qualities in the result produced by their mixture. Again, the various colours seen depend on something quantitative, the length of the waves of light; they do not exist in the things themselves but are produced in the mind by the action of those waves. It seems that there might be only quantitative differences in the things themselves and the media through which they act upon us to produce the sensations of quality.

But a world containing extension, shapes, and movement without any of the secondary, *i.e.*, genuine, qualities is nothing but a nightmare that haunts the mind of the scientist after over-indulgence in mathematics. A world that had no secondary qualities would in no way be different from an absolute void, for there would be nothing to distinguish any material body from the empty space around it or from any neighbouring body. When all colours disappear in the blackness of night, all shapes and all differences of length vanish from our eyes at the same time, for nothing can have any outline that is not distinguished by some difference of quality from its surroundings. If you believe that such distinctions still exist in the things themselves you must suppose that they have some substitute for colour. Without that there could not be any movement in the world, for how could it be said that A was here one moment and B the next, if there were no qualitative difference between the two or between material bodies and empty space? If you do not admit the existence of a void anywhere you must suppose that the material bodies are marked off from one another by differences of quality; otherwise the world would be one continuous mass without any parts, for there can be no parts without outlines to separate them, and no outlines without quality. Such a world would be like a canvas covered with one colour only, without any difference even in the shading of that colour. On the other hand, if you believe in the possibility of empty space, you might suppose the different bodies to be marked off from one another by intervals of such space ; but even then you would have to grant the existence of some quality, even if it were one and the same quality, in all these bodies, in order to distinguish them from the surrounding void. To make a picture one must at least have white as well as black ; even for a geometrical diagram—and such the world is in the eyes of many scientists—both these are necessary. And it would not be enough to concede the existence of one quality alone in the world outside the human mind, in order to mark off matter from empty space. No one who thinks the matter out can believe in a world of entities various in quantity but all identical in quality and striking up now and then against other entities called minds, which convert these purely quantitative differences into the wide variety of qualities present in our sensations. The whole world must be of the same nature as our minds, which arise from it and are continuous with it, and must therefore have qualities, though they need not, of course, be everywhere the same as those in our minds. There may be, or rather must be, many others in the world which are beyond the reach of our imagination.

It is true that modern scientists never trouble themselves about the presence of secondary qualities in the world, and do not seem to fare any the worse for this. One would imagine that they supposed their electrons, waves of light, and fields of force to possess merely extension and velocity, mass and energy. But what are we to think of a wave of ether or of anything else if the wave is in no way distinguished from a void ? One might as well exhibit a blank canvas and call it a picture of " A storm at sea." One must hold either that these waves have colours or other secondary qualities of their own, or else that they do not exist at all except where there are coloured bodies to oscillate at a certain time and distance from the supposed sending out of a wave. This latter alternative implies action at a distance, for there will be nothing at all between the radiating body and the nearest object to it which is affected by the radiation. The ether was originally assumed by the scientists in order to avoid the idea of such action, but as the ether is not allowed any real qualities it is no more than a synonym for empty space.

The suggestion is often made, in the most solemn and impressive tones, that matter is nothing but energy, or even that it is motion. But for motion or for any form of energy there must be areas of space qualitatively distinguished from one another; these two terms simply indicate the relations of position or changes of distance between such areas. Without these latter they are like mathematical symbols which represent nothing. In the "universal blank" with which we are presented by the modern physicists there can be no change or relation anywhere; the form of the world would be just the same whatever we may suppose to be happening, and in that case it would be nonsense to say that anything happened at all.

This argument does not, of course, contradict what was said earlier in the chapter. There it was maintained that the colours we see, the particular instances of these colours, exist in the image of the external object impressed on the brain. But it is possible that other instances of these same colours sometimes exist in the external object itself, though it cannot always be so, for we see different colours at different distances or in an altered atmosphere when we are looking at the same object. It is certain that there must be some quality in the object itself, perhaps a quality of which we have no conception; a quality which at any rate differentiates it from its surroundings.

When any man has taken the trouble to prove for himself the existence of things other than his own sensations he may find it a harder task to prove the existence of other minds. Perhaps no one has ever seriously doubted whether there were any sensations and thoughts other than his own, and believed the rest of the world to be unconscious. But though the belief in the existence of other minds is universal, the universality of a belief is not in itself a proof, and obviously anyone would be arguing in a circle who wished to use it as such in this particular case, when he has to prove that there is any belief at all, or any other kind of thought or any sensation, outside his own consciousness. It is not enough to say that every man instinctively believes, or that he must believe, in the existence of other minds, for instincts have been known to be wrong, and men at different times have been told, especially by scientists, that they must believe many doctrines which later on they have been commanded to reject. To our remote ancestors it would have appeared absurd to doubt that the lightning was a sign of anger in heaven; one must not be too hasty in assuming that violent language is a sign of anger on earth. Descartes and Malebranche believed that the lower animals were unconscious automata, and that when they pursued or avoided one another they were not set in motion by hunger or fear but by the impulse communicated to their internal machinery from some other animal through the usual medium of sight or sound. If they had known of the evolution of mankind they would have found it difficult to fix the point at which consciousness began; but that is a difficulty which faces most philosophers. The Solipsist, who believes only in his own consciousness, if there is or ever was such a man, might borrow their arguments and apply them to his fellow-men, as well as to the lower animals. It may seem waste of time to set forth and refute such arguments, but there are two good reasons for doing so. In the first place, such a discussion will tend to make us critical of those "critical" philosophies, which, if carried out to their logical conclusion, would declare it impossible for any man to know that other minds existed besides his own; and, secondly, in refuting the Solipsist we shall have to use arguments which prove much more than the existence of minds in all living bodies.

We are often told that no knowledge is certain which goes beyond experience, but those who tell us so include in the term "experience" the perceptions of all mankind and not only those of the individual. Obviously they do not carry their scepticism far enough, since each man should properly begin with his own experience and work outward from that; in considering what knowledge is possible he must not assume at once the existence of any consciousness other than his own, but must begin, like Descartes, with the bare fact of his own being. Since he can never be directly aware of the experience of any other mind, how can he prove that any other mind exists? The first argument that occurs to us is drawn from analogy. Each of us is aware that all his sensations of touch are simultaneous with the contact of two bodies, and that one of the two is in every case the same; he is also aware that all his impulses and resolves are followed by motions of this particular body, which he consequently calls his own. He sees other bodies around him which look almost the same as his own, and act in a similar way; for instance, they, and they alone, avoid any such contact between themselves and others as would in the case of his own body be followed by pain. Now, as in his own case certain feelings intervene between the action of other bodies upon his own and the reaction of the latter, he may conclude, according to the usual argument, that feelings like his own exist in the interval between every similar action and reaction in the outer world. This argument is of the same nature as that which each man must use to prove the existence of any world outside his own consciousness. It consists in this, that when a series of events has often occurred together in our consciousness, and then one of them fails to appear before us with the appearance of the others, we must suppose that the missing member of the series exists somewhere, though unperceived by us.

This argument is sound so far as it goes, but could not properly be accepted by those who doubt the validity of human thought in " transcendental " regions, since for the individual the existence of any consciousness but his own " transcends " his experience; nor by those who doubt the absolute regularity of events, since they would have no right to assume that consciousness is always present whenever bodies like their own react in the same way as they do themselves. It should not even be used by those who believe that there are things without consciousness. To them—that is to say, to most men—the Solipsist might put the questions: " Where do you fix the dividing line between conscious and unconscious beings, and with what right do you fix it here rather than at any other point? What is the exact degree of similarity that must exist between the actions and reactions of other bodies and those of your own, before you will allow that consciousness exists in those other bodies? Everything in the world acts to a certain extent like you; even a stone, if it is struck, moves away from the object that strikes it. Why do you deny that consciousness exists between the action and reaction in that case?"

The objection raised by the Solipsist gains considerable force from the fact of the continuity of Nature. In the ascending scale of the different forms of existence there appears to be no gap such that one could suppose everything above it to be conscious and everything below it unconscious. Besides, the highest of all conscious beings have been gradually evolved, and as at one time there was no life on earth, it seems that they must have been evolved from non-living matter. Can you suppose that consciousness came suddenly into existence at any point in this gradual development, that up to this point there was only unconscious matter, taking ever more complicated forms, and that one of these forms next moment became conscious? If so, how could any man be sure that this point was not the moment at which he himself was born? For the difference between one man and all the rest is certainly not less than the difference between any two consecutive moments in the development of mankind from inorganic matter. The Solipsist, therefore, might believe that only his own body had reached the stage of evolution necessary for consciousness.

One cannot compare the transition from the unconscious to consciousness with the development of organic out of inorganic matter. Life is nothing but a complex of the movements of material bodies, and therefore not essentially different from the inorganic. The passage from the lower to the higher stage need not have been abrupt; if the mechanical theory of life is correct it must have been gradual. Even if it was not, it was only the substitution of a more complex group of movements for a simpler one.

It would be useless to argue that the action of all living beings exhibit purpose, and that they must therefore be conscious. You could not fix any precise moment for the first purposive action in the world, and suppose that up to that time mechanical laws had prevailed, to be superseded suddenly at one particular place by something new, an intention or will. Besides, if you suppose that unconscious existence is possible, could you prove that unconscious matter is incapable of performing actions similar to those which with you are due to conscious design? The characteristic of a purposive action is that it exists as an idea before it is carried out, as a miniature before it appears in life size. But the form in which the action exists first need not be a conscious form : it might be like the seed of a plant, which is usually assumed to be unconscious. However complicated may be the structure of the mind, there is no reason why matter should not take forms equally complicated : the conflict of motives might be paralleled by the conflict of forces, and choice or resolve might be merely the victory of the stronger force. The apparently purposive character of the actions of other living bodies might be due to the " survival of the fittest " ; those bodies which acted as though they were inspired by purposes would naturally be the most likely to survive, and the more highly organized they became, the better they could adapt themselves to surrounding conditions. We do not suppose that the colour protection of certain animals is due to any design on their part ; it might equally well have been formed if they had been unconscious. Even the development of the living body is not regarded as due to any design present from the beginning in the germ, and the only part of it believed to be conscious is the brain. But if there can be so complicated a process without consciousness, can we even be sure that consciousness is present in the brains of all living bodies ?

This brings us to another argument which might be used by the Solipsist. The brain is not so different from the other material bodies that one would expect to find it distinguished from all others by so essential a difference as that between consciousness and unconsciousness would be. Besides, at what precise point in the history of the brain are we to suppose it to become inspired with feeling ? The molecules of which it is composed are continually changing, and are ultimately derived from inanimate matter ; is it possible to imagine that each of them suddenly becomes conscious just because it combines with others to form that particular structure we call the brain? If you suppose that there was once no consciousness in them—and you must suppose this, if you believe everything outside living bodies to be unconscious, for once they formed no part of the body—you must hold that they passed at some time from an insentient to a sentient state, a change altogether different in kind from any other. For all other changes are simply alterations of quantity, *e.g.* size or motion, or of quality; that is to say, they are alterations of some attribute that the thing has already. But the passing from unconsciousness to consciousness would bring in something absolutely new. It is inconceivable that any alteration in quantity or quality, in size, motion, structure, or force, should produce in any thing consciousness, which is the awareness of all quantities and qualities alike. The change would be as great as that from non-being to being, a creation, in fact, rather than a change. It was natural, therefore, that to explain the origin of consciousness a new entity should be introduced, the individual soul, in which sensations are assumed to be produced by the action of the brain. And this view is still the only one possible for those who believe that there can be anything unconscious; they cannot, as I said, suppose that entities possessing extension, motion, and force become instinct with feeling merely because they adopt that particular formation called the brain, or that such entities produce sensations in the void, as it were—another theory once favoured by certain Materialists. On the other hand, the belief in individual souls—though not the Pantheistic belief in a soul of the universe—is met by some fatal objections. For instance, at what precise moment does the soul enter the body, and why at that moment particularly? At what point in the development of the world did souls begin to exist? If they possess extension, how do they differ from matter? And if they are unextended, how do they come to be confined to the brain, and remain unaffected by, and unaware of, the rest of the world, except through the medium of the brain?

But what is more important for our present argument is that we cannot refute the Solipsist by asserting the existence of a soul in every man. Each of us is directly aware of his own consciousness alone, and from that might deduce the presence of a soul in his body; but it would be impossible for him to prove the existence of a soul wherever there was life. The relation between the soul and the body—or between the psychical and the physical, to use terms more popular among the philosophers—has been discussed as often as any problem in metaphysics, and the theory which seems to be most favoured might be taken as a strong argument for Solipsism. According to this theory the movements of the brain and the processes of consciousness are parallel, but there is no interaction between the two sides; consciousness, therefore, does not in any way affect the movements of the body. To use a common phrase, the psychical and the physical are two "aspects" of one reality. The phrase does not help us much, and anyone who believes in this theory is powerless against the Solipsist, unless he also believes that every physical event throughout the world is accompanied by some form of consciousness, and that the one is impossible without the other. If not, how could he prove that alongside the physical "aspect" in other men, the movements in their brains and the consequent movements of the rest of their bodies, there was a psychical aspect, a series of sensations and thoughts? The two forms of the one reality might exist only in his own case, if it is not necessary that they should both exist everywhere.

It seems that the brain, with the afferent nerves which bring impulses to it from the outer world, and the efferent nerves through which it acts on that world, is sufficient by itself to account for all the actions of men, and that consciousness is an unnecessary luxury. The Solipsist might argue that even speech, which is taken to be the sign of a distinctively human intelligence, may be only the working of a machine, far more complicated, of course, than any we can make, but still only a machine. He would suggest that the elaborate structure of the auditory and vocal organs, and the brain itself, had been built up in the past without the assistance of consciousness, just like those parts of the body believed by most men to be unconscious, and had been inherited from one generation by another. The process of learning to speak one's own language he would take to be a series of automatical reactions to the sounds made by others, and no more a sign of hearing and thinking than an echo is. The photograph made upon the brain by this or that object becomes associated with the impression made upon it *viâ* the vibrations in the air when the name of that object is pronounced; while that impression is being fixed the imitative nature of the machine sets up a tendency in the brain to produce the same sound through the vocal chords; and this tendency, again, becomes associated with the photograph of the object, and is revived whenever the presence and action of the object revivifies the photograph. Other men, for the Solipsist, would be merely gramophones with a large number of records; for a gramophone can make remarks about the weather, a round of golf, or the sins of the Government as well as the average man.[1]

The molecules of the brain at one time formed parts of objects supposed to be devoid of consciousness, and obeyed mechanical laws. Of the three classes of thinkers who believe that unconscious beings exist, the Materialists imagine, or used to imagine, that the molecules themselves became conscious when they began to form parts of a brain; the Spiritualists hold that they awake into activity another entity, the soul; and the third school simply declares that feelings and thoughts arise in the void, so to speak, whenever a brain is formed. The first of these might be asked by the Solipsist, if he cared to argue with the machines around him, what need there was to assume that the molecules of the brain, while now acting apparently with a purpose, and no longer mechanically, should also be supposed to possess the further property of consciousness. To be conscious is simply to be aware of one's own states and actions; it is a simple attribute, which belongs to the barest sensations as much as to the highest thoughts and resolutions. What are called " higher forms of consciousness " are not so really, for there is only one form of consciousness; the epithets " higher " and " lower " belong rather to the different states of being of which one is conscious. In the same way there are not higher and lower forms of hearing, for hearing is the same whether the thing heard is a mere noise or the finest music: it is to these last that the terms " lower " and " higher " belong. Consciousness, therefore, if it is not as wide as existence, must be merely

[1] *Cf.* " The Book of the Machines," in Butler's *Erewhon*.

an attribute to certain higher forms of being and action. But is it necessary to assume that these higher forms are always accompanied by an awareness of themselves? You suppose that the shapes, motions, and colours of which we are aware in sensation can exist by themselves, without any consciousness of their existence; might you not also suppose that the image or plan of action of which one is conscious in forming an intention, and those kinds of energy of which one is conscious in emotions and will, can exist by themselves in the same way? It would not be necessary then to believe that when the brain begins to act on other principles than the laws of mechanics—if it ever does—it is necessarily aware of its action. It might form those images and exert those forces of which we are conscious in thought, emotion, and will, and yet have no consciousness of them. The Materialist, then, could not prove the existence of any feelings or thoughts except his own.

If with a powerful microscope one man could see every atom of another man's brain, would he observe any movement there that could not be explained by previous movements? If he observed none such how could he prove the existence of consciousness there, however purposive the actions starting from the brain might appear? If he did observe such movements would he be better able to explain them if he assumed the presence of consciousness? I do not see how he would, or what right he would have to make the assumption on such grounds. He would only be justified in saying that the molecules of the brain now moved in such a way that the actions starting from them now tended to the good of the whole organism of which they were parts. So do parts of the body which are usually supposed to be without feelings of any kind. If the Materialist tried to explain the apparently purposive nature of the movements of the brain by attributing it to the presence of consciousness there, he would have to suppose that each molecule was aware of its own position relative to the others, of the action which was to follow the movements of all the molecules, and the result it was to produce, and also of the extent to which it was itself to diverge from its normal movements. The whole plan of action, in fact, would have to be known to each molecule, just as every one of a number of men engaged in a common task must be aware of the whole procedure, unless he has his particular share assigned to him by a leader. According to the Materialist there is no such leader to direct the molecular movements of the brain, and, therefore, if he supposes the purposive action of the body to be due to the presence of a conscious intelligence, he must suppose this intelligence to exist entire in every molecule of the brain. But such a theory would evidently be absurd.

This difficulty is avoided by the Spiritualist—to use the most convenient term—who believes in individual souls directing the movements of the brain. He would meet the arguments of the Solipsist by saying that the motions of a living body could not be so intelligent as they are if there were not present in it a being conscious, through the brain, of the state of the body, and able to supervise the movements of all its parts. This would not be a convincing answer, for there would always remain the alternative possibility that the apparently purposive actions were due to the highly organized nature of the brain, which had developed during millions of years into a machine capable of acting for the good of the whole body, but had been evolved without conscious purpose, just as that highly complicated organ, the eye, is supposed to have been evolved. Paley argued that the organs of the body must have been put together by a conscious Being apart from them, who brought all their parts together, like a skilful workman, into a cunningly devised whole. If the Darwinians have overthrown that argument, they have also overthrown or rendered unnecessary the assumption that the brain, the most elaborate organism of all, always acts as it does because there is a conscious entity apart from it directing all its movements.

Besides the difficulties already raised against this assumption, difficulties regarding the origin of the individual soul, the precise moment at which souls entered the world, the precise moment at which each entered its body, and its mode of existence and relation to the organism during sleep, there is also the problem of the interaction of the soul and body, if these terms are intended to denote separate existences and not the oneness and the multiplicity of life and mind.

To repeat a question asked above, if a man could see all the molecules of another's brain, would he detect anything incalculable in any of their movements, anything which could not be deduced from the preceding movements? The Spiritualist must assume that he would, and that the deviations from the normal course of affairs, *i.e.*, from the path which the molecules would have followed if they had formed part of the world supposed to be unconscious, are due to the activity of the soul, its will, and its emotions. But a resolution or an emotion is for the Spiritualist something quite different from the movements of the molecules upon which they are assumed to act. In that case what is to decide whether the normal laws of "matter" are to prevail over a violent emotion, for instance, which tries to divert the molecules from following those laws, or whether the emotion is to prove the stronger? An answer to that question seems to me impossible, and is certainly not rendered easier by the Spiritualist, who is never tired of maintaining that the processes of the soul are not measurable like those of matter, so exactly calculated by the scientist. If the physical and mental events are incommensurable, how can the second have any influence on the first? No interaction is possible between entities that belong to such different orders of existence. Besides, one cannot understand why the soul should confine its action to the brain; it is not supposed to be spatial itself, with a size and shape of its own, so that there seems nothing to prevent it from exerting as great an influence all over the body, and even beyond, as it is assumed to exert on a particular part of the organism. But since we do not see such miracles, we must doubt whether there really is any non-spatial entity directing the movements of the brain, or rather what appears as the brain, and therefore cannot refute the Solipsist by asserting its existence.

We shall not get any better argument from the third class of thinkers who divide the world into conscious and unconscious beings, *i.e.*, from those who content themselves with saying that thoughts and sensations arise whenever a brain is formed, and then only. If the psychical and physical processes are regarded as moving on parallel lines without interaction, then, as we have seen, the Solipsist could never be refuted; for if you believe that it is not necessary for every physical event to have a psychical complement you cannot prove that the movements of every brain are accompanied by consciousness. If, on the other hand, you suppose that there is interaction between the two series of events, that an emotion or resolve acts upon the brain and so upon the external bodies, you are met by the same difficulties as the believer in individual souls. For evidently you cannot escape these by avoiding the word " soul " and talking merely of the emotions and the will. To imagine consciousness as beginning at a certain moment to accompany the movements in the brain is just as hard as to imagine the soul entering the body; to think of an emotion as acting on the brain is just as hard as to think of the soul as doing so, if emotions and the movements of matter are incommensurable and belong, as it were, to different worlds. As long as you assume consciousness to be something comparatively new and exceptional in the world you are faced by insoluble problems regarding its origin and its relation to that part of the world which you believe unconscious; you cannot prove that its origin was not the moment of your birth, that you are not the one bright spot in a world of darkness.

There seems to me to be no force in the arguments directed against the Solipsist by Professor Taylor in his *Elements of Metaphysics*. After declaring that no proof of the existence of other minds can be drawn from the use of analogy he continues: " How then do we learn the existence of feeling, purposive experience outside our own? The answer is obvious. We learn it by the very same process by which we come to the clear consciousness of ourselves. ... It is by the process of putting our purposes into act that we come to be aware of them as our purposes, as the meaning of our lives, the secrets of what we want of the world. ... To realize your own ends you have to take notice of the partly coincident, partly conflicting, ends of your social fellows, precisely as you have to take note of your own. You cannot come to the knowledge of the one without coming by the same route and in the same degree to the knowledge of the other." [1] But we are not aware of the purposes of other men in the same way as we are of our own. We do not mistake our own intentions,

[1] *Elements of Metaphysics*, pp. 204, 205.

whereas we often mistake those of others. We know our own resolutions and the feelings that give rise to them, whereas we only infer those of others from their actions. If a man were conscious of his own feelings and of other men's in the same way, how could he distinguish at all between his own feelings and those of others? They would all be equally his.

A little farther on Professor Taylor tells us that, " to an enormous extent, it is by first repeating, without conscious aim of its own, significant purposive acts of others that a child first comes to behave with conscious significance itself. It is largely by learning what others mean when they utter a word or execute a movement that the child comes to know his own meaning in using the same word or performing the same movement." Is the child, then, conscious of other people's hunger before he is conscious of his own, and does he put food in his mouth because he has perceived the sensation of pleasure which others have had when they have done the same? If not, how can he learn what others mean by their actions? No doubt, most of the actions of children are originally imitative, but this could not prove to any child that there was any consciousness in those whom he imitates. He observes that when they point to a certain object they make a certain sound, and then does the same himself; but how can he be sure that when they point towards the object they perceive it as he does? He observes, too, that they avoid doing things which, if he did them, would be followed by pain, but might he not suppose that their bodies automatically avoided things which might injure them, without assuming that they ever had any consciousness of injury?

It does not seem to me that there is any greater force in the arguments advanced by Professor Alexander in his Gifford Lectures. He too denies that knowledge of other minds is derived from the use of analogy, maintaining that it is a direct experience. "The idea of a foreign consciousness, unless directly supplied by some experience to that effect, is something to which we have no clue in ourselves." [1] But is it true that we could not form the idea of any such thing without direct experience of it? If that were so, how could we form any conception of existence apart from our consciousness?

[1] *Time, Space, and Deity*, vol. ii. pp. 32-37.

Obviously we cannot have direct experience of any object as existing outside our sensations, of a table or tree as it is when unseen. Even if you suppose that it exists without our consciousness, you do not mean that we are ever directly aware of it as so existing. But as we certainly have an idea of such existence this must be obtained indirectly. Why, then, should not our idea of other minds be derived not from direct experience but from reasoning by analogy?

I think almost every man, if he troubled to consider the grounds of his belief, would say that he gained it from analogy and not from any direct experience. This is confirmed by the fact that uncivilized nations have often attributed consciousness to things which are generally believed to have none. Professor Alexander explains this as " an act of projection which is perfectly intelligible when the mysterious object, a foreign mind, has been discovered through such experiences as have been described," *i.e.*, through social experiences. " It is an extension of the notion of a foreign mind to things which behave in some ways like persons or ourselves." Our " direct experience " is evidently an inadequate guide; it informs us that there are foreign minds, but does not help us in determining where they are. As it does not warn men when they are wrong in attributing consciousness, how are they to know when they are right? If our social instincts assure us that there is consciousness in human bodies, do not his religious instincts assure the heathen who " bows down to wood and stone " that there is intelligent consciousness in his idols?

Professor Alexander admits that children and uncivilized men reason by analogy when they " extend the notion of a foreign mind to things which behave in some ways like persons or ourselves." But he declares that we are relying on direct experience when we apply it to human bodies, and presumably also when we attribute consciousness to the lower animals. This seems to me an altogether unreasonable distinction. Where does our direct experience end and our reasoning from analogy begin? Surely the cause which makes us attribute consciousness to other men is not different in kind from that which makes the savage think that the lightning is a sign of anger in heaven. The only reason why we have abandoned the latter belief is that the lightning is not consistent in its actions like a human being, *i.e.*, that the analogy is not complete, as it is between one human mind and another.

The social instincts depend on the belief in other minds; that belief is not grounded on the social instincts. It is true that some instincts are innate, especially in the lower animals, some of which have a natural terror of others. But these instincts are inherited from the experiences of other generations. Our belief in the existence of other minds may be so too; if so, it might seem that each man could argue from this that his ancestors at least had been conscious, since they had had this belief and passed it on to him. Yet even that would not be altogether justified. The truth might be that the bodies of his ancestors, while really unconscious, had always acted in such a way as though they were conscious of the existence of other minds; *i.e.*, that the instinct was in fact a certain inherited disposition of the brain which only became conscious in him. Unless he holds that feeling is universal he must admit that his ultimate origin far back in time was unconscious, and admitting that there was at any moment a transition from the insentient to the sentient he might, as I said, believe this to have been the moment of his birth. Certainly Professor Alexander's account of the origin of consciousness would justify him in believing that this might be so. To quote from that account, " It has then to be accepted as an empirical fact that a neural process of a certain level of development possesses the quality of consciousness and is thereby a mental process "; [1] and " it may still be open for discussion at what level in the brain structure consciousness is found." [2] Who could tell that he alone had not reached the necessary level of development?

It has been argued that the Solipsist, in saying " I am aware only of my own sensations and thoughts," implies the existence of other minds, for his use of the words " I " and " my " involves a distinction between himself and other persons. But even if this is so it is not necessary for him to use those words at all in order to express his meaning. He might simply say: " There is in the world one body, the states and movements of which are always accompanied by sensations, which do not occur when other bodies act or are affected in

[1] *Op. cit.*, vol. ii. p. 5.   [2] *Op. cit.*, vol. ii. p. 6.

a similar way." And there is in fact no reason why he should not use the term " I " to distinguish the series of states of consciousness from the other events in the world, as a term to denote the one mind that existed. Each man must, as I said, know his own consciousness in a different way from that in which he knows the consciousness of other men, for otherwise he could make no distinction between the two. The first kind of knowledge is direct, the second is an inference, and the theory of our imaginary Solipsist is that the inference is not justified.

For one who believes that consciousness is not universal there seems to be no argument left that can be used against the Solipsist, except the argument from common sense, which of course involves a vicious circle, since he has to prove first that sense, or sensation, is common, and not confined to himself. The critical philosophers, who are never weary of telling us that a man can only know his own thoughts and feelings, those of other men, and, to a less degree, the feelings of the lower animals, seldom trouble to explain how, if their theories and criticisms are true, he can know anything but the first. If they mention the subject at all they generally do what the theologians have so often been ridiculed for doing and tell the reader that it is not a matter for argument ; he must believe. If the problem had been put before Hume he could only have answered that this belief was a matter not of reason, but of faith, and Kant could only have made it a fourth " postulate of the practical reason." I suppose the neo-Kantians would have to tell us that we must act " as if " the belief in the existence of other minds were true, and leave it at that, without any very firm conviction that the belief is correct. Just as in the early days of modern philosophy the unorthodox wrote long volumes criticizing the doctrines of the Church and ended by professing entire submission to its authority, so the critical philosophers of later days use arguments which, if carried out to their natural conclusion, would be fatal to the doctrines of common sense, and then refer us to common sense as the supreme arbiter.

It is worth noting that every argument for morality advanced by the Utilitarians would have equal force if addressed to a man who believed that he was the only conscious being in the world. On their principles this belief should not trouble at all anyone who felt compelled to accept it, for precisely the same consequences to himself would follow all his actions even if all other men were unconscious machines ; and if morality is really nothing but " enlightened self-interest " the consequences to himself are all that any man considers. The Utilitarian theory in ethics corresponds exactly to Solipsism in metaphysics and is equally absurd ; yet it has been seriously defended by thinkers in all ages, whereas it is improbable that any man has really believed other men to be unconscious, even when his metaphysical theories should have led a philosopher to that conclusion.

I do not see how the Solipsist could be refuted by anyone who supposes the world to consist of two kinds of beings, conscious and unconscious. But that division of the world is quite indefensible. It implies that at a certain moment in the history of the world a thing which had previously possessed only extension and motion suddenly felt its own existence, or else came to be accompanied by a separate entity which felt it, and that the same event occurs at a certain moment whenever the unconscious elements of matter form themselves into a living body. This would evidently be a breach of the law of cause and effect, for the movements of material bodies at one instant should only lead to similar movements at the next, with the normal transference of velocities, whereas there is in this case the introduction of something new, essentially different from extension and motion. This is equally impossible, whether you suppose it to have occurred at the origin of all life, or at the origin of your life only. Besides, there is a continuous transition from one form of being to another, and we cannot define exactly what it is in their behaviour that entitles certain entities to be regarded as conscious. This difficulty becomes obvious to anyone who considers the question whether plants have feeling. It seems that they must, since there is so little difference between them and the lowest species of animals. But after admitting the presence of feeling in plants one finds it difficult to stop anywhere, and in fact there is no reason why one should stop.

It has been shown that the qualities called " secondary,"

colour, sound, or others like them, must exist everywhere with the "primary" qualities, or rather quantities, *i.e.*, extension, shape, and motion. We must now go farther and say that the secondary qualities must everywhere be accompanied by consciousness. In what way could an unseen colour exist, or an unheard sound, or an unfelt hardness? The idea of such a thing is to my mind quite meaningless. It is the sensations themselves that are red, for instance, or loud, or hard, just as a sensation of sweetness or bitterness is simply a sweet or bitter sensation. Try to imagine a red or a blue as it would be in itself, and you will find that you always think of it as it exists in the mind; otherwise you can only think of something colourless, which acquires colour when perceived.

Our belief that the secondary qualities can exist apart from consciousness is due to the idea that the qualities we see belong to the external thing itself; since we have to believe that thing to remain even when we are not conscious of it, we assume that those qualities we attribute to it remain also, though unperceived. But these qualities really exist in the brain and are continually giving place to new ones there; we have therefore no ground for maintaining that they can exist apart from consciousness. There is in fact no ground for believing that existence apart from consciousness has any meaning at all, or that any form of being essentially different from our own is possible.

All the difficulties which meet those who limit consciousness in any way would also make the position of the Solipsist impossible. He would have to explain how his consciousness came to be restricted to a certain area in a perfectly continuous world; why it began at one moment rather than another; and why the innumerable elements of his brain, which are continually being replaced, become every one of them conscious immediately they begin to be parts of that structure. His theory only derives its force from that individualism which sets up a quite arbitrary barrier between each mind and the rest of the universe.

The main reason for the general denial of consciousness in the inorganic world is the absence of any indication of purpose there. But obviously purpose and consciousness are not identical; we do not suppose ourselves to be unconscious when we give ourselves up to a state of mere feeling, or to a train of thought which does not aim at any conclusion. On the other hand, if unconscious existence were possible at all, there might be, as I said before, purposive actions unaccompanied by any consciousness. For there might be as many forms of insentient as of sentient existence, and among the former might be one that corresponded to conscious purpose, and produced the same results. If we are to judge the nature of other beings from their likeness to ourselves we cannot stop after proving, from the resemblance of the actions of some among them to our own, that some of them have intelligence and will. From the inaction of others we can infer with just as good ground that they are in the same state as we are when inactive, *i.e.*, in a state of mere feeling. There can be no absolute difference between us and the rest of the world, but only a difference of degree, of consciousness more or less intense, more or less highly organized. There are wide enough differences even in our own life, as that between intense thought or strained attention and the merely passive state when a man closes his eyes and is aware of little else beyond a sense of fatigue or the warmth of his body. This last condition approximates to that of the things we call inanimate, except that in the man there is always some degree of thought, until he falls asleep.

It will be objected that in sleep we are unconscious, and that since our bodies still exist during that time, unconscious existence must be possible. But sleep implies only the absence of thought, and not of feeling. The objection may be fairly met by the theory that there are different levels of consciousness, a theory first advanced by Fechner, who in his *Tagesansicht gegenüber der Nachtansicht* worked out more fully than any other the doctrine that consciousness is universal. According to him, in sleep we sink to the level of the surrounding world, supposed to be unconscious, but really possessing a consciousness less intense and more uniform than ours is when we are awake. In dreams we rise a little above that level, and the highest plane of all is of course our waking state. The same idea as Fechner's is contained in such phrases as "subliminal consciousness," or "subconscious" or even "unconscious

THE POSSIBILITY OF KNOWLEDGE 57

mind"; for by these last two phrases can only be meant a state of feeling too low or too uniform to attract the attention. But the use of such terms is unfortunate; the phrase "unconscious mind," on which von Hartmann founded a whole philosophy, can only be called a contradiction in terms. The correct phrase would be "mind unconscious of itself."

The five senses are the higher and more vivid forms of consciousness that break in upon a lower and duller form, the general feeling of the body, a feeling of which we are seldom aware, our attention being wholly occupied with the ever-changing sights and sounds, or with our thoughts. This general feeling is not only too low to attract our thought, which moves on a higher level of consciousness, but also too uniform to interrupt the current of our ideas, which is only diverted by a violent or abrupt change of sensation. The more vivid and varying sensations are like the pictures thrown on the screen by the cinematograph. The screen does not fill up all our sight space, and therefore we must see other parts of the theatre, but we cannot be said to be aware of them. Again, when reading a book, we see other things besides the pages, but pay no heed to them. So together with the five senses there is an area of fainter consciousness which does not draw our attention. We are not aware of the warmth of the body, except when it is considerably increased in any part or diminished, or when as far as possible we free ourselves from the more intense forms of consciousness. It is not to be supposed that between the cold and heat which attract our attention there is a neutral state of no consciousness at all; rather there is a uniform state of feeling which is seldom noticed except when it undergoes a change. For our attention is drawn not only by the intensity of a feeling but by the change from one state to another, and also by the contrast between the state of one part of the body and the rest. Heat that is noticeable enough when it exists in one part only is no longer noticed when it is spread over all the body. But we cannot suppose that the feeling has ceased, though it no longer draws our attention. Again, a continuous and uniform sound after a time comes to be unheeded, though it remains there all the while.

We come thus to the conclusion that the whole world is conscious. We are surrounded by consciousness, which may be, as I said, less intense than our own, but, on the other hand, may be very much more so, and be unnoticed for the same reason as that which prevents us from noticing the motion of the earth, though we observe the slower motions upon it. Our minds might be like bubbles at rest in the centre of an enormous maelstrom. The inanimate appearance of many of the objects we see should not deceive us, for the brain, too, would not seem to a being from another planet the most likely seat of consciousness, certainly not of that world of thoughts and feelings which every man is. We know what the reality is of that which appears to others as the brain; we must infer that something similar, though less complicated, less highly organized, is the reality of that which appears as a stone or a tree.

We have answered the Solipsist by denying that consciousness can ever have come out of an unconscious world, that unconscious existence is even conceivable. But when a man has proved to himself that feeling exists everywhere, and that there are other highly organised centres of thought and sensation, can he also prove that the thoughts and sensations there are so like his own as he generally assumes them to be? Can he be sure that when others say they see something they call "blue" or "red" they have the same sensation as he has when he looks in the same direction? There must, certainly, be something identical in all "blue" objects which produces that colour in his sensations, but might not this property, whatever it is, produce in the consciousness of others an entirely different colour? It would be hard for him to judge whether he was mistaken or not, for he cannot compare his sensations with theirs; all he knows is that they point or refer to a number of things and call them "blue," things which always produce in him the same colour-sensation, so that the word has become associated with it from his childhood. Suppose that the Martians came to earth, and their eyes were so formed that trees looked red to them and pillar-boxes green; suppose that they saw a different colour for every colour of ours; how could we know the difference. We should teach them to call the trees and the grass "green," and the

THE POSSIBILITY OF KNOWLEDGE 59

pillar-boxes and Socialistic flags "red," but all the time they might be associating with each of these words a colour quite different from the one we mean. If they called both the trees and the pillar-boxes "green" we should know that their eyes saw differently from ours—it was in this way that we first learned the existence of colour-blindness—but so long as they saw a separate colour for every one that we see we should continue to think that their sensations were the same as ours. They might see colours of which we had no conception, they might even have sensations altogether different from those of colour, but with the same number of varieties, and yet we could not know this. It might seem that each man is in the same position towards his fellows as we should all be towards these Martians. He cannot *see* that the same set of objects, which produces the sight of red in him, produces that sensation in others as well, or even that it produces any colour sensation at all.

The reason why he takes this for granted is that he supposes the colour to exist in the thing itself, at a certain distance from him, and not in his sensations. When he is driven to abandon that idea by such arguments as those already given earlier in the chapter, he will find it hard to prove that he and other men mean the same thing by the word "blue" or "red." He could not prove it at all if he accepted the principles of Hume or Kant or any of their followers to-day. The main argument for it seems to me to be the uniformity of Nature; the fact, everywhere else apparent, that the same forces produce in similar entities the same results suggests that this is also true here. The brains of all men are alike in structure and composed of the same elements; it follows that the realities of which they are the appearances are also alike. If we supposed that there were individual souls on which our brains acted we could not be certain that these souls were not different in nature, so that the same force would produce in them different sensations. But grant that the whole consciousness of the world is one soul, of which human brains and all other perceptible things are the phenomena, and it is then reasonable to infer that where the phenomena are alike, the states of consciousness which they represent are not less so. Besides, the elements of every brain, as of the rest of the body, are continually being replaced by new ones from the world around; that is, there is a continual replacing of those conscious entities, parts of the universal consciousness, which form any man, and are in fact the reality which appears as his brain. These new elements from the outer world of consciousness are always of the same nature as the old, for each man throughout his life has the same set of colours and other qualities in sensation. He may infer, then, that all the conscious entities are so far alike that whenever they are united in an organism which appears as a brain their consciousness is of the same quality. To put it shortly, each man in his life is many " brains " in turn, all representing the same kind of sensations and thoughts; the sameness of these could only be a coincidence, if they were not identical in all other " brains " as well.

It would be strange, too, that the innumerable elements of any one " brain," ultimately derived from different parts of the world, should only contain a limited number of colours, that at every moment such multitudes of them should contain one and the same colour, if others, similarly derived, could contain a different set. There would be no likelihood that the same quality should exist in any two, if there were not the same range or scale of qualities for both; for if any two in the same circumstances, under the influence of the same forces, can exhibit different qualities, there would be no reason why any two should exhibit the same. The possibilities of difference would be infinite. There would be no reason why any elements of the same " brain " should be at all alike.

What consciousness may be like in bodies less complex than the human we have no sure means of knowing, for where the structure and the forces brought to bear on it are different we cannot tell what qualities may exist, higher or lower in the scale than ours. Thought is so complex that it requires an elaborate organism like that which appears as the human brain, but it is possible, even probable, that such exist on other worlds in space, or have been, or will be, for it would be absurd to think that the conditions necessary for their formation can only have been realized on this planet. It is probable, too, that sensations like ours exist even on the earth, outside the realm of life, for there is no reason to believe that all of them demand any especially complex organism. If we must not commit the "pathetic fallacy" of attributing to trees, rivers, and mountains emotions like our own, still more should we guard against the idea that they are merely objects for the human mind to see and use, or masses of atoms without quality or feeling.

APPENDIX

In his Gifford Lectures on *Time, Space, and Deity* (bk. iii. ch. vii. and viii.), Professor Alexander maintains the theory that we have a direct perception of external bodies outside us, and do not merely see images of them in the mind or brain. He distinguishes appearances into three classes: real appearances, which belong to the thing itself, the tree or house seen; mere appearances, which arise from the combination of this thing with others; and illusory appearances, due to the intrusion of the mind of the observer into the observation. An example of the first is the size or brightness of an object seen at any distance, small or great; of the second, the blue colour of a distant mountain; of the third, the colours seen by contrast, as when a grey patch by contrast with a red ground appears green.

As regards the first kind of appearances, he maintains that the lower brightness of a light seen from a distance is really contained within the light, and that the smaller size of a plate seen from a distance belongs to the plate itself; neither the lower brightness nor the smaller size belongs to a mental image of the real thing. But the fainter light of a lamp seen far off cannot be "contained within" the real light in such a way that we could see it apart from the rest. To imagine this is to break up the simple intensity of the light into two sections, one of which is seen and the other not. These two must be quite distinct, since one of them is so related to the mind that it can be seen and the other stands in no such relation. But evidently there can be no such division of the intensity.

Farther on we read that the smaller size of the plate as seen from a distance "is a portion of the real geometrical size of the plate." We are not to take it as a portion of the plate in the ordinary sense, for obviously we see the complete round figure, on a smaller scale, and the plate is not made up of smaller figures of its own shape. We are to suppose that we see half of the plate, for example, yet not any particular half, but rather half of its size in the abstract. This is to treat the plate as a mathematical entity rather than a concrete thing, as the general idea of a circle eight inches or so in diameter. It seems to follow from this that we do not see a half of any particular plate, but of a size and shape which exists equally in many plates, just as when we consider geometrical figures we do not consider them as existing in any particular thing but in many.

Besides, if we are to take " part of the plate " in this geometrical sense we meet with the same objection as before, when we were considering the intensity of a light. The geometrical size cannot exist in two distinct sections such that one stands in the relation to the mind necessary for being seen and the other outside that relation. It is difficult to make the objection clearer, because the whole theory itself suffers from so much obscurity. I do not understand how a state of the brain here can determine what part we shall see of an extent or an intensity over there, and the difficulty is still greater if you suppose that we do not see any particular part of the object. But everything is clear enough when we accept the theory that what we see is not the object itself but a representation of it in the brain.

The introduction of the element of time does not serve to explain why, if we perceive the object itself, we perceive it in different sizes. It is true that if a man closes and then opens his eyes and sees the complete circle of a plate in front of him, then the farther he is standing from it the less is the interval of time between his seeing the centre and his seeing the rim; the light-wave from the centre always arrives first, if he sees the full circle, but the farther he is away, the shorter the time between its arrival and that of the light-waves from the rim. From this Professor Alexander infers that " while it is still the whole disc which is seen in its full geometrical extent, that extent looks smaller because it is filled with the qualitied events of illumination, and is only apprehended through them. We see a smaller disc because the disc occupies less time under the conditions of vision."[1] There might be some force in this argument if we only perceived the first

[1] *Time, Space, and Deity*, vol. ii. pp. 196, 197.

light-wave from each part of the plate ; then we should see each part at a different time, and the farther we were away the less would be the time taken up by the arrival of all the waves, one from each point. But when there are light-waves arriving simultaneously from every part, how can it make any difference that the interval between the starting of the waves from the centre and the starting of those from the rim which arrive at the same time as the former becomes less and less, the farther we are standing from the plate ? We do not continue to take together in turn a wave from the centre and a wave from the rim which bears the same number as the other in the series to which it belongs.

To come to the " mere appearances," arising from the combination of a particular object with other things, we may take the instance of a mountain which appears blue from a distance through a haze, or the different colours of the sun seen at different times. "The colour of the distant mountain is not the colour of the mountain alone, but of the mountain and the atmosphere whose haze modifies the colour." But the haze does not of course modify the colour of the mountain itself ; its own colour and that of the mountain exist quite apart from one another in reality, and the blue we see is not to be found there. The two colours, those of the atmosphere and of the mountain, cannot be contained within the one actually seen. Or if you suppose that they are so contained you must admit that they do not appear as existing in different positions but together. If so, we do not see the particular instances of those two colours—for the instances are only particularized by their different positions in space—but those two colours in general. We see something that does not belong to this mountain or to this part of the atmosphere more than it belongs to many like them. This is the logical conclusion from the idea that our perception of the colour is distinct and separate from our perception of position, and that consequently we can misplace the colour.

As an instance of the third class of appearances, those which he calls illusory, Professor Alexander takes the green colour seen by contrast on a piece of grey paper lying on a red ground. He maintains that the illusory object here is as much non-mental as the " real " appearances, for there is green in the world, though not in the paper, and it is this green which we see. " The appropriate response of the mind to green is the kind of sensory act which the mind is at the moment performing, and accordingly it sees green." [1] The light-waves set up in the brain the state necessary for the perception of this colour, and the perception inevitably follows. But it is not asserted that we see the green existing in any particular object, and so it seems obvious that we must perceive green in general, or at least some colour in general, some shade of green which may exist in many places. Professor Alexander will not admit this suggestion, for " the act is a sensational act, and has its individuality, determined by its spatial extent and situation." But if the spatial extent and situation here belong to the mind, they cannot give any individuality to the colour, which according to this theory is non-mental. And they cannot belong to the colour, for the situation of the colour is certainly not where we see it, in the grey paper. Besides, the same spatial extent of colour may exist in many places, so that it cannot be individualized in that way.

This explanation of the illusion suggests that the mind looks straight at the position of the grey paper but squints, though in no definite direction, when looking for its colour. It is a curious theory, and must inspire us with a general distrust of all our sensations of colour. How can we ever know that when we suppose ourselves to see a colour in any object we are not seeing a colour which really exists somewhere else in the universe? The action of the object, *viâ* the light-waves, may set up in the brain the state necessary for the perception of *some* colour, but how can we be sure that it is the colour of the object itself? Everything we see might produce in the mind the " appropriate response " to some colour other than its own. It might even have no colour at all but some other quality, and yet produce the response appropriate to green or red and the consequent perception of one of these. In eyes and brains differently constructed from our own it might produce quite a different reaction, and consequently a different sensation.

The difficulty is due to the general obscurity which this theory creates in the relation between the brain and the object.

[1] *Op. cit.*, vol. ii. p. 214.

How can a state of the brain here produce, or rather be, direct consciousness of an object lying some yards or miles away? There is no continuity between the two, for the consciousness is not supposed to spread all along the light-waves between the distant object and the eye. We see a red colour, for instance, but what ground have we for saying that it is the red of an object in front of us rather than of one that lies behind us or in a different country. The object may determine the colours we shall see, and by its action on the brain fix their extent and relative position, but cannot assure us that it is its own particular instances of these colours that become visible to us. For though it contains certain shapes of blue and red, for instance, yet our perception of these shapes is not directly due to their existence in the object but to the fact that an area of the brain itself is so shaped as to perceive just that extent in each direction and no more. The brain might really be seeing the blue or red in some larger object, but owing to the limitations imposed upon it might cut out of that larger object the figure actually seen.

It is evident that there must be in the brain something corresponding to every detail of all that is actually seen of the object before us; otherwise there would be no reason why our perceptions should be more complete at one time than another. Besides, the sight of something we have seen before could only call up the memory of the previous occasion if it had then left an impression of itself upon the brain, or else, to adopt Professor Alexander's theory, disposed the brain now in precisely such a way that it could become conscious of having seen it at another time. When you reflect how small a detail may identify such an object for us you must admit that the brain contains a very faithful copy of the original. It seems unlikely that we should be unconscious of this copy and see directly the original over there. Are we to suppose that the brain contains no secondary qualities for us to observe, but only the general form of consciousness, the details of which are supplied by a distant object? If so, it would have nothing to differentiate its parts, for no distinction is possible without secondary qualities. The brain is frequently described by Professor Alexander as a complex of movements, but there can be no movements without colour or something like colour to distinguish the moving object from others or from the void.

This argument might be met by a flat denial. " It is not true that the extension of a material thing is impossible without secondary qualities, as Berkeley taught." [1] If so, it would not be true of motion either. Indeed, Professor Alexander distinctly asserts that " secondary qualities are thus a set of new qualities which movements of a certain order of complexity have taken on, or which emerge from them." [2] His theory is that secondary qualities only arise where the motions have reached a certain order of complexity, and that consciousness arises when a certain higher order has been reached. Both parts of the theory seem to me impossible. I cannot form any idea of shapes, sizes, or movements without colour or something like it, any more than I could imagine a picture on a blank canvas. Such an idea is as inconceivable as that other, still popular among some scientists, of waves in a perfectly homogeneous ether.

It is equally strange to suppose that when the motions in a particular area reach a certain complexity there arises a consciousness, not of any secondary qualities within that area—for they are replaced by consciousness—but of qualities existing at some distance from it. Consciousness is something that can accompany every quantity or quality, and is therefore essentially different from either. A transition from unconsciousness seems to me as impossible as a transition from pure quantity to quality. It is conceivable that there may be a change from one secondary quality to another when the motion of any object reaches a certain velocity. In that case nothing is added to the world. There is a scale of qualities in the world parallel to the degrees of motion. But a universe consisting wholly of quantities cannot suddenly have a new element, quality, added to it when the quantities reach a certain complexity ; nor could it, after consisting wholly of quantities and qualities, have another new element added to it which accompanied these, *i.e.* consciousness, whenever the complexity reached a still higher degree.

It may be remarked that Professor Alexander's account of consciousness gives us no valid reason for believing that

[1] *Op. cit.*, vol. ii. p. 61. [2] *Op. cit.*, vol. ii. p. 59.

consciousness exists in all brains. No man could be sure that his own brain was not the only one in which the "complexity of motions" had reached the necessary degree. The arguments I have already put into the mouth of the Solipsist apply with particular force to such a theory. Wherever in the scale of complexities the dividing line between consciousness and unconsciousness may lie, the transition must be very abrupt, and it would be impossible to tell which brains possessed just that extra degree of complexity which made all the difference.

The main argument advanced by Professor Alexander in favour of his theory is that it allows for the possibility of knowledge. He "cannot help confessing how much simpler it would be, and how much laborious explanation it would save, if only it were true that our intuitions and sensations were mental as is commonly supposed, and how easy it is compared with our procedure to refer all these variations in part to the mind or its body."[1] But he objects that if the easier theory were true "we should then be living in a world of sensations and of images," and should have no test to show us how much of the sensations represented any element of the real things, and how much was due to the mind. We cannot discriminate by means of other sensations, for we must doubt these too; the only possible test is direct perception of the real things. But his own theory certainly allows some influence of the mind on our sensations, when we see the distant mountain as blue or the sun as red, and though this may be explained as due to the combination of the atmosphere with the mountain or sun, it must certainly be the mind that combines the colours into one. And how are we to know that the particular state of the atmosphere is not necessary for the perception of the true colour of the real object?

If we hold that the shapes and colours we see exist in the brain, we are admitting that they exist in a real object just as much as if we hold that they belong to a tree or hill. The latter theory does not make the field of sensation any wider, for it is admitted that in any case we only see part of the size of the tree and a certain degree of its colour. The important

[1] *Op. cit.*, vol. ii. p. 199.

question is not whether we see anything real—for the brain, or what appears to others as the brain, is a real object as much as the tree or hill—but how we can know that anything else exists but the thing or part of the thing seen at the moment. Granting that the immediate object of sensation is the tree, or rather part of its size and a certain degree of its colour, how does this assure us that anything else exists, or that what we see now will continue to exist when we no longer see it? Certainly we cannot tell from sensation itself that the tree has an existence independent of sensation; supposing that it had, we could not know this from the mere fact that our perception of the tree was direct. Might not the real reason why we cease to perceive it after a time be simply this, that it ceased to exist? The only sound argument for believing that the objects we see remain when unseen is that the order apparent amid the disorder of their appearances would be impossible if they were not fragments of a large world, and if their discontinuous appearance were not events in a continuous existence. It is, in fact, just the same argument as I have already given for believing that other things exist besides those actually seen, even though these latter exist only in the brain. The supposition, then, that the shapes, sizes, and colours seen exist in the brain is just as good a foundation for knowledge as the supposition that they exist in the "real thing," the tree or hill, and, as Professor Alexander admits, it is very much simpler.

CHAPTER III

THE NATURE AND FORMS OF CONSCIOUSNESS

WE commonly speak as though there were two entities in sensation, the perceiver, or the act of perceiving, and the object of perception. The most elementary form of this idea is the belief that something vaguely called the mind exists in the head, and, looking through the eyes as through windows, sees things more or less distant. When this belief is abandoned it is supposed that the mind has before it a representation of the distant " real thing," or at least a picture formed by the action of the " real thing " *viâ* the light-waves and the nerves, whether like it or not. There is still some vagueness in the use of the word " mind," for sometimes it is taken to mean only the perceiver, the " subject " of sensation, sometimes to include also the object or " sensum," as it is often called. But this is not an important point, so long as it is clear which meaning is adopted in any particular argument. What is important is the dualism that distinguishes two sides in sensation, the subject and the object or sensum.

It is true that not very much is said nowadays about the former of these. The " subject " has become as unpopular in modern philosophy as the individual " soul," in the metaphysical sense of that word, and probably for the same reasons. If there are many separate minds in the world there must be so many separate subjects, and the origin of these and their entering into relation with the objects are as hard to understand as the origin of souls and their entry into bodies. At what moment in the history of the world did these subjects begin to exist, and at what moment in the history of each body does each particular subject come into being? Why at one moment rather than another? Why does it observe only these particular objects at any one time, and if the objects or sensa continue to exist when unobserved why does the subject cease to observe them ? Extension, it is thought, belongs only to the objects ; the subject must be non-spatial. How, then, can it be confined to the observation of objects within a particular area ? It is true that according to one theory the visual objects present to any mind are not continuous with the rest of the world but form a separate or " private " space. For reasons I shall give later on I do not agree with this theory; but even if it were true, I see no reason why any subject should observe only one such space.

We have also to ask whether the objects of one mind are always the same, like a number of pieces of coloured glass shifted about to form various designs, or new ones are continually presented. In the former case one would naturally identify the object with the brain, for the object is certainly extended and must be exceedingly complex to display so great a variety. If so, we cannot, of course, accept the theory just mentioned, that the objects seen by any mind form a "private" space, for the brain is obviously continuous with the rest of the spatial world. On the other hand, if new sensa are continually presented to us in sensation, the relation between them and the subject or sentient is much less intelligible. If they did not exist before they were sensed their creation is a mystery ; and if they did, their entering into relation with the sentient is equally hard to understand. For before they became objects to it they cannot have stood in any relation to it at all, since the subject is non-spatial ; and if one thing now stands in no relation to another it can never enter into communication with it, since there can be no conditions to fix the moment when it shall do so. The two would exist in different worlds. So there would be nothing to decide at what moment or by what sentient any object should be observed.

These objections are only valid against the theory that there are many subjects. They have no force against anyone who holds that consciousness is universal, and that there is but one subject of this consciousness ; for then there is no question of its origin, and as the whole world is continually its object there can be no entering of particular objects into relation with it at a particular time.

But the " subject," as I said, has become unpopular. It is

still disputed whether there are two elements in sensation, but the question is now put in this form, to quote from Professor Broad: "Are sensations analyzable into act of sensing and sensum?"[1] This question invites another; if there is an act of sensing, what is it that acts? There must surely be a sentient as well as a sensum. Every verb must have a "subject" in the grammatical sense, whether it has an object or not, and to speak of an act without an agent is a misuse of language. But if there is something that acts, *i.e.*, senses, we must call this the subject of sensation, and are thus brought back to the theory already discussed. Certainly that theory is more in accordance with popular belief, for the average man would declare that he was aware of himself as observing, not less than of the object observed. At any rate he would insist that an "act of sensing" was meaningless without a sentient. It is true that he might be brought to doubt the first assertion by such arguments as these: "If you are aware of yourself in sensation, as well as of the object, surely you yourself must then be an object of awareness. There are, then, three elements in sensation: you as perceiving yourself, you as perceived by yourself to be sensing, and the object of your sensation. Do you admit the existence of all three? And what is it that you perceive, when you perceive yourself to be having a sensation? The self in sensation appears to be void of all qualities, for these belong to the object; it merely acts, *i.e.*, senses. But how can you perceive an entity that has no qualities?"

Similar questions might be addressed to anyone who divides sensation into act of sensing and sensum, or object. Is there in sensation a consciousness of the act of sensing, as well as that act itself and its object? And what is this act of which there is consciousness? What additional element comes into existence when the object begins to be sensed? If it is something added to the object itself, a new quality, we cannot call it an act at all. But unless you admit the existence of a sentient there is nothing else to which this new element can belong as an attribute. It is often enough debated whether the sensum can exist without being sensed, but little is said of the more important question, on which the answer to the

[1] *Scientific Thought*, p. 254.

other depends, what this "act of sensing" means. Without the existence of a subject as well as an object it seems to me meaningless. The only attempt at an explanation I have seen is that made by Professor Broad. He suggests that "'getting sensed' may just mean 'coming into such relations with the somatic sense-history as to form a general sense-history.'"[1] The somatic or bodily sensations, he holds, may perhaps not be distinguishable into act of sensing and sensum, as are the sensations imparted from without, *e.g.* those of sight and hearing. The objects of these latter sensations, such as a patch of green or a note of music, "get sensed" when they become associated with the inner, bodily feelings, and the only known way in which they can become associated with these feelings is by occurring at the same time, " falling into a single Specious Present." Of this theory it may be remarked that " act of sensing " does not seem an appropriate term. There is no act directed upon the sensum ; all that happens is that the latter enters into relation with certain feelings of the body, and this entering into relation involves nothing more than existence at the same time. For what else is implied in the words " falling into a single Specious Present " ? If the sensa of sight and hearing were spatially continuous with the sensations of the body the theory would be clearer. But if there is nothing but co-existence in time how can particular sensa of sight and hearing become connected with the inner feelings of this body rather than that ? They are simultaneous with some feelings in every living body, or rather in everything that exists ; some further relation seems needed to unite them with one body in particular. In any case this co-existence is an inadequate reason for analyzing a sensation into act of sensing and sensum.

There seems, then, no ground for dividing a sensation into two elements, unless it be into objects and a universal subject of sensations. If consciousness exists everywhere it is improbable that there are a number of subjects, each observing a definite area, so that these areas fit together. The division of sensation into two elements arises from the connection of the five senses with that more complex form of consciousness, thought, or else with the inner consciousness generally, *i.e.*

[1] *Op. cit.*, p. 521.

thought and the feelings of the body. It may be asked what is meant by " inner " and " outer " consciousness. I think that the use of these terms may be explained and justified in this way. Our thoughts form a connected, self-determined series, and are generally accompanied by a uniform feeling of the state of the body, mainly of its temperature, a feeling that changes seldom or gradually. That is to say, there are very few abrupt transitions in thought or bodily feeling, and the two together form what we mean by the self. But the objects of the five senses—for I include touch as distinct from a feeling of temperature—are neither connected with one another nor uniform, and so their appearance is an interruption in the harmony of the self. One may compare thought to a picture, the feeling of the body to a simple frame, and the external sensations to Futuristic designs on the wall-paper around it. The picture and the frame harmonize together into a whole much more than the wall-paper harmonizes with them; the paper, in fact, is much the most " external." This explanation seems to me confirmed by the variations in our feelings of inwardness and outwardness. The music we hear often appears to us after a while to be as much a part of ourselves as our thoughts ; it does not seem to come from outside. This is probably because the music, like thought, is a " connected, self-determined series," one sound appearing as the natural consequence of the sounds before it. Again, when we have heard the same sound for a long time it does not appear as something external, because it is as uniform as the feeling of the body. When we subdue our thoughts, too, and give ourselves up to contemplation of a picture or landscape we make no distinction of " inner " and " outer." And in these cases I do not think we have any idea that there are two elements in the sensation, subject or act of sensing and object or sensum. On the other hand, an abrupt change in the bodily feeling, breaking its uniformity, though not caused by anything outside the body, appears to us just as external as an object of sight or a blow. It is true that the change may appear to take place in the body—though this is not always so in dreams—yet it appears as external to the self. In that case we do analyze the sensation into feeler or feeling and the thing felt.

Another reason why we divide sensation into two elements

is the belief of each man that the things he sees exist " over there," while he himself exists here. When he abandons the belief in the spatial separation of perceiver and perceived he is less inclined to make the division. But the chief cause, as I said, is the association of the five senses with the self, *i.e.*, the thought and bodily feeling. The two elements do not exist in the sensation; they are the sensation and the self as thus defined. This theory resembles Professor Broad's, but adds thought to the feeling of the body, and must now add co-existence in space to co-existence in time as another necessary form of association. The attributing of existence in space to thought and sensation is something of a paradox in philosophy, but seems to me justified for several reasons.

If our sensations and thoughts do not exist in one space, how can they become associated together in what we call one mind? Co-existence in time, as I said, is obviously not enough. Are they united by being present to one subject or soul? But the belief that there are individual subjects or souls is exposed to all the difficulties I have mentioned already. What else is there that can unite particular sights with particular sounds, or both with a certain series of thoughts? If sensations and thoughts were purely qualitative one would expect to find all the sounds of one quality all over the world combined into one mind, and all those of another quality into another; the phenomena of sight would never be associated with those of hearing, but the various colours would form a separate series of minds or conscious units. The sensations of red all over the world would be much more closely united in one state of consciousness than any sensation of red with any sound. In order to account for the way in which the events of consciousness are combined we must suppose that there is something quantitative in them as well as quality; and as that quantitative element is obviously not intensity, for sensations of the same intensity are not necessarily joined together, it must be extension, *i.e.*, the smallness of the extent or distance between them, their continuity in space.

The causes of any man's sensations exist within a limited area. But this fact, of course, would not join the sensations together and make them the sensations of one man, if these did not also co-exist within a certain region. Otherwise why should not the same mind at the same time hear the ringing of a bell in Moscow and see the Statue of Liberty at New York? At least it might hear a bell in Moscow at the same time as one in New York, the two sensations being of the same kind. For if the two sensations did not exist in space, as their causes do, but were purely qualitative, what could it matter how far apart their causes were? But in fact we only experience sensations caused by events within the same limited area. If you imagine that the sensations themselves exist out of space, they lose this one form of unity, co-existence in space, and certainly they have no other, since in other respects they are quite different and disconnected.

It seems to me quite clear from this that the sensations of each man exist in the centre of the area within which their causes exist, and consequently that they all have extension. For a similar reason it follows that this is true of our thoughts also. Why should a particular series of thoughts be affected only by sensations within the same restricted area, if they themselves were outside the spatial world? If thoughts were purely qualitative one would expect to find them affected only by sensations that had the same qualitative relation to one another or to the thoughts themselves, whereas they are continually interrupted by quite irrelevant sights and sounds that happen to be near together. Again, our thoughts and purposes, like any extended bodies, can only act upon the same limited area, and this limitation is unintelligible if they do not exist anywhere in particular. How can they change the mutual relations and the movements of extended bodies, if they themselves have no place or extension?

Again, the memory of a sound often calls up the memory of a sight or feeling associated with it. Since there is no likeness between the sight and sound the recall of the latter is hard to understand, unless there is some non-qualitative relation between the two. It can be explained by assuming that the memory-images of both exist in the same area of the brain, and the belief that memories do exist in the brain is strongly supported by the way in which they are affected by injuries to that organism. If memory-images, then, exist at a certain place the same may safely be inferred of the original sensations.

There is another argument used, if I remember right, by Ribot, to prove that sensations and thoughts must exist in space. Just as proximity in space is necessary to combine sensations of different qualities into one mind, so separation in space is needed to distribute sensations identical in quality into different minds. If there is no such separation, how is one mind distinct from another? There must be something to distinguish them, and if this is not their distance from one another in space it must be something qualitative. Perhaps no two minds have consisted at any time of exactly the same sensations and thoughts, but it is not inconceivable that there should be two thus identical in quality. Most men would be quite ready to believe that it had often happened. In such a case could we speak of "two minds" any longer? If there is no distinction, either by distance in space or by difference of quality, the "two" are obviously one and the same thing.[1] Again, suppose that the minds were only slightly different in their qualitative character; if they are not separated from one another by distance in space we must infer that a slight change in quality would make them one, and that is incredible. It would imply that only a small and unessential difference had made them two before; that essentially they were one. Even if you do not admit that the whole of any mind is ever identical with any other in quality, you must admit that parts of two minds—for instance, a sound in each—may sometimes be the same. In that case are there two sounds or one? Surely, if there is no separation in space, there is only one sound, which is related to two sets of accompanying sensations and thoughts. This would, of course, be true also of the same thought in two minds. If there were no separation in space, it would be literally one and the same thought; it could not even be called two instances of the same thought, since there would be nothing to distinguish the instances. The thought would be in relation with two distinct series of thoughts and sensations, but there is nothing to prevent one thing from standing in a relation to many different sets of things.

---

[1] It is interesting to recall here the Leibnitzian principle of "the identity of indiscernibles," and the 5th Proposition of Spinoza's *Ethics*, that there cannot be two substances with the same attribute.

If you believe that there can be two thoughts or sensations of the same quality, or two instances of the same thought or sensation, you must suppose that they are distinguished and made two by existence in different places, by their distance from one another. It is useless to say that they may be distinguished by belonging to different minds, for how are the minds distinguished except by having, or rather being, different thoughts and sensations? You may imagine that besides the thoughts and sensations there are subjects which form and experience them, but as the subjects have nothing in themselves to distinguish them—since they are different from the entities they form and experience—there is nothing to mark them off from one another and make them many. There could only be one.

A similar argument might be advanced against the theory that there are "private" spaces, *i.e.*, that each mind has before it in sensation a space of its own, not contained within a wider space including all others. If that were true, how could these spaces be distinguished from one another? Both their extent and their contents, the shapes and the colours within them, might be the same. If one were larger than another, then they would be at least partly the same: the one would be included within the other. And could one suppose that the two spaces were distinguished by their quality, *i.e.*, by the patches of colour in them, when one knew that these colours might at any moment become the same, in which event there would be no longer any distinction, and the two would become one? There is nothing to prevent two men from having exactly the same sensation, and even if this had never actually happened, it is quite certain that two men often have sensations very nearly the same. That being so, it surely cannot be the very slight difference that makes their "private" spaces two. They must be distinguished from one another by separation in a wider space. To speak of two spaces as "private" is not to distinguish them, but to make them identical, by giving them a common attribute; or rather, since the word "private" is purely negative, it is to remove any means of distinguishing them, or any reason for doing so. It is paradoxical but true that their union in one space is the only thing that makes them two.

To return to the subject of the existence of minds in space, it is certain, if space exists at all, that spatial entities cause our sensations. The idea of causality implies a relation in time; the cause immediately precedes the effect. But I do not see how there can be any temporal relation unless there is also co-existence in space. One event is simultaneous with another, because the two are parts of one state of a whole. When you think of an event taking place in India at the same time as an event in the United States, you imagine a picture or rather a series of pictures of the whole world stretched out before you, and the two events as included as one in the series. If one of two events existed in space and the other not, they would be parts of different worlds, and the statement that one came before the other, or at the same time, could have no meaning. It may be replied that we perceive a sight and a sound to be simultaneous, although we perceive no spatial relation between them. I do not believe this: I think we have an idea of the space around us as being filled with the sound, though just because it seems to exist everywhere around us we do not " place " it so definitely as the colours and shapes presented to us by sight. We cannot be content with saying that they are simultaneous because they are both parts of one state of one mind, for we must explain what it is that makes the mind or its state one. In any case such an argument could not, on the usual theory, apply to the relation between cause and sensation, since the cause is not a state of the mind to which the sensation belongs, unless you suppose that they are both parts of a universal mind. It is true that they are so, for the world is one and everywhere conscious. But the events in this mind could not form a single time series unless they were united by existence in the same space, since there is no other form of union that could make events everywhere parts of one state of one and the same thing. If, then, sensations and the events which we describe as their causes did not co-exist in space we could not say that these events immediately preceded sensations, and consequently we should have no right to say that they caused these. For causality is impossible where there is no relation in time.

The community of time which most men believe to unite

our minds and the rest of the world is interesting from another point of view. If there were no such community, if the events in each mind formed a separate time series, how should we explain the connection between the consciousness of to-day and that of to-morrow? It is generally supposed that in the interval caused by sleep there is no consciousness of any kind. If that were so, and if the events in each man's mind formed a private time, and were not contained within the one " public " time of the whole world, how could there be any interval of time between his thoughts and sensations just before he falls asleep and those he has as soon as he awakes? It would be as though all movement in the world were to cease and then begin again; would there be any time between the cessation and the recommencement of motion? Evidently there could be none, for time is meaningless apart from movement and events. I ought not even to have spoken of " ceasing " and " beginning again," for there would be no pause. The whole supposition is in fact, though it might not seem so, a contradiction in terms. For a similar reason a pause in consciousness during sleep would also be impossible, if that consciousness formed a " private " time. There could not be a part of that private time in which nothing happened; events are necessary for time, but what event would there be during sleep?

Such a consciousness could never begin or end, for that would imply an earlier and a later time at which it did not exist, and that is impossible, for the only time is the series of movements in the mind. These considerations, which will seem metaphysical in the worst sense of the word to those who believe in one universal time, have real force against some philosophies. For instance, I do not see how Kant could have explained the interruption of consciousness which is generally supposed to occur during sleep, since for him there is no universal time; in fact he would have a harder task than others, for he regards time as a form imposed by the mind on the states of consciousness. But all individualists in philosophy may well be asked what meaning they can give to the interruption, for if there are many minds, essentially separate, one general or " public " time is impossible. They might escape this difficulty by accepting the theory that all minds are conscious to some extent even during sleep, which I believe to be true. But they would find it impossible to explain the origin of a mind, or its ending, if they believed it to end.

Those who believe that there is one " public " time—which does not imply that differences in measuring it are impossible—must hold that all events are temporally related. But a temporal relation is impossible without co-existence in space ; and I think all men do more or less consciously suppose different minds to be so united with one another and with the rest of the world. Each has a feeling that not only the body but the thoughts and sensations of his neighbour exist " over there," and that the inhabitants of different countries not only move but think in those countries.

The action of the mind upon the body is also unintelligible if they do not both exist in space. In that case one would expect to find each of them moving in its own world, unaffected by the other. According to the doctrine of psycho-physical parallelism that is what actually happens ; the efferent nerves along which our action passes to the outer world are not moved by our thoughts but by a physical process in the brain corresponding to our thoughts. But how can there be any correspondence or parallelism of spatial and non-spatial entities ? The extension and movement of the former are essential elements of their existence, and if the two worlds are to correspond there must be something in the mind analogous to extension. But of extension it may be said with truth :

> None but itself can be its parallel.

Instead of attributing to the mind some property similar at all points to spatiality, it is the simplest course to suppose that the mind is spatial.

The fact that sensations of hearing, for instance, do not appear to be spatial, may well be attributed to the structure of the auditory organs, which prevents us from perceiving two sounds side by side and confuses many sounds into one. If sight presented to us a series of colours existing only one at a time, a series of flashes of light differing in intensity, we should never have come to regard these colours as extended. Yet for all that they would be so, for to have spatial sensations it is not necessary to be aware in thought of their extension. We may represent the senses to ourselves as five small windows in a dark room. Through one of them we can see many shapes and colours side by side, or one above the other; through the others we can only see one colour at a time, and no shape except that of the window itself, which always remains the same. In their case, therefore, the idea of extension does not arise, for that requires juxtaposition and the comparison of shapes and sizes. We cannot perceive any spatial relation between the windows, for to do that it would be necessary that our attention should be able to pass continuously from one to the other, and though there must be some form of consciousness in the interval between them, it may be supposed that this is too low to attract our thought, or too confused for such passage. It is like the darkened but not wholly dark room which is seen but not noticed when our attention is occupied with the figures on the lighted screen. Perhaps we could observe the intervals of darker consciousness between the five senses if there were any passages across them, nerves to link the areas of clearer consciousness; but the want of these makes it impossible.

It is an even greater paradox to suggest that not only is all consciousness spatial, but if " material bodies "—which on our theory, of course, are all areas of consciousness—are atomic in structure, the same must be true of minds. But it is a logical conclusion from the generally accepted doctrine that material bodies are the causes of our sensations. If the brain is a multitude of minute elements, then, even if you believe the mind not to be the reality which appears as the brain, but to undergo its action, you must suppose that each minute element acts upon the mind. Could all their activities be combined into one simple result, producing a state of consciousness in which there was nothing corresponding to the multiplicity of distinct causes? It is true that the attraction exerted by many atoms on one produces a simple result, the one path which the atom follows. But it would seem strange that the elements of matter, which must possess some quality themselves and be distinguished from one another by intervals of empty space or of some extended quality, should produce a continuous patch of one colour. If they themselves with their various qualities are the objects of our sensations, these obviously cannot be continuous; if they create the objects, why are not these as discrete as their creators? Is the simplicity of the result due to their concentrating their activities on one simple substance, as they do in attracting each atom? I cannot imagine what sort of relation there could be between this simple substance and the many elements, unless it were that of subject and objects. If the substance is spatial, one would expect that only the usual relations between extended bodies would obtain between it and the others. If it is not spatial, why is it affected only by the events within a limited area? The theory that the "individual mind" is such an entity is exposed to all the criticisms already brought against the belief in "individual subjects." Besides, if many atoms could combine to produce simple, continuous sensations of five kinds, it would seem more natural that all their actions upon the mind should unite to form a single result, one kind of sensation alone; that at least those which cause our sensations of sight should at each moment produce only one colour.

There appears to be a certain delicacy among modern philosophers which prevents them from bringing their theories of mind into sharp contact with the theories of matter favoured by natural science. Those who hold that we see directly the "real tree" or the "real table" do not take into consideration the fact that if they and the scientists are right we must perceive directly a countless swarm of atoms. This must also be true, of course, if it is the brain, or rather the reality appearing to others as the brain, that is the immediate object of sense. Certainly it is permissible to argue that the atomic theory is false and that the matter forming the tree or table or brain is continuous, but one must not ignore the subject altogether. A great many hard things have been said of the atoms; some, reversing the famous saying of Democritus, declare them to be "merely conventions," convenient symbols without any reality corresponding to them in the external world. Such a use of the word "symbol" is meaningless; and the atomic theory is only convenient because it helps us to account for the facts, which is as good an argument as one could have for its truth. It might, indeed, be called the only argument for the existence of anything. I do not believe that Nature has formed a conspiracy to deceive us into the idea

NATURE AND FORMS OF CONSCIOUSNESS 83

that there are atoms. But those who accept the current theories of matter must try to explain the relation between its ultimate elements and the human mind.

If they also admit that consciousness is universal they will define matter, if they keep the word at all, as the less intense or less complex areas of consciousness outside the minds of living beings, and hold that all consciousness, including these minds, is composed of innumerable spatial elements, all alike parts of one and the same Being and here and there joined in closer and more organic union than is found in most of the universe. The presence of countless elements in every one of our sensations and thoughts will not easily be admitted, but without that admission it is impossible to form an idea of the human mind that can be fitted to the scientists' picture of the rest of the world. It does not follow that if there are really so many entities in consciousness we ought to be able to perceive them directly, since for perception it is necessary that we should be able to fix our attention upon the object, and our attention cannot be called into activity by each one of these entities singly. Besides, the elements of consciousness are in continual movement; but only those things can be observed which for some time are at rest, or in their movement continually leave some trace behind of their previous course. We do not see the shape of a moving ball; what we see is a line of colour of a certain thickness. If the ball left in our sight space no images of itself in its previous positions we should not see any definite outline at all; it is the line of these images we see, because for a time, however short, they occupy the same part of our sight space, *i.e.*, they are at rest there. There can be no instantaneous sight, for an instant is no time at all; we cannot, then, see the shape of the ball " at each instant " of the movement. Now the atoms of consciousness are never at rest, but leave no trace of previous positions in their movement, and therefore it is not possible to observe them singly; we can only see and feel an aggregate of them as a whole, for only aggregates of them are at rest for any time.

Of sensation in general, then, it may be said that it is not composed of sentient, *i.e.*, subject, or act of sensing on one side and sensum or object on another; and of consciousness in general, that it is spatial and composed of innumerable elements too small to be directly observed. The reasons why we infer the causes of our sensations to be spatial and atomistic are derived from the sensations themselves; it would be strange if they could give us information about properties which they did not themselves possess. And as it is not to be believed that human consciousness arises from the void, as we must take it to be an extract from the rest of the world, which existed before it and exists around it, the natural conclusion is that it is of the same character.

With regard to particular senses there are several points to be considered. One of them resembles a subject mentioned in the previous chapter; it is the question whether we have in sight any direct perception of a third dimension. Is there a sense of distance outwards from us, as there is of the distance between two objects, *i.e.*, patches of colour, that are side by side, or one above the other? It may be asked also whether there is a sense of solidity, but this is really the same question, for no one imagines that we experience in sight the depth or thickness of a globe, for instance, along a straight line outwards from the eye. There is certainly no appearance of one part directly behind another. But it might seem that one part of the globe, which appears not directly behind but to the right or left of another, also appears farther off.

This is not the same as the question whether a man has a direct perception of the " real " distance between him and an external object. The parts of a carefully shaded disc may look just like the parts of a globe, and a smooth wall may be so coloured as to look as though it contained figures in relief. In such cases it might be said that there was a sense of distance in the visual image, although the distance did not belong to the real world outside our consciousness. It is true that the consideration of such cases will probably shake most men in their belief that sight has a third dimension. But most men have at some time in their lives discovered that things which do not exist in the outer world may really exist in sensation, so that they may be prepared to admit that the visual image of a disc varies in distance, although the disc itself does not.

Those who deny that in the visual image there is a third

dimension, outward distance, argue that the belief in its presence is due to previous sensations of touch and movement. These have informed us that an object on which the light is distributed in a certain way, as on a globe, is spherical, and not a disc, *i.e.*, that one part of it is farther off than another. A man does not directly see different distances of different parts of the globe, but has a feeling that he could touch some parts of it sooner and more easily than others. So, too, if he sees a tree along a road, there is in the visual image no sense of the distance between him and the tree. But from the size and clearness or faintness of the image he has a feeling of the effort that would be needed to reach it, since he has walked to a tree that presented the same size and clearness to him before. A blind man might have the same idea of the distance of the objects around him. And if it were possible for a man's arms and legs to become suddenly lengthened his perception of the distance of objects would change in time, although their images in sight remained the same.

On the other hand, it is maintained that a sense of outward distance in sight is an obvious fact of experience. It may be due to the effect produced on the mind by previous feelings of touch and movement, but it is certainly visual, and not identical with the memory of those feelings, or with the sense of effort necessary.

I agree with the former view, for these reasons :—

1. The light-waves from a distant object cannot, when they affect the retina, convey any information of the distance over which they have travelled. They may impress upon it images side by side or one above the other, and the impressions they make may vary in clearness, but there can be no more indication of distance in these than there is in the effect produced by any material object upon another. The impact of a bullet does not depend upon the distance it has travelled, but on its velocity in the moment before it strikes. The rest of its course makes no difference except indirectly, by affecting this velocity. The effect would be just the same if it had been shot out from a shorter distance but with less force. If sight, then, depends on the way in which the retina is affected, it cannot contain any sign of outward distance. Some who admit this argue that our previous experiences of

touch and movement actually affect the sensations of sight, and do not only produce an idea of distance accompanying the sensations. Professor Broad, for instance, suggests that "the physiological conditions of any visual sensation include (a) a set of brain-states which correspond by transmission to the events in an excited area of the retina; and (b) certain brain-states which are independent of the present retinal stimulus. Among the latter are traces left by past experiences of sight, touch, movement, etc.; and these play an important part in determining the particular visual distance that a given visual sensum shall have."[1] In this case the experience of distance is a part of the sensation not given from without but from within, and it becomes difficult to distinguish such a part from an idea that accompanies the sensation. It is often absent from the sensation, and we can always exclude it at will by turning our attention away without turning our eyes; we then still have the same sizes and colours before us, but none of them appears farther off than another. It seems to me that only the sizes and shapes, of which we cannot be rid by any purely mental effort, should be called parts of the sensation, and that the distance, the presence of which to our minds depends on the attention, should be called an idea.

2. If I look down a road at a line of lamp-posts or trees, it is not a sensation of distance that tells me that they stand at equal intervals from one another, that the fifth, for instance, is just so much farther off from me than the fourth, as the tenth is farther off than the ninth. The clearness or faintness of the images of the lamp-posts gives me some idea of their distances, but my knowledge mainly comes from the fact that their highest and lowest points lie along two straight lines converging together. The idea of the equality of distance is derived from this element of the sensation, and not from any equality of distance in it.

I may put it in another way by saying that all our ideas of the distances of objects from us are derived from the same properties of sensation as those which we find in a picture, *i.e.*, from size, intensity of colouring, and perspective. That is to say, it comes from nothing that is not two-dimensional. But if there really were any outward distances in sensation,

[1] *Scientific Thought*, p. 297.

surely we should appeal to these in order to judge of the equality of such distances, and not form our judgment from the two-dimensional elements of sight.

3. When we speak of a sensation of outward distance we must answer the question: " Distance from what point ? " From the body ? But if any images have an appearance of distance, so have those of any part of the body we can see. From what point do their images in sight appear to be distant ? As for the parts of the body we cannot see, obviously none of them can be the starting-point from which we see distance. To meet this objection Professor Broad suggests that " we should distinguish between visual *depth* and visual distance. Depth is a visual quality, not a sensible relation. Visual distance is a sensible relation between two visual sensa, *founded upon* the difference of their respective visual depths." [1] But if depth is a quality, can one talk of the " distance " between two objects which differ in their depth ? We do not talk of the " distance " between two objects that differ in any other quality, as between two roses of which one is redder than the other. Such a definition agrees even less with the popular theory than the view which substitutes for the " sensation " of distance an idea, due to previous sensations of touch, sight, and movement. The popular theory maintains that we see distance outward from something which is certainly not one of the objects seen ; it is true that it never attempts to define what that " something " is, but contents itself with the vague phrase " from here." This supports the view that the sense of distance does not exist in sight, but is an accompanying feeling of the effort, the movement, that would be needed by the beholder in order to touch the object, or to see its " real " size. It is a feeling for which sight is not necessary, for a blind man might have it towards the objects in a room or street with which he was familiar.

4. Even if we did fix on some object A, presumably a part of the body, and declare that it was distance from this object that we meant when we talked of seeing the distance of other objects B, C, D, we could not mean that we actually saw the interval between A and the others as we see the interval

[1] *Op. cit.*, p. 298.

between two bodies that stand side by side, or one above the other. Certainly we do not see the distance to a wall as we see that between two pictures on the wall. In the former case we cannot look along and measure directly with our eyes the amount of space between. It follows that sight must be two-dimensional, and all talk of outward distance in sight is meaningless, except in a very " Pickwickian " sense.

What has been said of sight must be equally true of hearing. And of course the perception of distance in hearing can only depend on the intensity of the sound and on our knowledge of the objects in the neighbourhood. Voices heard from a considerable height " sound " quite near simply because they sound as clearly as though they were speaking a few feet away; there is nothing else in the sensation itself to tell of distance but this clearness. It is accompanied by the ideas of the size and clearness with which the speakers would appear to us if we could see them, and of the amount of movement necessary before we could reach them. This account of the matter seems so evident as to furnish an additional argument to those who deny that " the sense of distance " in sight is anything but an idea produced by previous sensations of sight, touch, and the movement of our bodies.

To come next to the sense of external movement, there are the same changes of position in our sight space when we turn round as there would be if the whole scene before us began to move round us in a circle. What difference would there be between our sensations in these two cases ? In the first, but not in the second, we have the feeling of the movement of our own bodies, and that seems to be the decisive factor in the distinction we make. In the second case we often have a feeling of the movement of our eyes as they follow the moving object, but this feeling is not always present. Between the visual sensations there is no difference at all. How entirely the sense of external movement depends on the absence of any feeling of bodily movement is evident from the fact that when we are in a moving train or aeroplane and have no such feeling the objects passed seem to be moving, and not we ourselves. If you turn your head from side to side in front of a window-pane, defects in the glass may displace some of the objects seen from a lower to a higher position in your sight space ; they will then seem to move upwards, simply because you have no feeling of lowering your head or any other movement of yours that would account for the vertical displacement. But you are aware of the movement of your head from side to side, and therefore the objects do not seem to move horizontally, though their position in your sight space may shift from left to right. From this it is clear that we have an idea rather than a sensation of external movement, as of outward distance. When we turn our heads the objects change from position to position in our visual space, but we have an idea of places, not identical with those of our visual space, in which the objects remain fixed ; when the head is kept still but the objects move we have the idea that they change their position not only in our visual space but in a wider space independent of it, in which our visual space itself can move. Without this idea of a space independent of our sensations we could not draw any distinction between the two cases. The feeling of bodily movement cannot have created the distinction for us, but determines our use of it.

To pass from the perception of space to that of time, it may be asked whether in memory we see the past directly or have before us only images of past events. This corresponds to the question whether in sight we have a direct sensation of the real things themselves or only of their images in the brain, and as Bergson points out, whatever answer we give to the one will determine our answer to the other. I have already given the reasons for believing that the immediate objects of our sensations are not the things themselves but their impressions on the brain, and the same line of argument will prove that the objects of our memories are not the past events but the traces they have left in our minds.

If we perceived the past event itself why should it appear so faint in our memory ? It is a long way off in time, but either it still exists there in all its vividness, or does not exist at all ; you must not imagine it as still existing in its own time, but growing ever fainter and fainter. As the distance between a man looking at a tree and the tree itself does not affect the latter in any way, so the time between us and an event cannot make this any the less intense. It would seem, then, that all the objects of our memories should be as clear as when they were present to our sensations. For reasons similar to those given in the appendix to the previous chapter, it is impossible to suppose that we see a part of their intensity. And if you hold that the present state of the brain modifies and determines the perception of past events, you have to assume that there is in the brain something corresponding to every detail of the event so far as it is remembered. If so, it is much more natural to suppose that it is this model in the brain that we perceive, and not the event itself.

Besides, how can a man now perceive an event existing then, across the gap of time separating observer and observed? There are some who divide memory into a present act and a past object, a division which seems to me inconceivable. For instance, Professor Alexander tells us that "remembering and expecting do occur at the present, but we are not entitled, therefore, to declare their objects simultaneous with the present. To be apprehended as a memory in the act of remembering simultaneously with an act of present perception is not to be apprehended as simultaneous with the 'present' object. The simple deliverance of experience is that it is apprehended as past."[1] From this we gather that the act of remembering is present, while the memory, *i.e.*, the object of the act, is past. But what meaning has the word "act" here? It is evidently open to the same criticism as the phrase "act of sensing," which I have already considered. Normally a transitive action implies that a certain state of one thing is followed by a certain state of another, but that is certainly not true here. Is there a subject which perceives the memory-object, and if so what properties has this subject? It is not necessary to repeat the arguments against the existence of such an entity. On the other hand, if we accepted as true the sentences just quoted, we could not explain "act of remembering" in the same way as the "act of sensing." The latter we took to mean the temporal and spatial co-existence of the sensum with the more uniform and permanent feelings of the body and with thought. But we are not allowed to assume any such co-existence of the memory-object

[1] *Time, Space, and Deity*, vol. i. p. 117.

with those forms of consciousness, for it is distant from them both in time and space. I can find no meaning, then, in this dualism of past memory-object and present act of remembering.

Again, if we perceived the object as past surely we should have to perceive the interval of time between it and us as we are now, and it is quite evident that we do not. Even if we did, we should only perceive it as distant, not as past. There is no attribute of " pastness " that can belong to an event ; to say that the present becomes past is in fact meaningless, for we cannot mean by this that the event exchanges one predicate for another. It cannot have existed in the past as present, and also exist in the present as past. Each event exists in its own time, and not in any other as past or future. The belief that there is such a thing as pastness or futurity is one of the many absurdities into which the idea of succession in time leads us. Even if we did perceive the real past, then we could not perceive it *as* " past." There will be more to say on this subject when we come to consider the idea of succession in time.

Our present thoughts and actions are evidently affected by our memories, and that not only by the act of remembering, an act always the same, but by the various objects or contents of memory. How would that be possible if the objects existed in the past, at a distance in time from our present thoughts and actions ? "The burnt child dreads the fire," but if the real object of its memory is the past sensation of burning, which does not exist now, how can that sensation influence the child's mind and hands now ? A movement may act upon another movement which follows it immediately, but how can a distant event suddenly wake into activity, an activity exerted upon the present across a gulf of time ? Besides, those who hold that the object of memory is a past event also hold that the object of sensation is the actual thing or person outside us, not an image in the brain. From this theory it follows that the real object of memory is often not something that occurred in us at a past moment, for all that occurred in us was just the act of perceiving, an act which is the same in all perceptions. What differentiates our perceptions, and consequently our memories, is the real thing or person at some distance from us. When any recollection, then, causes a present action, the cause is always two stages removed from us; it is distant from us in time, and distant from the place where we were at that time. It is not simply far off from us along the same street, but some way round a distant corner. We are not allowed to say that the past object imprinted an image of itself upon the brain, and that this image has remained; we are to believe that it acts upon us now directly, not through any representation of itself. But such action at a distance is quite incredible.

Professor Bergson's account of memory may seem to be relevant here, but is not in fact the same as that just criticized. I have left the discussion of his *Matière et Mémoire* to a later chapter dealing with his philosophy in general.

CHAPTER IV

SUBSTANCE AND PERSONALITY

I. WE speak of a thing as "having" certain qualities, for which it may substitute others while itself remaining the same. For instance, the colour of a leaf goes through several changes during the year, and yet we regard it as the same leaf in spring, summer, and autumn. The size of every living body increases and its elements change, yet most of us, ignorant and forgetful of metabolism, suppose that every man retains at least that one garment throughout life. If the thing itself, then, remains the same throughout the changes of its qualities, its colour and size, it must be distinct from these; in fact this is implied in our saying that it "has" or "possesses" them. But what is the thing itself, as distinct from its qualities? Could it continue to exist if it had none? All that we ever experience is a variety of colours, hardnesses, shapes, sizes, etc., which are said to belong to things; we never come across the entities to which they are said to belong. Instead of saying that a "thing" occupies a certain space, why should we not say that a colour or some other quality occupies it? For we have seen that there must be qualities in space wherever we suppose "things" to exist; otherwise these "things" could not be distinguished from one another or from the void around them, if there is a void. What need or right have we to suppose anything to exist there, except a certain quality or qualities extended over a definite area, or, to put it in another way, a certain extent of some quality?

The "thing" is regarded as a single entity holding several qualities together; at least that is what is implied in the subject and predicate form of ordinary language. But in that case we cannot, of course, call the objects we see "things," for these are not single entities but collections of many elements, atoms, brought close together for a time. If there were some one entity that united these elements and entitled us to speak of them in the singular, what would become of this when they dispersed? The only real things, apart from the world taken as a whole, are those which by massing together form a visible object, *i.e.*, the ultimate elements of matter, whatever name we may give to them. And there is no evidence that each of these consists of more than one quality occupying a certain space.[1] But even if there were several qualities occupying the same area this would not prove that there was one " thing " or " substance " which possessed and united them all. For the fact that in motion they all changed their place together would merely be due to the fact that, as they were all in the same area originally, the same force was brought to bear upon them, with the same results in the velocity and direction of movement of all. All that is needed for their unity, then, is existence in the same place.

If several qualities could be united merely by the fact that they were all possessed by one " thing," there would be no reason why they should all have to exist in one particular area of space before we could attribute them to the same possessor. Why should it not " have " one quality here and another a thousand miles away? As we do not imagine this to be possible, we must infer that the essential property implied in " belonging to one thing " is co-existence in space.

The idea of a " thing " possessing several qualities is partly due to the different impressions produced indirectly by one and the same external body on our different senses. We imagine all these qualities to exist " over there," in the tree or house or whatever it may be. As has already been shown, that is not true; the colour and other qualities attributed to the external object really exist here, in the mind of the observer. This is true even of hardness and softness, which to many seem most evidently to belong to the object. The sensation of hardness is nothing but the feeling of the energy we are exerting, joined with the feeling that it is impossible to move

---

[1] *Cf.* Professor Alexander, *Time, Space, and Deity*, vol. i. p. 275: " The qualities of a substance do not interpenetrate. . . ."

farther the finger or hand or other part of the body in contact with the object.

Another reason for the belief in things apart from qualities is that the former alone are thought to be capable of acting upon one another. But all that is implied in action is that a certain state of A under definite conditions and according to a definite law is followed by a certain state of B, and this might apply to the changes of qualities as easily as to those mysterious entities called " things " which are said to possess them. By " state of A " I mean nothing but the quality existing in a particular place A, which is succeeded by another or alters its place when there is an alteration of quality at B, or when a certain extent of some quality comes into contact with A. When we say that one thing acts upon another, all that we see is an extent of colour changing its place, or vanishing altogether and leaving another in its stead, and all changes are of the same kind. If a state of A, *i.e.*, of a particular extent of some quality, is followed by a certain state of B, this is just the same as the change of A itself from the state a^1 to a^2. We do not talk of a force passing from a^1 to a^2, nor should we talk of a force passing from A to B. It is commonly asserted that a man feels the transition of force from himself to things, but obviously that is impossible; to do that he would have to feel the force first in himself and then in the thing on which he was acting. All that he does feel is a movement in himself, or a certain state or quality of consciousness. The same is true of the idea that a man feels a force directed from some object upon himself; the shock is not the feeling of that object or of its state but of something in himself.

But the notion that there is something besides qualities is very firmly rooted in the human mind through its three strata of language, logic, and metaphysics. It is in this notion that we can most easily trace the connection between the three, for the " noun " or " substantive " and " adjective " of grammar obviously correspond to the " subject " and " predicate " of logic, and to the " substance " and " attribute " or " thing " and " quality " of the metaphysicians. The pairs of words are only different expressions of one and the same conception. The idea of a " substance " or " thing " appears to be confirmed by the fact that the quality, a colour, for instance, in a certain space changes after a certain time, while the size and shape remain the same. One colour passes out of existence there and another takes its place; yet we cannot suppose that nothing of what was there before remains now; it would be strange that another colour of the same size and shape should always appear the instant after the old one has gone. But that which remains throughout the change need not be a " substance " distinct from any quality. When, for instance, the colour green departs and yellow appears in its place, that which is common to both of them, colour in general, as opposed to its particular forms, remains all the time. It is this that is the true substance underlying the changes. So, too, if colour gave place to some other quality, the universal, quality in general, would be permanent. Again, if different qualities existed in one place, we should say that this universal existed in certain of its forms there, as it exists in every place. We should not need to suppose any other entity as uniting them.

Akin to the doctrine of things that " have " qualities is the belief that there are individual souls which " have " sensations and thoughts. The word " soul " is not popular among metaphysicians nowadays, but other words such as " mind " or " subject " or " ego " or " self " have been used in a way which either implies the same meaning or else has no meaning at all. If you talk of a mind or subject that combines its perceptions into a concept evidently you are distinguishing it from that upon which it works. The sheer force of every-day language compels men to make the metaphysical subject a logical subject too, and so a substance, with thoughts and sensations as its predicates. But is the mind anything but the series of thoughts, emotions, sensations, and memories co-existing in space, determined by one another and their surroundings, and raised and distinguished from their surroundings, which are also conscious, by the greater intensity and complexity of their consciousness? That they do exist in space I have argued in the previous chapter. All the thoughts and sensations of any mind are the result of events —light-waves, sound-waves, etc.—directed upon a particular area. What other form of co-existence is possible besides their co-existence in one place, their likeness of quality and intensity, which, as I said, distinguishes them from their immediate surroundings, including the sleeping memories? I have already pointed out the objections to the idea that there is an individual soul or subject for every mind; the origin of such an entity and its limitation to a particular area would be unintelligible mysteries. Besides, as it is supposed to experience and unify many sensations and thoughts, it must be distinct from all these. Its only character is to be the subject of different forms of consciousness; that is to say, in itself it has no differentiæ. One soul or subject, then, will be exactly like another. There will be nothing to distinguish this one from that, for they are not supposed to exist at different places, in which case they would have to be extended, and not merely " have " extension as a quality, *i.e.*, something different from themselves. It follows that there cannot be many in the world but only one. The same argument might of course be applied to all the " things " regarded as different from their qualities.

The fifth Proposition of Bk. I. of Spinoza's *Ethics* may be quoted here in support and illustration of the argument. " In the nature of things, two or more things may not be granted having the same nature or attribute. Proof: If several distinct substances are given, they must be distinguished one from the other either by the difference of their attributes or their modifications (prev. Prop.). If, then, they are to be distinguished by the difference of their attributes, two or more cannot be granted having the same attribute. But if they are to be distinguished by the difference of their modifications, since a substance is prior in its nature to its modifications (Prop. 1), therefore let the modifications be laid aside and let the substance itself be considered in itself, that is (Def. 3 and 6) truly considered, and it could not then be distinguished from another, that is (prev. Prop.) two or more substances cannot have the same nature or attribute." [1] Thoughts and sensations are the modifications of the self; its attribute is to be the subject of thought and sensation, and in this, its essential nature, it cannot be distinguished from another. Therefore there cannot be many selves, and from

[1] Spinoza's *Ethics*, tr. by A. Boyle.

the same line of argument it follows that there cannot be many things, if these are different from the qualities they are said to possess.

The phrase I have used above, "a series of thoughts and sensations," is certainly misleading if it is taken to imply that there is nothing permanent, that when one sensation goes nothing of it is left, except traces of it in the memory, and something wholly new comes into its place. If that were so there could be no relation of time between the two events; in order that they may be members of one and the same time series there must be something that lasts throughout both. All continuity implies that two or more events in time or extents in space are in some respect homogeneous and therefore one. There is something permanent throughout the series of thoughts and sensations, but this is not an entity distinct from them; it is their common element, consciousness in general. Here again it is the universal that is the true substance. In so far as the stream of consciousness takes different forms we must use the plural and speak of thoughts and sensations; in so far as it is all consciousness we must call it one.

This common quality exists everywhere, and what we call "individual minds" are only the more intense and more highly organised areas; they are not absolutely separate any more than the mountains are from the earth. Each of them is cut off from the others in so far as there are wide areas of lower consciousness between them; so, too, the waking consciousness of to-day is cut off from yesterday's and to-morrow's by an interval of sleep. But in its fundamental nature it is one not only with other human minds but with the whole world. There is not in each mind a separate unit which "has" these particular sensations and thoughts; there is nothing that distinguishes men from the rest of the world except the character of their consciousness, or from one another except differences in the forms of the common human character and their separation in space.

II. If we thus deny that there are many subjects having qualities, including the forms of consciousness, sensations, and thoughts, as their predicates, and resolve all persons and things into certain qualities occupying particular areas of space, we

SUBSTANCE AND PERSONALITY

cannot attach so much importance to the individual as before. Wherever any two things or persons have, or rather are, the same quality, they are one and the same, except as regards position in space. And difference of position cannot be regarded as an absolute distinction, for what we usually call " one thing " occupies different places in turn, without losing, in our opinion, its essential unity. In so far, then, as anything individual exists, it is chiefly made so by some particular difference of quality. This brings us to the very ancient problem, how far qualities are individual. It is a problem that has continually recurred in philosophy ever since the time of Plato. To mention two of the most recent instances, it is discussed in Mr Russell's *Problems of Philosophy* and in Croce's *Logica*. I have spoken like a Platonist of "colour in general" and "consciousness in general," thus accepting the doctrine that there are " universals " or common qualities. It is a doctrine confirmed by the languages of all civilized nations at least, for each has a word for colour as well as for red, blue, yellow, etc., for quality as well as for colour, taste, and warmth, for consciousness as well as for sensations, thoughts, and emotions. The average man, though he may not know it, is so decided a Realist, in the mediæval sense, that he would find it hard to understand what the Nominalists meant. If you told him that there was really no common element in red, blue, and green, distinguishing them from sounds or temperatures, he would certainly accuse you of talking metaphysics, which from him is a polite synonym for nonsense. I should use some other synonym myself, but otherwise I confess that I should agree with him. It seems to me just as evident that there are universals, or common elements in many qualities, as that there are distinguishing elements.

The existence of universals is sometimes denied on the ground that there are no two instances of the same quality, the same colour, for example; there is always some slight difference, though we may not observe it. There is no evidence at all to confirm this, and every appearance of the contrary. Again, it is said that the colours shade off into one another, so that it would be impossible to decide exactly in how many places blue or red exists. But it is not necessary that the universal should always exist completely wherever it may be;

it may exist partially in some places, along with another also existing there partially. For instance, we may say that both the universals red and yellow are present in the colour orange. Everyone admits that colours are like one another, and likeness can only mean partial identity. You may ask what common element there is in a pillar-box, a complexion, and the setting sun, which we all called red, and infer that there is no such quality as redness belonging to these and other objects. But if there is nothing common to them why do we apply to them all the same adjective? Other colours may be associated with the redness, but that does not disprove the existence of such a common quality there.

Even if one did not admit that different colours were universals, one would have to admit that colour and sound were. In each of these there is evidently a general element distinguishing it from the other, and there is no shading off from the qualities perceived by sight to those perceived by hearing. Still more evidently are quality and quantity universals. There must be something found in all qualities, colour, sound, temperature, and the rest, which distinguishes them from any quantity. And both quality and quantity are forms of being or existence in general, which stands at the head of the hierarchy of universals. This is not simply an abstraction, if by abstraction is meant something unreal existing only as an idea. For we can say that everything in the world is an addition to the sum of being, a phrase which would be meaningless if there were no common property shared by each thing with all others. There can be no addition of things which are in no respect the same. If anything absolutely new were credited, different from all forms of existence hitherto known, there would be more, not of any particular form of being, but of being in general. And whatever is capable of becoming more or less must be considered a reality.

You cannot even use the word "many" without meaning "many instances of the same thing." The plural always implies an identity, the same thing repeated in many existences. Even in using such vague terms as "things" or "beings" we are thinking of the objects so described as in some respect the same; otherwise we should not use the same term for them. But they could not be the same in any respect if they were not all forms of existence in general, as colours are forms of colour, the universal.

In Croce's *Logica*, which is mainly concerned with the problem of universals or "*concetti*"—a term which does not imply that the universals are merely subjective,—a distinction is made between pure concepts and pseudo-concepts, *i.e.*, genuine and false universals. The latter, to which no reality corresponds, are of two kinds, the abstract and the empirical. The abstract concepts include those of mathematics, the idea of a triangle, for instance, or of a plane or line ; these do not represent anything real, for everything in space must have three dimensions, whereas a plane has only two, and a line only one. The empirical concepts include those of particular colours and particular species of animals. These are condemned as pseudo-concepts on the ground that they are not universal and that it is impossible to draw any dividing line between the colours or classes. There is properly no class of beings that can be called " men," for the human race has been developed from lower forms of life and it would be impossible to say definitely at what point men appeared. There is too much continuity in the world now, and there was too much in the past, to allow us to talk of fixed and clearly marked species. The divisions of this kind that we make in Nature are useful for practical purposes, but have no absolute reality.

This seems to leave us with very few concepts that can be called " pure " and represent real universals. Those mentioned by Croce are " quality," " development," " beauty," and " final cause," or their opposites, " quantity," " immobility," " individual pleasure," and " the mechanical." In each of the four pairs one or other of the opposite terms is universal, and both may be. One might object that of the second pair development may be only a temporary phenomenon, while immobility is nothing positive ; that beauty can only exist for a mind like the human, and that the individual pleasure caused by the objects we call beautiful only exists in such minds. This would leave us with the first and fourth pairs as the only true universals. But if one may call the common element in two or more things a " universal "—an incorrect term but convenient, since we do not use " generals " in that philosophic sense—we shall find it easier to give instances. Pleasure and pain, for instance, do not exist everywhere in the world, but they may be counted as true universals, or "pure concepts," for they are not abstractions like points and lines, and even though they may both be present in the same feeling, they are sharply distinguished from one another. This may be denied, but the denial could only be due to a confusion of thought. The pleasure may be very faint, and only just rise above the level of an indifferent feeling, but for all that it is as much a pleasure as the greatest, and equally distinguished from the slightest pain. So a line may be only a millimetre long, little more than a point, and yet is no less a line than one extending for miles.

Even the "pseudo-concepts" must represent some reality, for otherwise they would be of no use for practical purposes, whereas their usefulness is admitted. If you regard them as nothing but names or ideas you cannot explain why it is that we call some objects by the same name or class them under the same general idea, for you are supposing that there is nothing in the objects themselves to make us do so. It is true that in some cases, as with the animal species, any divisions we make may be arbitrary. But the main force of the doctrine of universals consists in recognizing that there is more or less identity in all things that exist. The common element in A and B may not be exactly the same in amount as that in B and C; so in classifying the forms of life it may be arbitrary to fix upon a certain amount of identity as marking off certain animals into a distinct species. For the identity between A^1 and A^n, the two extremes of what we call one species, may be no greater than that between A^n and B^1, a member of a "different species." But from that it is absurd to conclude, with some individualists, that there is nothing common to any two things, in which case all things would be equally unlike.

When any colour changes, passing through a series of intermediate states a^1, a^2, $a^3 \ldots$, the state a^2 or a^3 is not something absolutely new; a^2 is almost wholly identical with a^1, and a^3 with a^2. Since, then, we admit that two successive colours in the same place are mainly identical, we should admit that two colours in different places may be so too. This will seem to most people so obvious as not to need discussion. Yet it has been virtually denied by the individualists in philosophy, and the deductions to be drawn from it may not be so readily accepted, for they make havoc of the ordinary ideas of identity and personality.

If, as I have said, a " thing " is a certain quality occupying a particular space, there are two forms of identity possible. We speak of " the same thing " when the place occupied and the shape remain the same, though the quality changes, or when there is a continuous change of place, *i.e.*, a movement. For instance, a thing which changes its colour is called the same, because its position, size, and shape are relatively permanent. At the same time it must be remembered that the colour generally changes by degrees, not abruptly, and that in any case the qualitative change is not absolute, for even if red gives place to blue, colour still remains. The other kind of identity, the more important kind, is that of quality. And since one and the same, or practically the same, quality can exist in different places, there is no reason why we should not say that the same thing exists in different places. If A and B are of the same colour, *i.e.*, are the same colour, then they are the same thing existing here and there. If the colour is slightly different, they may be called the same thing, or states of the same thing, as much as a^1 and a^2, successive states of a changing A.

It is one of the fundamental ideas of the human mind that the same thing cannot exist in two places at once, but can exist at different times, and in different places at those times. Whether this is true or false depends simply on our definition of a " thing," and if, as I said, the essence of a thing is a certain quality it may be regarded as multiplied in space as truly as in time, especially when the same quality exists at many places in the same form. The main reason why we make the distinction between many existences in space and many in time is that the parts of time at which " the same thing " exists are continuous, whereas the parts of space at which one quality or kind of being exists are separated by others containing different qualities or kinds, or by empty space. But continuity is only one form of identity and not essential. If a quality appeared at a certain place, disappeared from existence, and after a time reappeared in the same place, we should be quite justified in calling its two existences states of the same thing. That is just what happens to our waking consciousness, interrupted as it is by sleep. And if a quality is found at a certain time, and beyond an interval of space in which it does not exist is found again at the same time, in this case too there are two existences of the same thing. This might be said even if times and places were both different and discontinuous.

All this is so likely to be condemned as metaphysical quibbling that it will be worth while before going farther to point out how it bears on, and is supported by, a doctrine still accepted by a great part of the human race. The doctrine of reincarnation is generally regarded in Europe as a harmless eccentricity, but is the fixed belief of many millions in the East, and certainly deserves some consideration, unless our thoughts are to be bounded by geographical limits. If the essence of a man is his character, if he is his character, then as often as that reappears we may quite truly say that the man is born again. If any man regards himself as a reincarnation of Napoleon, for instance, one might condemn his taste, but could offer no objection on philosophical grounds, provided that he thinks and acts as Napoleon would have thought and acted at the present time. You will not agree with this, if you believe that there is in every man an individual soul which has the character and is distinct from it. But even then one soul could only be distinguished from another by its character, and if that is the same in two cases, we should be right in saying that the soul reappeared. However, we may leave this subject for a while; it is simpler to consider the identity of things before that of persons, for with the former we do not have to take memory into account.

The importance of continuity in space and time as a factor in identity has been very much exaggerated. If the shape, size, and colour in a particular area are continually replaced by others, or even if the colour alone changes, we have much less reason for talking of " the same thing " than if we find the same shape, size, and colour in two different places. Continuity in itself is not essential, but it is true that it is generally accompanied by identity in more important

SUBSTANCE AND PERSONALITY

respects, *i.e.*, in the three just mentioned. Yet this may exist without continuity, for there are obviously innumerable objects all over the world where the shape, size, and colour are the same, or as much the same as " one thing " remains in the course of its existence. Two copies A and B of the same book when new are much more identical with one another than A is identical with the A of a few years hence, if it is much handled. This is true even of composite things. And if you come to the real things of which they are temporary collections, *i.e.*, to the ultimate or penultimate elements of matter, you will find an even greater identity in the atoms scattered over far-distant parts of space.

The ideal of science is to establish this principle; that what we call " many things " at different places can only differ from one another to the same extent as any one of them can differ from its own state at an earlier or later time. The velocities of the particles of matter are not the same, but then the velocity of each of them changes; their size, their gravitational influence at any distance, the velocity with which they propagate light, and the qualities through which they can pass are the same everywhere. Unless we accept this as true, the amount of uniformity we have so far discovered in the world can only be regarded as an extraordinary series of coincidences. Either it must be complete, or there is no reason why it should be found anywhere, for there could be no limit to the possibilities of difference. We are justified, then, in assuming that the identity is as great as I have said, and this identity can only be explained by supposing that one thing exists in many places at once as it exists at many times in one place or many, and that its sameness is therefore no stranger in the first case than in the second. As it extends throughout all time, so it is scattered over all space. But perhaps one should not call this an explanation so much as a simple statement of what is implied in such identity of nature.

How unimportant continuity is in itself is evident from this, that we regard as one and the same throughout life a body of which the materials are often replaced by others. It is computed that after seven years not an element remains in the human organism which was there at the beginning of that period; in this respect we die and are reborn several times during life. But the body retains its general form, and that is enough to justify us in calling it the same. Certainly the fact that the change is gradual causes the identity of form, but this continuity of change is not necessary, since without it two bodies may be as much alike as one remains like itself.

The identity of the human body, then, is an identity of form; it has no continuity except continuity of change, and this is not essential except in so far as it preserves the form. The existence of the human mind, too, is not continuous, for it is interrupted every night by sleep. It is true that, since consciousness is universal, it is not altogether destroyed in the brain by sleep, but is reduced to a lower level of feeling, like that possessed by the lower forms of being, living or inanimate. But that kind of continuity exists between separate minds, which are only the high mountains on the continuous surface of sentient being. Personal consciousness is certainly interrupted by sleep. It would seem that here too the identity must be one of form or character. But there is a general idea that memory gives the mind a kind of identity which no " unconscious " thing can possess; that it proves the mind to be one and the same throughout life in a more genuine sense than it could be in virtue of its character alone.

Memories are the images of past experiences, generally sunk to a lower level of consciousness than the human or personal, but occasionally raised to that level again. There is no evidence of continuity here, for all the elements of the memory may change as do those of the body, while the form remains as before. The memories are stored in the brain—the reality which appears as the brain—and that is not continuous, since its elements are superseded by others, as are those of other parts of the human organism. It follows that here too there is only an identity of form. The picture that is lighted up when we remember may be only a copy from the original. All this has a very dogmatic sound, and it has often been denied, as by Professor Bergson in his *Matière et Mémoire*, that memories exist in the brain, although it is admitted that injuries to the brain destroy the memory. Professor Bergson's criticisms and the possible answers to them are given in a later chapter. But it may be said here that if the memories do not exist in the brain, their influence on it, and consequently on our actions, becomes unintelligible. Extra-spatial entities cannot act on something that exists in space. Besides, according to the view set forth in *Matière et Mémoire*, it seems that memory must be identified with the past, itself still existing, every detail of it, in the present. In that case there seems no reason why the slightest resemblance between present and past should not call up the memory of the latter, or why the memory should often be so faint when it comes.

It is supposed that memory gives us a direct assurance of personal identity. But we could not have such a direct assurance unless we could be directly aware at once of past and present existence, and that is obviously impossible. In remembering a recent event a man thinks, no doubt, that he is the same man who had that experience, but this belief does not by any means prove that he is so, nor does it show how he could be so, which is just what we want to discover. The natural tendency of each man is to think that his body is the same in its materials as it was ten years ago, and this we know to be false. The connection established by memory may be no closer than that between two men when a thought is conveyed by speech from one to the other. All that occurs in recollection is that a present sensation awakes a similar image within, or the image of a sensation previously associated with one similar to the present, and that these images are believed to represent something which happened in the past. We do not directly perceive the past, any more than we perceive directly an object ten yards distant.

Even if we were directly aware of the past the inference that he who sees the object now is the same as he who saw it on the remembered occasion might be mistaken. Certainly we are often wrong in the inference that the thing seen now is the same, in virtue of continuity of position, as the thing seen at some former time. Besides, our memories are not always accompanied by a feeling of identity. The experiences of the boy of ten, when remembered after twenty years, seem quite alien from the man of thirty, though the boy and man are called the same person. The only identity established by memory is an identity of quality or form, and that is the most important kind. Each man retains through life, or a great part of it, the same memories, as he retains the same habits and traits of character. Nothing is gained by supposing that the memories "belong to" some permanent entity distinct alike from them and from all sensations and thoughts. As for continuity, existing as they do in the brain they are only continuous in the same degree as any other part of the body. The image awakened by the present sensation may be only a copy of a copy. Yet in so far as the form and quality are the same, it is the original.

Neither memory, then, nor continuity can make the man of to-day the same as the man of yesterday, except in so far as either involves or causes identity of form and character, the only thing essential. Some of our memories fade away, all grow more or less alien from us, the continuity of personal consciousness is broken by sleep, the elements of the body are superseded by others, but the character and some memories are permanent. Yet even the character and form do not remain in all respects the same; it is hard to trace the likeness between the man of seventy and the youth of fifty years before. In some respects the former is identical with all old men, more identical with them than with the youth of twenty supposed to have been the same person. In a sense he may be called old age itself, existing in a particular form and place. But whatever identity he has with the youth of twenty consists in his character, form, and memories.[1]

III. It follows from this that in so far as "two men" have, or rather are, the same character, form, and memories they are not two but one. They are as much, or almost as much, one as any man is one with himself at different periods of his life. It must not be supposed that the identity of what we call "one person" is something different in kind from any possible identity of what we call "two persons." Our ordinary ideas of individuality are altogether too rigid.

---

[1] *Cf.* Mach, *Analysis of Sensations* (tr. by C. M. Williams), p. 4. "The ego is as little absolutely permanent as the body. That which we so much dread in death, the annihilation of our permanency, actually occurs in life in abundant measure. That which is most valued by us remains preserved in countless copies, or in cases of exceptional excellence, is even preserved of itself."

But they have always been accompanied by others which in some measure counteract them; ideas expressed not only in philosophy but in the two forms of human thought most akin to it, religion and poetry, and even in some phrases of everyday language. They are often regarded as metaphors, and to most men the word "metaphor" is a polite synonym for "fiction"; but they are as literally true as anything we admit to be a fact. It is worth while to notice some of these popular ideas, not usually considered metaphysical, which confirm the theory of personality given above.

In the old mythologies certain qualities common to many men, certain types of mankind, found in many places and at many times, were treated as individuals and deified. Something of the same tendency may be observed even now, though with our less vivid imagination or intelligence we are content to talk of the "war spirit," or "the spirit of justice," or to personify "Labour" or "Art" with a capital letter. We have not yet promoted "Labour" to divine honours, but it is to be supposed that we mean something when we use the singular noun instead of the humbler plural "labourers." The use of it could not be justified if we did not regard it as the name of a single individual. But there is nothing to prevent us from using it so, for all labourers as such are not less one and the same than what we call "one man" at different periods of his life. Indeed, the first kind of identity is in some respects greater than the other.

It is not necessary to give many illustrations of this tendency in the ancient religions. Half Olympus was peopled with human types personified. When many men were seized with the same impulse it was the most natural thing in the world to ignore the distinctions between them, which had practically disappeared, and consider the whole mass as many bodies, or even as one body, possessed by one soul, like the Oriental gods with their many hands. So, too, when men of the same type were found in many places it was natural to suppose that they were in mind at least one and the same person, or were derived from, or inspired by, a common original. Every village blacksmith, for instance, was taken to be one of the incarnations or the descendants of Vulcan, and every doctor in the city was believed to have something of Æsculapius in him. This was only one of the elements of primitive religion, but it was certainly the most intelligent, and is interesting as showing how the Greeks, Romans, and other peoples rose above the limited idea of personality which prevails nowadays. At the same time that limited idea was strong enough even then to make them attribute to the universal type or person a particular human form, distinct from the many human forms in which it exists. The confining of the universal within a particular time or place or shape is a common perversion of human thought. Plato, at least in his later theory, and the extreme Realists made the same mistake when they placed the " Idea " or the " Universal " in a world of its own, like the heaven of religion, not in the many parts of the world where it really exists.

I have already mentioned another form of religion, or popular belief, in which the same wider notion of personality is contained. The doctrine of reincarnation or transmigration must certainly have been suggested by the fact that the same character reappears in different generations. This is most clearly seen in Buddhism, which distinctly teaches that the character is the person, and denies the existence of any soul to which the character belongs. To the Western mind the belief in reincarnation has almost always appeared strange and even inconceivable, for that belief ignores the memory, which we assume to be an essential element of personality. It is to be observed, by the way, that in the East not only the individual but the national memory, *i.e.*, the national history, is held of slight importance. On the other hand, we overestimate the importance of both, absolutely and also relatively, to that of the general memory of mankind. The memory is only one element of personality, and the others may exist without it. We do not attribute it to inanimate things or even to all animals, and yet we regard them as the same at different times. Nor is it so individual as is thought, for the same or practically the same memories may exist in many men; memories of what we call the same event, and also of events so like one another as to be essentially the same. Those which any man considers to be his private property are really more or less identical with those of every other, just as his character is more or less identical with theirs.

The only Western philosopher in modern times who has taken the doctrine of reincarnation seriously is Schopenhauer, who preferred the religions of the Hindu and the Buddhist to any other, not excepting Christianity. He interprets it in the way just described, and in his chief work, *Die Welt als Wille und Vorstellung*, vol. 2, ch. xli, gives the following illustration, among others, to show that it applies as much to animals as to men: " If I see an animal going away, without my observing where it goes, and then see another come forward, without my observing whence it comes; if both have the same form, the same nature, and the same character, and are different only in their material elements, which in any case are continually changed and renewed even during the life of each of them; it is an obvious assumption that what disappears and what comes in its place are essentially one and the same being, which has only suffered a slight change, a renewal of the form of its existence, and that death is for the species only what sleep is for the individual." He might have added that the material elements too are one and the same thing in many places. But there could be no clearer explanation of Eastern philosophy than the words I have just quoted.

To come next to Christianity, it is quite evident that its fundamental doctrines are inconsistent with the common idea of personality. This is especially true of the doctrine of the Atonement, which has exercised the minds of the theologians more than any other. It is impossible to justify unless it is admitted that every Christian is in a real and not simply metaphorical sense one with Christ. But every article of the Christian faith cuts right across that individualism which dominates our elementary metaphysics. I hope to develop that idea later on, but it is worth while to note here how many phrases in the New Testament, particularly in the Gospel of St. John and the Epistles of St. Paul, while fully in accord with the Christian philosophy, are quite contrary to the popular dogma that every man is a being essentially distinct and separate from every other. They express a kind of Christian Pantheism, limited to the Church, to which Christ stands in the same relation as the God of Spinoza to the world. The believer is not merely told, as he is nowadays, to act like Christ, but to live in him; or again, Christ is not merely said to inspire the Christian, but to be in him, a phrase which evidently contradicts the common idea of personality, and is therefore now diluted into something much weaker. But that is only another instance of the dilution of Christianity due to the individualism of the Western mind. To the modern believer Christianity is simply a historical event limited in space and time, and Christ a person essentially distinct from all others, one who lived for thirty-three years in Palestine and now only has the same kind of relation to mankind as any man may have to another, or is at least just as external. This may be denied, but in fact the rigidity of the popular idea of personality makes any other belief impossible. But if St. Paul may be taken as an example, those who lived nearest to the life of Christ thought of it as a historical event much less than we do; there are very few references to it in the Epistles. The life of Christ in the Church interested them far more, and their view of his personality was certainly what would now be called mystical.

The idea of a personality wider than the individual man is common, of course, in literature and art. " Man," " Nature," and " Life " are not abstractions for the poet, if by " abstraction " you mean something unreal. They are not less real than the individual man; in fact, the latter deserves much more than they to be called an abstraction, in the sense that the individual is not in reality clearly distinct from the rest of the world. It is true that poetry describes the individual as well as the universal; an epic or drama that represented only types of character without particular traits such as are found in every man would be condemned as untrue to life, as a psychological treatise rather than literature. At the same time it must describe something universal, for otherwise the expression " true to life " would have no meaning. If the characters were wholly individual we should have no standard by which to judge them. One may even apply to literature a principle similar to that which I have mentioned as governing science; that the persons described must only differ from one another and from real men to the same extent as one man can differ from himself at various times. That is to say, each of them should be what every man is capable of becoming; otherwise not every man would be able to understand the truth of the character introduced into the epic or play.

The tendency to personification in poetry is too well known to need quotation. It varies from the mechanical figures of Gray to the ethereal world of Shelley, a world which is real enough, though we have not all the eyes to see it. But poetry suffers from the same defect as religion, in that it describes the universal as existing in one particular shape, instead of existing in many shapes, times, and places. An emotion, anger or love, may quite rightly be regarded as a single entity not less real and individual than those series of conscious states in which particular instances of it occur, *i.e.*, those series we call men. Each man when angry is a particular instance of anger, and is as much identical with all angry men as he is with himself when possessed by some other feeling; in the first case there is identity of emotion, in the second of character. But in poetry and art it is of course necessary, however unphilosophic, to treat Anger or Love not as a person existing in many persons, but as outside them, with an individual body. The same is true of all allegories, whether in verse or prose. Literature, like religion, in order to become popular has to make these concessions to the popular mode of thinking.

When we speak of a great author as "immortal" we attach to the adjective a meaning which robs it of most of its force; we intend only to say that the influence of his works is permanent. But we can give the word a much more genuine sense. Whenever one reads a book by some writer now dead, his thought, the most important part of him, lives again; he comes back to life in no metaphorical sense but as really as if his body were by some miracle revived. The earliest poets of Greece live again in any man who reads the Iliad or the Odyssey with feeling and intelligence; the same words, the same rhythm, the same pictures and emotions enter his mind that came first into being three thousand years ago; or rather they are his mind for the time, since the mind is not a separate unit watching a procession of thoughts go by, nor a vessel into which thoughts enter. The fact that they are now linked together in a series with others with which they were not linked before does not detract anything from their essential identity, and though they may not exist now with the same vividness as before, yet they do exist again. The sympathetic reader of a poem is one with the poet in a more genuine sense than he is one with the business man of a few hours ago, though we say that the reader and the business man are the same person.

But the immortality I have just described is not peculiar to great authors and to those teachers whose words have been recorded. It belongs to all men, and not only to thoughts but to sensations. The main features of a landscape may remain the same for thousands of years, and when any man looks at it to-day there comes into being again the sensation of the Roman who looked at it in Cæsar's time. It is not true to say that it is a different man who sees it; if he looks at it without any personal thought, for that moment the sensation is the man. Again, when many people hear a piece of music played they become for the time one sensation in many places; each of them is in a real sense one with the composer and with all others who have heard that piece before, or are hearing it at the same time as he. So, too, we often say of a crowd that it feels or acts " as one man "; it would be true to say that for the moment it is one man.

The same thoughts and emotions reappear in generation after generation, and those which we call the most personal are the least different on the various occasions when they arise, with whatever series of conscious states they may from time to time be linked. Each of them is more truly one and the same thing in its different manifestations than it is one with the other members of the series to which it is attached. This is no less true of nationality; the Englishman and Frenchman who despise each other as foreign are in their mutual contempt more akin to each other than either is to his more broad-minded fellow-countrymen. The spirit of patriotism assuming the form of an Englishman fights against itself as taking the form of a German. So the " I," the self-consciousness, is in quality, and therefore essentially, one and the same in all men, the same feeling or idea existing in many times and places, but in one man is a foreigner to itself as existing in another, and often at war with itself, as one man may be at war with himself in thought. Men are most identical when each has the strongest and most intimate sense of his personality, for that sense is everywhere the same.

Individualism thrives on our clear perception of relatively small differences and on our blindness to fundamental identity. A slight idiosyncrasy draws far more attention than those much more important respects in which all men are the same. We live on a deep and solid basis of identity but observe only the projections from it, as we live on the earth and notice only what rises above the surface. The most conspicuous of those human mountains we call great men or outstanding personalities seem to dwarf their neighbours, but what they share with them is much greater than the differences. Again, no man ever quite realizes that the sensations, thoughts, and emotions of his fellow-men are the same in kind as his own. If he did, he could not draw so sharp a dividing line between his consciousness and theirs. Why is it that a man is not as much affected by the pleasure or pain a few yards away as by that pleasure or pain a few hours or days away which he regards as destined to be his own? He is not directly aware of the sensation over there, but he is not directly aware of the future sensation either. It is true that there may be a greater continuity of consciousness in the one case than in the other, but not if the future pleasure or pain is to come on the following day, so that the series of thoughts and sensations, of personal, waking sensations, is interrupted by sleep. I do not think that the distinction made is always directly due to the idea that one and the same soul which is thinking of the pleasure or pain now will experience it some time hence. For it is made by men who have no belief, or no clear belief in any individual soul, apart from the thoughts and sensations. But the idea of personality is probably an inherited relic of that belief, which may therefore be the original cause of the distinction.

To return to that belief for a moment, it would be impossible for those who identified the person with the soul to prove that the soul of yesterday was the same as that of to-day. They maintain that a soul comes into being at the birth of every man, but if it can come into being it can also cease to be; why should we not suppose, then, that it ceases to be when a man falls asleep, and that a new one is created when he awakes, as when he was born? The existence of memory could not disprove this, for the new soul might have inherited the memories belonging to that of yesterday, as every new soul inherits a great part of the characters of the parents. The man of yesterday might be the parent of the man of to-day. I admit that the term " new soul " is inappropriate, for if the soul is something apart from the sensations and thoughts it is said to have, there can be nothing to distinguish that of yesterday from that of to-day. But this would be no less true of all the " individual souls, " which could only be many in respect of their positions in space, and must be essentially one. Or rather, since they are not themselves extended, they cannot even be distinguished by their places. On the other hand, you do not make it any easier to prove the identity of the man of to-day and the man of yesterday if, while maintaining the usual idea of personality, you follow the present fashion and avoid any use of the word " soul." You only become much more obscure.

The fact that the elements of the brain and the rest of the body remain the same during the night affords no better foundation for the idea of personality. If Nature had so arranged that the process of metabolism, instead of taking seven years to change all the constituents of the body, were to take only seven hours, it is not likely that our sense of identity would be any the less, provided that the form were preserved. Certainly if the change were to take place during sleep in one night our memories would not be affected, for we can remember events that occurred more than seven years ago, when the elements of the body were different. The man of forty supposes himself to be the same as the man of thirty, in spite of that change.

There seems even less connection between present and future than between present and past, for in the former case there is no memory now. That form of connection will be established, but is not there yet. Hazlitt, in a little-known metaphysical essay, of which he seems to have been prouder than of any other of his writings, declared the cause of unselfishness to be this, that the bond between the present thoughts and future sensations of any man was hardly, if at all, closer than the bond between his present thoughts and the future sensations of his fellows. His chief argument was the fact which I have just mentioned, that there is no memory to link up present and future; nothing, therefore, to identify him who is thinking of a pleasure or pain now with him who will feel it to-morrow. Yet even the most unselfish of us certainly draws a distinction between the sensations which he thinks that he will feel, and those which he thinks will be felt by other men. The distinction may have much less ground in reality than he thinks, but we have to explain why he supposes it to be so great. Why does the idea of one pleasure or pain act more powerfully upon the mind than the idea of another equally great, and not farther removed in time? Evidently he in whom the idea arises must believe that one and the same entity—himself—foresees the first sensation and will feel it, and, as I have said, that belief logically implies belief in a soul, whether he is aware of that implication or not. For that reason he imagines himself as already feeling the sensation, and the imagination creates a pleasure or pain now. In the more sympathetic minds, of course, even the imagination of another's feelings creates feelings similar to them, and the distinction between self and others, though it does not disappear, comes near to the vanishing point. It is conceivable that in the course of time the sense of personality, as well as the sense of nationality, will dwindle to something very much smaller than it is nowadays. The self is not something fixed and absolute, separated by an impassable barrier from all others, but can be made practically as continuous with them as its own thoughts and sensations are with one another. So when a good orator is making a speech, the connection between two successive thoughts in his mind is not closer or more intimate than that between the first of his thoughts and its repetition in his hearers' minds.

We read of "multiple personality" in what we call "one man"; the division of Man into many men is another instance of multiple personality. There is this difference, that in the first case the persons exist at separate times, in the second at separate places. But the persons at different places are more closely united than those belonging to "one man," which succeeded one another in time, for there is interaction between the former alone, and these are also often more akin to one another.

To sum up, there is no reason why we should restrict the term " one individual " or " self " to each man separately. We might apply it to the whole universe, which is everywhere conscious, continuous, and essentially identical in character; or to the whole of mankind, where the identity of character is still greater. On the other hand, we might narrow it down to the life of one man during one day, for continuity in the specifically human consciousness is broken by sleep. For certain reasons we happen to have applied it to one particular form of consciousness existing in a particular time, or series of times, $i.e.$, days, and within a certain limited area of space. It has already been explained what those reasons are; sameness of character, continuity of space and movement through space, and memory. But these reasons are either inadequate or would justify us in regarding Man, not less than a particular man, as an individual or self. That is to say, our thoughts may as truly be called thoughts of Man as of men, for they are as much phases of the general human consciousness, which exists at many times and in many places, as of particular characters. Again, they might be called thoughts of the philosopher, the politician, or the artist in all men; a special form of consciousness, which exists in many minds, is as much a person as Smith, Jones, or Robinson. For the essential thing that makes one person of a series of thoughts and sensations is the character, and if a special type of character is found in many minds that too may quite rightly be personified. Even the old mythology, which limited such personified types to a particular form, is better than the restriction of personality to the individual man.

CHAPTER V

THE UNITY OF THE WORLD

1. THE idea which most men have of the world, when they are not influenced by religion, represents it as a number of things which simply happen to be there, each standing by itself as a separate centre of existence. Most men, that is to say, are firm believers in the metaphysical creed known as Pluralism. The clearest and most philosophical form of this creed, so far at least as it concerns the material universe, is the atomistic theory, which has remained in essentials the same from the time of Leucippus and Democritus to the present day. Whatever name may be given to the ultimate elements of matter, they are regarded as primarily distinct from one another, separate starting-points of existence. Yet at the same time they are considered to act upon one another, to be of the same size, or almost the same, and governed by the same laws, to possess in themselves or produce in our sensations the same qualities, and to exist in the same Space and Time. The objections which may be brought against this theory may with obvious adaptations be turned against any form of Pluralism, *i.e.*, against any metaphysical system which declares the world to be essentially many beings and not one.

We will take first the most popular form of the atomistic theory, which attributes extension to the atoms. I use the last word simply as a convenient term for the ultimate particles of matter, whatever they may be; the old atom, it is true, has been shown to be composed of electrons, but it seems that the electron in its turn may be proved to be composite. Whatever the elements of which matter is formed, it would be generally assumed that they must be extended, for without that they could not exist in space at all. If you suppose them to be movements in the ether, like the vortex-rings in Lord Kelvin's theory, you must admit that movement implies a change of place or of relation to others, and that is impossible if there were not a definite extent of some quality to undergo the change. Without different qualities there could be no alteration of any kind in the universe, and if the qualities are to exist in space they must obviously be extended. This would readily be granted, and so too, I think, would be the statement that the atoms must be the same or almost the same in extent. The older atomists certainly supposed that there was a difference in shape, but at the same time declared that all the atoms were exceedingly small compared with the bodies we can see, and there would be no reason why they should be so if they were not alike in size. If they differed much in that respect it is evident that some of them might be as large as the composite bodies we see, formed of masses of atoms. In fact, if any difference were possible, it would be strange that any two of them should be at all alike ; one might be as small as the smallest object the microscope can discover, another as large as the earth, a third as large as the solar system, and so on in proportion. There might be an infinite variety of atoms, each being enormously different in size from any other. But a world like ours can only exist if they are alike in size, and so the popular theory supposes them to be.

It might be objected that the similarity is only to be found in our world, the earth or the solar system, because those which are alike would naturally come together to form one body. But this does not explain why, if a difference is possible, any of them should be alike. The existence of so many identical or almost identical atoms as those which compose our world could only be the strangest of coincidences. Besides, no one seriously supposes that in other parts of the universe there may be atoms as large as the whole earth.

The Relativist, again, might condemn our argument on the ground that the size of everything varies for any observer according as it changes its rate of motion relatively to him. But that objection is not fatal to the idea that the atoms are identical. That idea may be stated in this way : that the more the atoms resemble one another in their rate of motion relatively to any one body, the more they appear alike in size as judged from that body. If they were all moving with the same velocity, their size too would appear the same; as it is, they appear smaller in proportion as they surpass any given velocity and larger as they fall below it. For this they must be just as identical as though size were something absolute. Besides, the differences in apparent size according to the theory of relativity could only be small, and that theory does not answer the question why we do not find atoms as large as visible objects, a house or mountain, for instance.

This likeness or identity of the atoms in their extension would be impossible if they were separate starting-points or centres of existence, not many existences of one and the same thing, like the many existences of one thing in time. I have already pointed out that the ideal of science is to establish that the ultimate realities can only differ from one another as much as any one of them can differ now from its past or future existence. They are as much states of one thing, then, as are the successive states of anything that we commonly regard as one. It is true that the existences in space are not continuous, as are the successive existences in time, but that does not make them any the less repetitions of one thing.

This argument has equal force if you regard the atom not as an extended body but as a centre of force, a theory preferred by some atomists, as by Kant. It is a strange and inconsistent theory, for it holds that every atom refrains from occupying or trying to occupy a space itself, but manifests its activity by keeping all others out of a certain space; an unnecessary and even impossible form of activity, if no other can enter that space or even makes the attempt. The only intelligible meaning of the theory is that the atom, while extended, is not fixed in extent but elastic, with a force increasing as it is driven towards its centre. Even then the theory is open to objection, and in any case our argument holds, for the amount of force possessed by all the atoms must be the same, since they are the same, or nearly the same, in extent. We do not expect to come across one possessing a force sufficient to expand it over a space as large as the earth or the solar system.

We assume, too, that gravitation is the same everywhere throughout the universe. The attracting power of every body —or, if you prefer, the curvature of space around it—is in the same proportion to its size and density. But if the elements of matter were essentially distinct there would be nothing to prevent a body of the same size as the earth from exerting the same force as another equal in size to the sun. The sameness of the velocity of light would also be unaccountable on the pluralistic theory. So, indeed, would be every law of nature, for there would be no reason why a number of primarily independent beings should conform to the same rules of action.

What has been said of the quantitative nature of the atoms, their size and force, may also be said of their qualities. It is true that the colours we see and the sounds we hear may exist only in human minds, but there must be similar qualities in the outer world. For a purely quantitative world would be perfectly homogeneous, like space, and could not produce any variety of qualities in our mind; in fact it would be nothing but a blank, and even distinctions of quantity would be impossible. And there must be the same similarity between the qualities of the outer world as between those which we experience in sensation, for if all the first differed from one another to an indefinite extent, no two of the effects they produce, *i.e.*, our sensations, would be like one another. Besides, the whole world consists of states of consciousness more or less intense, and since our sensations are so much alike we may judge the part from the whole and believe that there is the same uniformity throughout the rest of the universe. But this uniformity could be nothing but a series of coincidences if the world were a number of fundamentally separate beings. If that were so, why should any two have the same quality or go through the same set of qualities, when the possibilities of difference were infinite?

A similar argument may be addressed to the "spiritual Pluralists," who believe only in a number of self-existent minds. Why these minds should have sensations of the same kind, perceive the same colours, and hear the same sounds, would be unintelligible if they were really separate units. Each man might have in sensation a different set of colours, or even sensations altogether different in kind. If minds were not parts of one mind but self-existent, why should any two of them have the same five senses, when an infinite variety of completely different qualities is conceivable? This identity of nature is always taken for granted, as though it needed no explanation, or remains quite unnoticed. But it is fatal to the pluralistic theory. And whatever form that theory takes our argument may be adapted to meet it. Whatever you suppose the ultimate realities to be, the similarity of their nature would be an unexplained mystery if they were separate centres of being and not phases or repetitions of one existence. You cannot attribute it to interaction, for interaction presupposes a likeness of nature. Besides, the same cause would not produce the same effect if the things on which it acted were fundamentally distinct and different. Nor can we explain the uniformity by supposing that our world was formed by a gradual sorting out of the entities most resembling one another from a much larger number and their association in a separate system. We may still ask why any two should resemble each other in the least. Those who offer such a suggestion cannot have understood the possibilities of difference.

Another form of the unity of the world is the co-existence of all its parts in one space. It would be impossible, as I said in a previous chapter, that there should be many extended things unless they were correlated in an all-including extent; without that there could be no distance between them to distinguish them. There could not be two of equal size and of the same quality; if you try to imagine such a pair, you will find that you are representing them to yourself as separated by an interval of space, or are imagining the same thing twice, that is to say, separating them in time. If you supposed that there were two of the same size but different in quality, you would be imagining two qualities in the same space; or if you give them different sizes, you then have two qualities, of which one occupies a part of the space filled by the other. One extent cannot be outside of, or different from, another unless both are parts of one whole. From this follows at once the necessity of an all-containing Space.

The meaning of "Space" has always been, and still is, a favourite problem of the metaphysicians. Sometimes it has been called a relation between things, but the term "relation" does not explain anything. There are two kinds of entities known by that name; one implies the presence or absence of a common property, as do all comparisons and contrasts, and the other a distance between two things or their contact, either in space or time. All the manifold relations between all forms of being can be resolved into one or other or both of these two classes. What, then, is the relation described as co-existence in one Space? We cannot define it without referring to Space itself, for that includes both the common property of all bodies, *i.e.*, the extension over which they are spread, and the distances between them. The very words we use to describe relations " between " things are derived from the idea of a universal Space, and it is preposterous, therefore, to describe the latter itself as a relation.

The theory of Relativity is supposed to have fulfilled a famous prayer and " annihilated Space and Time," because it allows for no fixed points by which absolute motion might be judged, and without fixed points it is inferred that there can be no " absolute Space." But what I mean by " the one Space " is the world itself, as extended and continuous, apart from all its qualities. It has no points or parts other than the things themselves and the areas between them, and throughout its extent is as continuous as any one of those things. If you deny its existence because it is measured and divided differently by different observers, you must deny the existence of any one body, because its size and shape are not the same for two observers moving relatively to each other. The spatial unity of the world consists in its continuity, and in the fact that no body can change relatively to another without changing relatively to all the rest.

But the reality of Space has been denied for other reasons than those just mentioned. Ever since the time of Kant, whose own theory had been anticipated by that of Leibnitz, it has been held by many that Space has no objective existence, and is nothing but a form imposed on the matter given in sensation. It does not belong to the world of " things in themselves." But if these things are the causes of our sensations, as even Kant admitted—though at the same time he inconsistently denied that the category of cause and effect could be applied to that transcendental world—then there must be something in them corresponding to Space. For the mind, even supposing that it imposed a spatial form on the effects, the sense-images, produced by the things in themselves, certainly does not impose the particular order in which the images appear, or their particular sizes and distances from one another. It would have no motive for imposing one order rather than another, so that this could only be a matter of chance, and it would be a mere coincidence if any two minds, or the same mind on any two occasions, attributed the same relative sizes and positions to the objects seen. The order, sizes, and distances must, therefore, be determined by the cause of our sensations, the real world. But if this were not spatial there would be nothing in it to explain why it produces its effects upon our minds in this particular spatial order. The mutual relations between the effects would be quite arbitrary if they depended on nothing in the cause. Therefore, in this case too there would be no reason why the spatial relations between any two things should appear the same to different minds, or to the same mind on different occasions; why a certain house, for instance, should always appear at the same distance from another whenever we pass it. Unless there is something permanent in the cause to account for the sameness of its effects on different occasions, this sameness would be unaccountable. And if this permanent thing is not a proportion and relation between parts of the cause, *i.e.*, the real things, similar to the proportion and relation between the parts of the effect, our experience, there is no ground for calling the real things the causes of the spatial order in our experience, or even for believing that they exist. We assume their existence only for the purpose of explaining why our sensations are so consistent, and the assumption will not serve our purpose if we suppose that there is no correspondence between cause and effect. For instance, if, with Berkeley, you hold that the " thing in itself " is the mind of God, you must also hold that there are in God ideas of the relative sizes and distances from one another of all the bodies we see, not only as they appear to us, but as we believe them to be in reality. Otherwise there could not be produced in our minds by fragments the picture of a far wider world than that of our sensations. But how could this ideal Space in the mind of God be different from the real Space as we conceive it?

From the same argument it may be proved that the real world contains elements exactly corresponding to the three dimensions, and in fact all the properties of Space. If so, it is hardly worth while to attempt a distinction between Space and something that corresponds to it exactly in all respects. The argument, it may be observed, holds good against all those modified forms of scepticism which are known as "critical" or "positive" philosophies. Anyone who believes that there are causes of his sensations—and everyone believes that except the Solipsist, the only consistent sceptic—must grant that there is some likeness between causes and effects, a relation and correspondence between the former parallel to that found among the latter. If he does not, what conceivable motive has he for believing in any cause of his sensations at all? As an explanation of the origin of our experience Kant's non-spatial and non-temporal "thing in itself" is as useful as the Jabberwock.

Even if you did not admit that the external world is spatial you would have to admit that something is so, if it were only our sensations, and consequently that Space does exist. For if the mind "imposes a spatial form" on its sensations, which are a part of itself, then obviously these must be spatial; otherwise the phrase is meaningless. In any case it seems as obvious that a sensation of extension is extended as that a sensation of bitterness is bitter. Even those who deny that colours or any of the secondary qualities exist in the outer world admit that they do exist, since they are evidently present in our consciousness, and the same is true of Space. This being so, all the arguments against its reality, including the antinomies of Kant, must be worthless. We cannot evade the antinomies by declaring Space to be unreal; we must accept either the thesis or the antithesis and hold the criticism of it to be unsound. The reasons which prevent us from believing Space to be finite apply equally well to the space of our sensations, the extent of the images in the brain. We must believe that these sensations are bounded by others, themselves spatial, though less vivid and varied, by an area of vague feeling like the feeling of touch or the warmth of the body. Thus we are forced to regard the extent of our sensations as part of a wider Space. If we did not so regard it we should not draw any distinction between a change in our sensations caused by the movement of some external object and that due to our own movement.

Those who believe in a number of self-existent minds and not in a spatial world will find it impossible to explain why the sensations of these minds should all take the same spatial form and be of the same extent; for the height and breadth of our visual sensations might vary indefinitely, as I said before of the atoms, if the many minds were fundamentally separate existences. But we suppose that in fact the picture given in sight is of the same size in all men, just as it always is in us; we suppose that when we see another man standing near certain objects and turning his eyes in their direction he sees no more and no less of them than we should in the same position. This implies that we take his visual space to be no greater and no less than ours.

A pluralistic theory is inconsistent also with the unity of Time. If there were many self-existent beings, each passing through a series of states, why should this particular state of A, rather than that, be regarded as simultaneous with this particular state of B? Surely A and B would each have a Time of its own, *i.e.*, the series of events going on within it, and it would be meaningless to say that an event in one coincided in time with an event in another. When many minds have the same or almost the same sensations, that does not by itself entitle us to say that these sensations are simultaneous. In declaring that two events may happen at the same time we are declaring that they are parts of one event; not states of two essentially different things but parts of one state of one thing, just as the thoughts of them in our mind are parts of one idea. We picture them as given to us with others in a single sensation or ideal image; without that the notion of simultaneity would be impossible, and so would be the reality of it, if the events themselves were not associated in one being as the images of them are associated in one mind.

We call events simultaneous when their effects in sensation are parts of one state of our consciousness. Owing to this it has been declared that there is no such unity of Time in the events themselves, that this is only an appearance due to the unity of the mind. But this denial of the one Time is open to the same criticism as the denial of the one Space. If two events did not exist simultaneously, why should the effects of certain events a, b, c appear together in sensation rather than the effects of a, d, g? It cannot be our minds that cause the events to appear simultaneous, for there can be nothing in our minds to make them fix on these events as simultaneous rather than on those. And there would be no reason why many minds should fix on the same events as occurring together, if these did not occur together in reality and consequently produce their effects together in those minds. The unity of Time must therefore be attributed to the whole world and not only to events in human consciousness. Here again it may be noted that Kant's antinomies, if they were valid against a Time independent of the human mind, would be equally so against the time series in each consciousness, and make it difficult for us to believe either that it had a beginning or that it had no beginning. For I do not see how it could be denied that our sensations and thoughts do constitute a time series, if the form of time be imposed by the mind upon its own state.

The theory of Relativity has not weakened but only complicated the argument from the unity of Time. It is true that bodies moving relatively to one another will not find the same set of events contemporaneous, and therefore it is impossible to prove that there is such a thing as absolute simultaneity. But there must be some temporal, or rather spatio-temporal, relation between the states of all parts of the world, otherwise the flashes of light sent out from two points A and B would not necessarily arrive together at both C and D, two points at rest relatively to one another and equally distant from both A and B. Nor should we be able to calculate how the temporal relation between two events would appear to observers on a body moving relatively to ourselves. Just as we believe that there is some real relation between the parts of any object we see, though it appears different to others, so we must judge of events in time, though they may appear simultaneous to one observer and successive to another.

Yet another reason why we cannot accept the pluralistic theory is that interaction between many existences would be impossible if they were not phases in the existence of one. Otherwise each would remain within its own sphere of being and could not go beyond to affect events within another sphere. As Lotze pointed out in his *Metaphysics* and elsewhere, we cannot suppose that a force or influence detaches itself from A and passes over to B. Even if A could create a force outside itself, a "vibration in the ether," for instance, why should that force affect B, which can know nothing about it? If the two were essentially separate they would be separate worlds, each with a series of events going on within it, and blind to anything that happens in the other. If a state of A is to affect a state of B, the relation between them must be just like that between a^1 and a^2, which we admit to be states of one thing, A. The nature of a^2 depends on the nature of a^1 because they are existences of the same thing, and it is for just this reason that the state of B depends on the state of A and *vice versâ*. They are phases of the same thing existing in different places, as a^1 and a^2 are phases of the same thing existing at different times, and therefore the mutual dependence is no more surprising in the one case than in the other.

It has been shown that things are not separate entities that have qualities, but are the qualities themselves filling certain extents of space, and that the same quality, whether particular or universal, may exist in many places. This is another form of the unity of the world, but little need be said of it here, as it has already been sufficiently explained. Even if you did not admit that there was one space containing all extents, you could not deny that all these are forms of a common entity, extension in general. So too every colour is a form of colour, the universal, and colour itself is a form of quality. And both extension, or quantity, and quality are forms of being, which stands at the head of the hierarchy of universals. If, then, it is the particular qualities that are the real things or substances, not the supposed possessors of these qualities, it follows that the same title may be given also to the universals, to quality or to being in general. The *Deus sive Natura* of Spinoza, it may be remarked, is just this latter with its universal forms or "attributes," consciousness and extension, and its particular forms or "modifications."

The old materialism which regarded the world, with every

mind in it, as made up of a number of independent atoms is of course impossible now, though common enough in the eighteenth and nineteenth centuries. The mind could have no unity if it were really a number of self-existent beings, since each of these would evidently have a consciousness of its own apart from the others. This has been the chief argument for the existence of an individual soul, which would explain why each man is one consciousness and not many. It does not seem to me that Kant destroyed this argument, for his criticism was directed against the idea that the "soul-substance" was needed to unify successive sensations. But that was not the ground on which the philosophers before Kant maintained the existence of such a substance. As they believed that the material world was composed of a number of self-existent atoms, even those who supposed matter to be capable of consciousness could not explain how in a multitude of such entities there could at any time be one consciousness. The problem was not the unification of successive sensations but the unity of any one sensation. They inferred that the mind could not be made up of many self-existent entities of any kind, material or not; it must be essentially one through all its parts. The reasoning is quite sound, but it does not prove the existence of a separate soul in each man; the unity might be due to the presence of one soul throughout the world. Owing to the objections already mentioned against the belief in individual souls the latter is the only possible theory. No form of Pluralism, whether material or spiritual, can be maintained.

A general argument against all forms of that doctrine is that the "many self-existent beings" could only be repetitions of the same thing in different circumstances, like the successive states of any one of them. You cannot even use the word "many" without meaning many existences of one entity, whatever it may be. For it must be repeated that time is not the only medium in which one thing may have many existences; it may have them simultaneously in many places and attached to different groups of conscious states. The use of any plural implies that we are thinking of the objects so described as in some respect the same thing. We could not call them by one name, or include them in one concept, if we did not regard them as one thing multiplied in space.

Some form of unity in the world has been admitted by all philosophers who have believed knowledge of the real world to be possible, except by Leibnitz, whose Monadism is a *reductio ad absurdum* of the pluralistic theory. But one of the two great schools of thought has always regarded this unity as a secondary thing, as a likeness or other relation between separate substances. These are supposed to be fundamentally distinct, many beings which in the development of their existence somehow come into contact with one another. But, as we have seen, the similarity and interaction between them make such a theory impossible. If they started as distinct, as many, each of them would naturally develop a separate world, a Space and a Time not including the others, and qualities all its own. They could only come into contact with one another if they already formed parts of one Space. It is useless to call the unity of the world a " relation " between different things and suppose that Pluralism is still possible, for a " relation " means nothing unless it means identity or partial identity of quality—and therefore of being—or else existence in the same Space. A and B and the space between them are not three separate things, nor does the space between A and B exist in either or both of them as a property of theirs; for if the relation to B were included within the sphere of A's existence it is evident that this sphere would have to include B itself. A and B and the distance that separates them can only be parts of the one all-including Space. And a similar remark applies to all forms of relation, which must be contained, together with the terms they connect, within one being, just as, when we think of the relation, the ideas of the relation itself and the terms are contained within one mind.

II. Nothing but purely intellectual considerations can decide whether the world is essentially one or many. But the advocates of a pluralistic theory have sometimes based their opposition to Pantheism or Absolutism on the ground that it admits no independence or free will in human minds or in any other part of the universe; that it leaves no room for individualism since it denies the existence of any reality outside of, or distinct from, the One. But what is meant by " free will " ? If it means that the actions of each man depend on his character, such freedom is not disputed by any determinist. But the character does not spring out of the void at birth, and if it did, I do not see what satisfaction that could give to our feelings. It would then be a matter of chance, and no man could prefer to be what he is through chance rather than through causes existing before his birth and around him now. Or if the character does not come all at once from the void, but is gradually formed, yet not by any previous or external causes, in this case too its formation must be due to chance, through slight additions or modifications that occur by chance every now and then. Such a description of its origin is no more satisfying than that which represents it as arising all at once from nowhere. If it were true, a man might at any moment change from a scoundrel to a hero or from a hero to a scoundrel, since there is no reason why modifications due merely to chance should always be slight.

The supposed problem of free will has called forth more idle words in philosophy than any other. Most of those who have discussed it have talked as though a man were something other than his character; as though he had existed before his birth without any character at all, and at birth, or in the course of his early years, either chose a character—which would be free will—or had one forced upon him by circumstances over which he had no control—which is supposed to be the theory of the determinists. Such ideas are due to the other which I have already criticized, the idea that there is a subject or substance which " possesses " various qualities and is distinct from them, a self which is distinct from the thoughts and sensations it is said to have. It seems to be imagined that a man stands outside his character, as it were, and if he is free must be able to change it if he likes, whereas if he is not free he cannot do so and therefore deserves our sympathy. Either theory is of course absurd. The only changes of character possible are due either to external causes, such as injuries to the brain, which have been known to bring about a complete revolution in a man's nature; or else to the development of one side of the character, of the good or evil which had existed before but only in a comparatively latent state. If you suppose that any state of the world, including human minds, does not correspond according to fixed laws with the preceding state—I use the word " preceding " only provisionally, since I do not believe the parts of time to be successive—then you are admitting chance into the world, and you can fix no limit to what might happen. For if one thing in the world, one human mind can act in any way without obeying a law, then anything and everything may do so, and it becomes purely a matter of chance whether things obey a law or not. Such an introduction of chance would not satisfy any demand of ethics, for the only freedom that any man desires is that his actions may follow from his character ; he does not trouble himself about the question how his character was formed.

Individualism is mainly an illusion which we have to take seriously in order to make the world interesting, but must not take too seriously. We cannot act the play with any enthusiasm unless we half believe in its reality. The same difficulty is felt by the religious man, who is convinced that the other world is alone worthy of our attention, alone real, and yet has to take some notice of this world too, and act as though it were of some importance. But there is, of course, some truth in individualism, although, like the spirit of nationality, it has been wildly exaggerated. It may readily be admitted that every part of the universe is in some respect unique, as is also every state of every part. I see no reason why anyone should consider this inadequate. To require that the fundamental being of each thing should be different from every other would be to require that it should be isolated from every other. That one body may stand in relation to others it must form part of the same space and be identical with them in so far as it too is extended ; that one mind may communicate with others it must be identical with them, $i.e.$, as mind, though this does not exclude all difference.

If we are to judge any philosophy by the measure in which it satisfies our moral or æsthetic sense, then Pantheism seems to be far superior to any pluralistic theory of the universe. If every man were a separate entity, not a form of the infinite Being, he could not be under any obligation to sacrifice himself or his pleasures for the sake of another. It would even be unjust and unnatural that he should do so. A distinct self, such as each man is imagined to be by the

Pluralists, would and should naturally act as such, *i.e.*, selfishly. For the action of everything ought to be consistent with the nature of its being. Each man would be for himself the centre of existence, and to go beyond one's own interests would be eccentric. In fact, as I said, to pass outside one's own sphere of existence and act upon others would be impossible if reality were as the Pluralists describe it. But supposing it were possible, then it would be right and rational that each man should act solely for the good of his own little world, his own life, since according to the philosophy here criticized there is no single, larger world and all-including life of which every man is a part. If in order to avoid a *bellum omnium contra omnes* he made an agreement to keep the peace with other men, this would be for an entirely selfish purpose. The ideal for him would be to follow his own interests himself while promoting unselfishness in others. Certainly the notion of moral obligations would be absurd and unnatural if there were only men and not Man, only a number of isolated beings and not God.

This may easily be seen if we take one instance of such obligations, namely patriotism. An Englishman does not feel any devotion towards the forty million inhabitants of his country as distinct selves, distinct from himself and from each other. He would not sacrifice himself for a collection of such entities, for an aggregate. England for him is one life, of which he and all his fellow-countrymen are parts; which includes his ancestors and theirs, all the countryside and all the towns and cities in the land. This life is certainly no abstraction but just as real a being as any one of the forty millions.

So all other moral obligations involve a belief in the unity of the family, of the state, of humanity, or of the whole universe. Kant's maxim, " Act in such a way that you could wish the principle of your action to become law for all mankind," implies that a man should not act as this particular individual, but as the universal spirit of mankind existing in this particular form. If he were not this in reality, he could not fairly be expected to act as such. Again, in all religions each man is required to follow, not his own will, but the will of God; that is, in proportion to his power he is to act as though he were God. This would not be reasonable on any other theory than that of Pantheism, for why should any man identify his will with that of a Power altogether distinct from himself? It contradicts the very idea of freedom. In attempting to justify this the individualists in religion, especially the Deists in the eighteenth century, quite consistently laid stress on the doctrine of future rewards and punishments. It would be only right and natural that one whose existence, if not the results of his activity, is limited to a certain sphere, *i.e.*, his soul and body, should limit his interests to that sphere. Therefore it had to be proved that in submitting his will to that of God and doing apparently unselfish deeds a man was after all doing a thing consistent with his nature and benefiting himself.

But the doctrine of future rewards and punishments is not popular nowadays as an incentive to virtue. With it has disappeared the only logical basis of morality for those who hold the Deistic theory of the world—which is the theory of most Christians—and for any pluralistic philosophy. For it is idle to declare, with the Utilitarians, that in bringing happiness to the world a man is always bringing happiness to himself. Nor can we say that in sacrificing himself for others he is preferring his own higher good before his lower good, for we have still to prove that his self-sacrifice is a good for him at all. From the moral standpoint, no doubt, a dead patriot is better than a living traitor. But we have not yet justified the moral standpoint, or proved that conscience is not a kind of hypnotism inherited from one generation to another, or akin to that feeling of uneasiness which many experience at any departure from the automatic routine of daily life, or from a long-established tradition, however unreasonable. Might it not have been a thing originally "invented by the monks to enslave the people," or, to adopt a more modern explanation, an instinct implanted by Nature for the good of the race at the expense of the individual? Why, then, as Croce asks in criticizing this theory, should the individual continue to follow this instinct when he has discovered its origin, if that is its origin? Why should he trouble about the good of the race?

Morality has in fact no more right than religion to make statements or demands in a dogmatical form; they must be proved to be reasonable. We must not accept or obey them simply because they agree with our feelings, for men's feelings have often led them to approve and follow the most grotesque superstitions and to feel uneasy when they have not followed them. Our feelings themselves must be shown to be consistent with reason, which is the only test we have. Otherwise we must either disregard them or leave a discord in the mind, or at least a lack of union, between the moral sense and the intellect. The latter course is generally followed by those who cannot make these two elements of their nature agree, but it is unsatisfactory, for at a time of moral conflict his reason will be likely to suggest to a man that his scruples after all may be no more sensible than those of the Jews who were uneasy when they had walked more than a mile on the Sabbath, or the Greeks who were conscience-stricken when they had omitted a sacrifice. However strong his moral feelings, he may continually be haunted by the idea that perhaps they have not a much more exalted ancestry behind them than the taboos of the Polynesians.

The only logical foundation of morality is Pantheism, for this alone makes it reasonable that a man, as far as his power allows, should act as God. Such action is what the moral law demands, but the demand would be unintelligible if a man were a wholly finite being. But if he is God and man, or, to use the language of Spinoza, God modified as this particular man, then it is not unnatural to require that he should live as part of a greater life, not as a separate existence. In that case he would be acting in accordance with his higher nature and defying the illusion which makes him appear to himself something fundamentally distinct from the rest of the world.

It has been objected that moral goodness, if this account of it were true, would only be another form of selfishness, for if all the world is one existence, anyone who does good to " others " must really be doing good to himself. But selfishness means nothing but a disregard for the interests of others in comparison with one's own; the word has no meaning at all where there are no others whose interests one might disregard. Besides, the doing of good to others is not virtuous simply for this reason, that they are others. It might be called an eccentricity if they were wholly alien from oneself, separated from one's own being with that absolute separation in which the Pluralists believe. Unselfishness would then be as great an aberration as the wandering of the earth out of its own orbit into that of another planet, or any other divergence from natural law. Certainly the doing of good to oneself would be just as excellent a thing as the doing of good to others, if it were not that the latter alone implies in the doer a recognition of his unity with the rest of the world. In the one case he is acting as a finite existence, in the other as God.

Against this it has been argued that " even if there be a sense in which we may treat individual men and women as being "manifestations" or "appearances" of an all-embracing Absolute, Ethics surely has to do with the " manifestations " or " appearances," and not with the unity. Ethics is concerned with the relations of these apparently different and mutually exclusive appearances." [1] Certainly they have to act in one sense as individuals, with a limited power, but need that prevent them from acting on the principle that they are individual phases of the Absolute ? Each day a man's actions are limited to that day, and divided from the morrow by sleep, but he acts in it as one whose existence is not so limited, as a self whose life will pass through many days. The Smith of to-day may act for the Smith of tomorrow, or of a year hence, owing to his belief in his essential identity at the different times. So each phase of the Absolute, though limited to a particular time and space, may act as essentially identical with all others, as the Absolute working in a particular sphere.

As for the objection that " the moral consciousness certainly knows nothing of any metaphysical identity between myself and my neighbour," that is true if we emphasize the word " metaphysical " and refer to the metaphysics of the philosophers. But in the first place the sentence quoted does not affect us here, for we are not considering why men act virtuously, but why they ought to do so. The origin of the virtues may have been selfish ; they may have arisen from the belief that the good of a tribe or state as a whole brought with it the good of every individual, and have been inculcated so carefully throughout the generations that at last their origin

[1] Dr Hastings Rashdall, *Theory of Good and Evil*, vol. ii. p. 102.

has been forgotten and men have come to act in accordance with them mechanically. That moral consciousness which does not consider the ground of its morality resembles the æsthetic consciousness; men admire a landscape or a picture without considering the reasons why it is admirable. Besides, though they may have no purely metaphysical notion of their essential unity in the Absolute, they have the idea in a less technical form. Religion implies it, in speaking of the brotherhood of men, and in a thousand other phrases; patriotism implies it, when a man considers his country as one being of which he is part, a permanent life within one phase of which he is included. Every organism in which many men are united and to which they devote themselves involves the identity of all in one respect or another, and all moral appeals such as that to " our common humanity " are founded on the identity of mankind.

The same may be said of the desire for knowledge. If each man were primarily distinct from the rest of the world, his interest in it, apart from any selfish purpose, would be unintelligible. His only rational course would be to learn just as much about it as would enable him to use it for his own advantage. Apart from that, why should he wish to have in his mind a correct image of the world? Is it because it is a good thing for him to have there a fine picture, a great and self-consistent idea, and because knowledge widens his mind? But in that case he need not trouble himself whether it is a correct picture or not; any philosophy might satisfy him, so long as it formed a great and harmonious system. And he might widen his mind by working out a purely imaginary world, by drawing up for himself an encyclopædia on the subject of fairies, for instance, just as much as by studying astronomy or history. So long as he had the idea of a world it would not matter whether there were really any world or not. For his own practical purposes a very rudimentary education would be sufficient, and for " improving his mind " the idea of a Utopia or a Paradise would be better than that of the world we live in. One motive of the desire for knowledge may be the desire to promote the welfare of mankind, but certainly that is not the only motive, nor should it be. Equally strong is that fellow-feeling with the rest of the world of which I have spoken before. We do not want to know about the world because it is the real world but because it is our world, that existence of which our own lives are parts. It is as natural that each man should be interested in this as that in the later years of his life he should take an interest in his own boyhood or youth.

Pantheism does not, of course, deny the existence of all individuality whatsoever. To say that all beings are forms or modifications of the universal consciousness is evidently to admit the reality of differences between them. And the differences are always more observable than the unity, though —or rather, because—they do not go so deep. For that reason it is all the more necessary that philosophy and religion should lay stress on the oneness of the world, in order to correct the chaotic idea which most men have of its nature. But philosophy does not confound all moral distinctions by attributing all acts to the one Being, for it only attributes them to this Being in so far as they are identical in character. For the worst actions ever committed had this in common with the best, that they were instances of the working of universal laws of Nature. The worst thought was identical with the best in this, that it too was a thought, and therefore on the same level of existence.

The word "Pantheism," which I have used as the antithesis to Pluralism, is certainly somewhat misleading, but there is unfortunately no more convenient word, for "Monism" is generally taken to express the opposite of Dualism, and thus gives the wrong meaning. The God of Pantheism is the one substrate of all things good or bad. He is all things, in so far as all are the same and obey the same laws, and is therefore unconcerned with moral good and evil, which imply a distinction. He is not the God of Christianity, for whom that distinction is all-important. The Pantheist could only be accused of confusing all moral distinctions if he identified these two completely. There is, however, nothing to prevent him from admitting the existence of the Christian God as one of the forms in which the Absolute lives, and that doctrine in fact has been accepted by some philosophers lately. But to discuss this point here would be to anticipate a later chapter on the general subject of religion.

CHAPTER VI

TIME AND SUCCESSION

THE idea of time has given rise to more puzzles than any other in philosophy, puzzles which have interested many who have otherwise avoided metaphysics. One of the most popular is the question whether the order of events might be taken the other way round, whether we can imagine beings of another world to whom our past would be future, and our future past. Such fancies are not taken seriously, but they give us a hint of the difficulties which are involved in the common notion of time and are discovered whenever we begin to think about that notion. I have already pointed out how inconsistent we are in our ideas of the past; we speak of it as non-existent now, as though it had been annihilated, yet we regard it with pride or regret, as though it still existed. And we cannot help looking upon it as still there behind us; history appears to us as a long line with an ever-advancing point, the present. On the other hand, the future appears as a void upon which that long line continually encroaches. Thus we draw a distinction between past and future, a distinction which would be impossible if neither existed, for there could not be two kinds of non-existence.

There are two arguments against the idea of succession in time. Wherever there is an irreversible order, a successive series such as we suppose events to form, each member of the series must include all those before it, as does every number in the series of numbers. Without that there could no more be an irreversible order in the parts of time than there is in the parts of space. But we usually suppose that each time exists by itself, and that the past does not exist in the time "now." Therefore the whole course of events might be taken the other way round, for there is nothing in the present to decide on

TIME AND SUCCESSION 141

which side lies the "past" and on which the "future." Memory cannot decide it, for memory-images exist in the present, and therefore cannot tell us whether the events they represent exist on this side of the present or on that. The idea that they must be caused by events in the past does not help us, for if the supposed cause does not exist when the effect occurs how can it be said to produce it?

Besides, cause and effect are always proportionate to one another, and if we were to take the whole course of events in the reverse order to that which we usually suppose it to follow, we should be able to explain everything equally well by natural laws. This statement is a paradox and needs development, but its truth should be readily understood by anyone who believes the world to be governed entirely by mechanical laws. Those who believe in biological or other laws which cannot be resolved into the mechanical may find a greater difficulty in accepting it, but I hope to show that even on their theory it is true. Every supposed effect in the world might equally well be taken for the cause of the event we suppose to cause it. This being so, even if you do believe events to follow the generally accepted order, you must at least admit the possibility of a world in which exactly the same events passed in the opposite direction, so that the images, the "memories" you have in your mind, would be images of the future. But how are we to know that this is not such a world?

To come to the second argument, if one half of time is past and the other future, and neither exists, what have we left that does exist? The "present," the time "now"? But if this "now" has no extension it is simply nothing at all. On the other hand, if it is extended, what is there to limit its extent? What is to prevent us from applying the term to the whole of time? Suppose you take each continuous movement to be the "now," how does that "now," or the movement itself, differ from a length of space, in which there is no succession? And if there is succession in it, then throughout the movement the time must be divided between the increasing "past" and the diminishing "future." But here again, if neither of these exists, there can be nothing left in the "now," *i.e.*, the movement, that does exist.

The belief that the parts of time form a successive series

is due to the existence in the present of images not belonging to the present, *i.e.*, to what we call " memory." It is not the fact of a " past " time that has produced these images ; rather it is the existence of these images that makes us call the events they represent " past." Since the images exist, we infer that the events must exist somewhere, as do the distant things of which we have images in sight. As we place the things at a distance from us in space, so we place the events at a distance from us in time. They do not exist now, and yet they do exist ; and from this paradox we form that curious idea of a " past " time which leads to such a mass of difficulties whenever we attempt to define its meaning. For if we say that neither the past nor the future exists, how are we to distinguish between the two ? And how can there be a time that " has been " ? Every event must exist in its own " present " and not at any other moment ; at no time can it exist in a state of " having been." Such difficulties as these lead to the conclusion that the " past " is really the creation of memory, a purely human creation. In a world where there were no minds like ours, and consequently no memories, everyone must recognize that time would be just like space, and there would be no distinction of " before " and " after." Like the distinctions of " left " and " right," " above " and " under," this is merely the work of human minds.

I. " Wherever there is an irreversible order, a successive series such as we suppose events to form, each member of the series must include all those before it, as does every number in the series of numbers." If there were any progress in the amount of existence, if the parts of time formed an ascending series of values, such that time fulfilled the above definition, then they would be like the series of numbers and might be called successive. But if they are like so many " ones," then we have no reason for saying that one of them comes before or after another. And according to the usual theory of time, no part of it exists any more or less than another, or includes any other within itself. If that is so, there is nothing in any part of it to mark whether that part comes before or after the time on either side of it.

If the time on neither side of the present exists, how can

we know which is past and which future? Each moment exists by itself and therefore can tell us nothing about the time outside it; it has no sign-post. At the moment B you say that A is past, but if A does not exist how can you know this? Certainly not from memory, for it is evident that you cannot directly see any time but the present, if no other time exists. And even if you could see it, how could you know it to be past rather than future? There is no such thing as a character of "pastness" which could belong to any event and be recognized in it.

In fact men do in a way contradict their own theory of time by supposing the past to exist now, though in the background, as memories exist in the background of present thoughts and sensations. They regard the series of "nows" as like the series of numbers. "Ten," for instance, means both a sum of units and the final unit in that sum, and it is only from a fusion of the two meanings that the idea of numbers as a successive series has been formed. So we regard every "now," or the world at every moment, both as a long line of events and as the final point in that line; and it is really the past, existing in the background, but still existing, which gives every moment its place in the supposed succession of moments. Annihilate the past as well as the future in your imagination, leave a blank on each side of the present, and you will see how impossible it is to regard the present as being added to either, as we say the present is added to the past. If we did not retain images of past events along with the present sensation, we could have no idea of succession, and if the world did not retain the past along with the present, there could be no succession in reality. Some may believe that the past is so retained; they may hold, with Professor Bergson, that the past has not ceased to exist, but has only ceased to act. Against such a theory most of the following arguments against succession in time will not apply. But it is better, as I hope to show, to abandon both conceptions of succession, and to regard the whole of time as a single "now" of which every "now" in the narrower sense is a part.

"Every event must exist in its own 'present' and not at any other moment; at no time can it exist in a state of 'having been.'" The idea that it can arises from the belief that "external" relations, *i.e.*, those of time and space, qualify the terms, whereas they really qualify the whole of which the terms are parts. When we say, for instance, that A is twenty miles from B, we must not think that A contains as a property of itself "being twenty miles distant from B." All that exists is a whole composed of three elements, A, twenty miles, B. If we supposed that the relation was included in A's existence we should have to suppose that the twenty miles were somehow included in it, since they are necessary for the relation. For the same reason all we can mean by saying "A occurs a year before B" is that there exists a whole period consisting of the event A *plus* a year, *plus* the event B. No such relation as "before B" can be included in the existence of A; it cannot be qualified by any relation of "having been" to B. This is still more obvious if neither exists when the other does, for how can either stand in a relation to something not yet or no longer existing?

To come to another point, the idea of "motion" or "passage" or of "change" will not save that of succession in time. Assuming motion to exist, I do not see what is to decide in which direction any movement proceeds. Unless an object adds something to itself by its movement, unless at the end it somehow has that movement included in its existence, there is nothing to distinguish the end of its movement from the beginning. Its passage must be just like a length of space, and "beginning" and "end" be as interchangeable as "right" and "left," or "up" and "down." Imagine yourself as watching a movement without at any time remembering the part of the movement already gone through; you would then have no idea of motion whatever. This is obvious from the fact that you could not have any idea of direction without remembering the earlier part of the movement, and without the idea of direction that of motion is impossible. In fact we always do retain a picture of the earlier part in our minds. But in the world apart from the human mind motion itself would be just as impossible as the idea of motion in the case just supposed, unless the past were continually retained along with the present, as the memories of former positions of the moving body are retained along with the sight of its present position. And certainly, even if motion existed, we could never know in which direction it proceeded, unless the past co-existed with the present and so could become an object of our perception. Otherwise we could only be aware of the present and could not know on which side lay the part of the motion that was past.

The same is true of change. We could never have formed the idea of this if we had not, along with the image of the present state, the image of that from which it is changing; otherwise we could not know the direction of the change, and without the knowledge of the direction how would the idea of change be possible? The idea is due to the co-existence of fainter images of other states with the vivid image of the present. But what is there to assure us that the fainter images represent past states, if neither past nor future exists? And if in the things themselves there is nothing corresponding to this co-existence of the images, if the past is not retained with the present, there can be no reality corresponding to the idea of change.

We should not find it difficult to take the movement of any atom in this direction rather than in that. But the whole complex history of the world consists only of an infinite number of such movements, and must therefore be equally reversible. The atoms are all in reality elements of consciousness more or less intense, and it is of a multitude of such elements that our minds, our thoughts and memories, consist, so that with those too there is no absolute "before" and "after." They are only irreversible in appearance, because the mind as a whole contains impressions of events on one side of the present, and thus in a manner contains the "past." But we cannot say that each of its elements contains any impression of the "past," any more than each atom of a photographic film contains such an impression. The movements of every element of the mind are reversible, and therefore the whole consciousness must be so.

Suppose that there had been only two atoms, and that these had met but once during the whole of time and exchanged their motions; time would have existed just as much in that case, but what could have qualified the period on one side of the moment when the two atoms met as "before" or "after" the other? Assume that the period A did come before the period B; how could a world in which this occurred be distinguished from a world in which the opposite was true? It must, I think, be clear to everyone that in the case supposed the terms "before" and "after" would be meaningless, and to apply either of them to this period or that would be as arbitrary as a use of the words "up" and "down," or "right" and "left," to express absolute distinctions in space. Only if we imagined a mind as present to watch the two atoms would "before" and "after" have any meaning, and even then they would have it only for the mind, and not absolutely. During the period B the mind might have in its "memory" an image of the motion during the period A, and would put this behind it as "past." But it would have no real justification for doing so, since the fact that during B it has within itself a representation of the movement during A does not in the least prove that A came first.

Those who believe that there are in the world biological as well as mechanical laws, or even that biological laws are universal, will not be so ready to believe that the whole course of events might equally well have happened in the opposite order. Certainly it seems grotesque to imagine a world in which men were born by coming out of the grave, and went through the whole of life backwards; where the punishment would come before the trial, and the crime last of all, if one can talk of a crime, the whole action being reversed. Yet for the mechanical theory of the universe it would be quite possible, assuming that there could be succession in time; without succession it would, of course, be as meaningless to say that events proceeded in the opposite direction as to say that they really follow the usually accepted order. Even the advocates of biological laws would have to admit the possibility of such a reversed world, if they believe time to be successive. They hold that life is a gradual development from inanimate matter, or at least from a less to a more elaborate organism, and that the inanimate or less complex structure must come before the more complex. But in the mere fact that the moment B came after the moment A what could there be to ensure that the state of any being at B would be more highly developed than its state at A ? What have " before " and " after " to do with a less or greater degree of perfection ? Obviously later time does not necessarily imply greater excellence, for then progress would be universal and unceasing. There is no reason whatever for supposing that a body must be more fully developed at a " later " moment than at an " earlier." If time were successive I could just as easily believe the opposite to be true ; I could see no reason why manhood should not come before infancy. The idea that the more complex state of a body comes after the less complex is due to the existence of the less complex in the other, or rather the existence of its image, the " memory." With the greater development of the body comes a greater number of " memories," by which I mean simply images of another time than the present—and memories, as I have explained, create the idea of the " past," so that a man supposes the boyhood of which he bears an image in his mind to be a " past " state of himself. But the nature of succession, as usually interpreted, does not make it necessary that there should be images of the past in the present state rather than of the future ; how can we be sure, then, that our " memories " represent the past ?

If there were succession in time, anti-biological laws would be just as possible as biological laws, and the degradation of the world as its progress. The carrying out of a resolve might come before the resolve itself, for the passing of the act into the will would be no more wonderful than the passing of will into act. Every stage in the process of willing and carrying out must occupy some part of time, and might as easily take place in the reverse order as a book might be printed backwards. Every thought might occur the other way round as easily as a syllogism might be written with the conclusion first. For there is nothing in " before " and " after " to prevent the reverse order, any more than there is in " right " and " left." But this is to say that there is no absolute " before " and " after," any more than there is an absolute " right " and " left " ; each pair of terms is a purely human construction.

Every law of Nature might be reversed, and therefore, assuming the reality of succession, we might imagine a world in which the same events occurred as in ours, but in the opposite order. The image or " memory " of a completed movement comes last with us; in that other world it would come first. One would have first the image of the whole movement, and lastly nothing but the sensation of the object at A, its starting-point in our world, but its goal in that other. In that case could there be any idea of movement at all? And if there could be, surely the inhabitant of such a world would take it in the wrong order, and at the moment when he had the image of the whole movement before him he would think the movement past, whereas it would be still before him. This is obvious, for among the events reversed in that other world would be our thoughts, and our counterparts there would "remember" what had not yet occurred, without suspecting that they were taking events in the wrong order. But how do we know that it is not we who are wrong? Since there might be a world in which such an error occurred, it might be ours.

It may make the argument clearer if you suppose, what is at least conceivable, that there is somewhere out in space a world which is an exact reproduction of ours, except that the counterpart there of our twentieth century took place while the Glacial Age was occurring here, and the counterpart there of our Glacial Age is taking place now. Imagine the whole course of our history, every thought and movement, to be reversed over there. Then during the Glacial Age here the men there, with the same thoughts and feelings as we are having now, would have looked back on their Glacial Age, though it is simultaneous with our present. What is to decide whether we or they are right in the order attributed to time? Should we not both be as wrong as an Englishman and Australian, each of whom insisted that the people on the other side of the earth were standing upside down?

Again, assuming that there were succession in time, it would be conceivable that there should be another time series which went in the opposite direction to ours, though the events in it were parallel to those of our time, so that this event in the one would be simultaneous with that in the other. If one direction is possible for time, the opposite direction must be equally so. There might, therefore, somewhere out in space be a series of events which reversed our order, so that of the three movements A, B, C, simultaneous with a, β, γ in our world, A came last, though a, the movement simultaneous with it here, came first of the three. We might even go farther. Granting for a moment that each man has a direct perception of events in his own mind as successive, how could he be sure that the events around him were proceeding in the same direction, that of the movements A, B, C, producing the sensations a, β, γ, A did not come last for the moving body, though the sensation a comes first for him ? How could he know that the sensations produced by those external events appeared in the same order to other men as to him, or that other men mean what he means by " memory " and " past," and do not rather refer to ideas of the " future " ? But it is simpler if we take any two bodies that come into contact on two occasions. It seems quite possible that the occasion which was first for A should be the second for B and *vice versâ*, if a succession of events is possible at all. The order of cause and effect might be different for the two, and the motion of A which for A itself was the cause of a certain motion of B might to B appear as the effect of that motion. This is certainly a paradox, but quite consistent with the idea of succession in time. It suggests, however, that that idea has no absolute value but is relative to the human mind.

Even those who believe time to be successive must admit that there might be a world in which events were not successive but just like the parts of space. Everything in it might be exactly the same as in ours, except that the event a would not be " before " or " after " b, but on one side of it. Time in that world might justly be called a fourth dimension. All the words and thoughts there would be the same as ours, just as the scenes spread out on the film of a cinematograph are the same as those seen " successively " on the screen. This is possible, since succession is not necessary for what we call the series of " causes " and " effects " ; two neighbouring events must be proportionate to one another, but this relation between them would be equally possible if there were no succession in time but only proximity. Therefore everything that has occurred, all our actions and thoughts, including those on time itself, might equally well have taken place in a non-successive time. The only difference that succession could make would be that our thoughts themselves would be successive; but the contents of our thoughts, as I said, would remain the same. This would be true of every idea, even of the idea that time is different from space in being successive.

The argument that succession in time, as usually explained, is necessary if there is to be any proportion between events can easily be proved unsound. Supposing that an event A " preceded " an event B, this would not entitle it to affect B in any way. For since on the ordinary theory of time it would not exist when B did, any more than B exists during A, the two occupy just the same position towards one another, and B might just as well be called the cause of A. But in fact neither could really be the cause, for how could one event direct the course of another when it no longer exists, or does not exist yet? How can the velocity and direction of A and B after contact be determined by their velocity and direction before, if the latter are swept into nothingness when the movement is over? It must be noted that the motion of A and B would have to be determined by the whole of their former motions; it could not be determined simply by the moment before, supposing a moment could exist, for in a moment, a point of time, there could be no velocity or direction at all. To use such phrases as the " motion of A passes into that of B " will not help us, for all that one can extract from them is the bare assertion, not a proof, that the motion of A precedes that of B. This is so evident that nowadays the notion of causality has been generally abandoned, and some such term as " invariable sequence " is used instead. All that is meant by the statement that " B is the effect of A " is that B always follows A. The doctrine of causality is thus reduced to the simple assertion that there is a sequence of events, and does not help us at all to understand this sequence, or to prove that it exists. The idea of succession in time is not necessary for belief in the laws of Nature, for this only requires that two neighbouring events shall be proportionate to one another, not that one should be considered as earlier than the other. And from this proportion between events it follows that there is no law of nature which could not be taken the other way round. " Cause " and " effect " being always equivalent, it is just as easy to suppose that the " effect " produces the " cause," since it has just as much power.

But there is a great deal in the world, it will be said, which implies the previous existence of something else. To take a very simple instance, the presence of two jagged fragments of stone exactly fitting into one another implies that they must once have formed a single block. It seems absurd to imagine the process reversed, to suppose that they exist separately first and afterwards unite. It would seem still more absurd to suppose that vibrations in the air proceed from hundreds of ears to a bell ringing; in that case, why should vibrations come from so many different quarters at the same time, and be so much alike? It is needless to multiply instances; the objection is clear enough.

But in the first place it would not hold good in a less complex world than ours. As I said before, if only two atoms had existed and had met but once and exchanged their motions, time would have existed just as much in that case; but what could have determined which part of it was before the other? Those who hold the usual theory of time would maintain that succession existed here too: but neither the time on this side of the contact nor the time on that would imply that the other must have preceded it. It seems, therefore, that succession, if it exists, has nothing to do with such cases as those mentioned above, where one event appears to imply another before it. They cannot be due to the reality of succession, supposing it is real, for its existence does not demand theirs. If succession in time can be proved at all, it must be capable of proof from the simplest instance in which it occurs, or might occur.

It is true that such cases as those mentioned above show one time or event to imply another; the existence of the two fragments of stone apart implies a time when they are one block. The present state of the world involves the existence somewhere of the states we call "past," for we cannot imagine it to be the only one; there are too many things in it which look as though they were due to one original, too many which look as though they were scattered parts of something once entire. We could never imagine, it will be said, that the present was the first state of the world, for it would be strange that a world should come into existence with so many things alike or capable of fitting into one another. But there is no reason, or at least not the same reason, to prevent us from imagining that it might be the last state, that the world might now end, or rather come to a full stop. But why should the states of the world which the present implies be taken to be past rather than future, if neither past nor future exist? I do not see how there could be any distinction between the two, or why either should affect the present more than the other. I could just as easily imagine that the state of the world now is due to what it will be as to what it has been; that it might be its first state, just as easily as that it might be its last, and that the resemblance and symmetry of many of its parts, the two fragments of stone, for instance, are due to a future union between them, just as easily as that they are due to one that is past. That is to say, one could take the course of events backwards and say that those states of things implied by the present state, those states usually believed to be past, are really future; one might suppose that the present is what it is because those states are to come, instead of supposing that it is so because they have already been.

Those who believe in succession but hold that the past does not exist do not realise altogether what this latter proposition involves. If the past does not exist now any more than the future, it cannot determine, any more than the future, the events happening now. On either side of these events there must be a void; nothing, therefore, that can condition their existence. Yet there is always the idea that though the past does not exist now, the fact that it has been somehow exists along with the present and determines it. But the fact that some other event or time has been cannot thus be retained alongside the present, and if it could there is no reason why it should modify the present more than the fact that a certain other time will be. In reality those who believe in succession do believe that the past exists somewhere now in the background of the present; they give it the same sort of shadowy existence as that of memory.

If the series of events were like a line of things in space one state of the world could imply another just as much as if they were successive, provided that each event corresponded with the one on either side according to the laws of Nature.

The present state might appear to imply the events on one side of it rather than those on the other, but this would not make it necessary for us to call one side " past " and the other " future."

It may be thought that the existence of the will indicates an absolute distinction between past and future. But in fact the will determines the one just as much as the other, and each equally determines the will. For if the will corresponds and stands in an exact equation with the past as well as with the future—and it must do that, if it does not just rise up out of the void, so to speak—how can you decide which it causes ? Surely it might be called the cause of the events to which it is future just as much as of those to which it is past, since there is no reason why the privilege of determining the present should belong to past events, if non-existent, rather than to future. But the will, it may be said, is a movement, and a movement in the direction of the events we call " future." This brings us back to a point already considered. How are we to know in which direction the will moves, and why should it be said to move in one direction rather than another ? It can only do so if throughout the movement one part of it, the past, exists, while the other does not. There can be no direction without progress, and no progress if nothing more exists at the " end " of the movement than at the " beginning."

One reason why we take the will to decide " future " events rather than " past " is that when the former exist the memory of the will exists too. And as the memory of the will exists, though in the background, with the present perception of the action, so we imagine the will itself as still existing, though in the background, with the action itself. But we remember the will as existing without the action, and therefore regard the present, when both exist, though the will is not now to the fore, as an increase of existence, and so as coming after the moment when the will was alone. Besides, the action appears, though it is not really so, to correspond to the will more closely than do the events in the mind just preceding the will. In the same way the picture on the canvas resembles the picture in the artist's mind more closely than the events which preceded that mental picture resemble it. Yet we call those events "causes" of the mental picture, and must suppose that they correspond to it as closely as the picture on the canvas does, since cause and effect are always proportionate. So the events preceding the will must be as proportionate to it as the action is, and might with just as much reason be supposed effects of the will.

Such arguments will not please those believers in "free will" who mean by that term that the will, or rather the whole world including the will, does not stand in exact proportion to what we call the "previous" state of things as well as to the "future," and could not be inferred from it by an intelligence aware of all the "previous" facts. But if the will is in any degree independent of the "previous" state, I do not see why the "following" action should not be equally independent of the will, so that, even apart from paralysis, the members of the body might refuse to obey the decrees of the mind. We could not then infer the nature of the will from the action, any more than from the previous state of things, and our neighbours might be animated by the most excellent intentions while performing the most terrible crimes. But the idea that the will stands in exact relation to the events on both sides of it in time, so that it may equally well be said to determine, and be determined by, either side, does not in the least detract from the goodness or badness of men's resolutions. They would be just as virtuous or vicious if they could not be carried out. Their origin and result have nothing to do with their merits. It will make no difference ethically if we deny succession in time. Those philosophers who regarded all events as parts of an eternal "now" to the mind of God, and past and future not as realities but as appearances to the human mind, never supposed themselves to be destroying all moral ideas by doing so.

Before leaving this part of the argument, it may be remarked that the idea of succession in time leads to a difficulty which is peculiar to the infinity of time and has no parallel in any difficulty arising from the infinity of space. It forms part of Kant's first antinomy, and has often been used as an argument for the belief that the world must have had a beginning. If there was no beginning of time, it is said, then an infinite number of events must have been completed in the past; but how can an infinite number ever be completed? The fallacy here lies in comparing the series of events with the successive series of numbers. If the former were really successive they would have to proceed just like a man counting; they would, as it were, count themselves, for otherwise nothing could mark one of them as before rather than after another. But it is impossible that an infinite number should have been counted in the past, for we should have to think of the future as counting on beyond the infinite number already reached. A simpler way of putting the difficulty is this. Every successive series must have a number one, and therefore if events were successive there must have been a beginning. On the other hand, if you believe that time is infinite backwards as well as forwards—or rather on one side of the present as well as on the other—you cannot conceive of it as successive, any more than space. Give up the idea of succession and you will find the infinity of time no harder to accept than the infinity of extension. We do not find any difficulty in believing space to be infinite on this side of any particular place as well as on that, for we can conceive that the extent on either side is infinite in one direction but finite in another, *i.e.*, at this particular place. It is true that Kant in his first antinomy argues against the infinity of space on the ground that there cannot be a completed infinity. But the word "completed" involves the idea of counting, which does not apply to space, the parts of which are not successive. This part of the antinomy is generally felt to be unsound, whereas that relating to time seems a real difficulty, since events are assumed to follow one another, just like numbers that are being counted, and each must therefore have some quasi-numerical value to mark its place in the series.

II. We regard time as a series of "moments," and "now" as separating past and future. But what is meant by either term, "moment" or "now"? Does either of these entities possess extension or not? If not, it must be like Euclid's "point," which has no magnitude; that is to say, it is nothing at all. There cannot be a part of time without extension, any more than there can be a part of space without any size. Whenever you think of a point or moment you are thinking of a part of space or time with a very small extent; if you reduce that extent to nothing what idea of those entities is left you? How could you imagine one point or moment next to another? Surely it would coincide with that other, and at any rate it would be impossible to imagine it as lying on this side rather than on that. And as the moment has no extension, an infinite number of moments would have to elapse before an event possessing any extension came to an end, and the ending of an infinite number is a contradiction in terms. If the moments are distinguished from one another we must regard them as capable of being counted in imagination, or as counting themselves, and certainly that could never be finished. You cannot assume, then, any such thing as a " present moment " if you deny it extension; and since past and future, on the hypothesis we are considering, do not exist, time can only be made up of three non-entities. To look at it in another way, since there can be nothing between past and future, the " now " being nothing at all, these two must make up the whole of time. Yet it seems that there must be something between them, to which they can be past and future respectively.

Assuming, on the other hand, that the present, the " now," has a certain extent, what limit can we set to it? The word " now " is applied to various lengths of time, to any period which possesses a certain uniformity, as to the present age, or to modern times as contrasted with mediæval. There is no reason why we should not apply it to the whole of time, for the course of the world is in some respects always uniform. As another meaning of the word psychology gives us the " specious present," *i.e.*, that amount of time which the mind grasps together. It is like the view of a procession through a narrow window, but the width of the window need not be supposed always the same. But this definition will not save the common notion of time as a series of successive events.

In the first place it could only be applied to time as viewed by the human mind, and not to time in itself. Imagine the course of the world before the existence of men; there could be no " specious present," and therefore no " now," and therefore no past or future. Or suppose you take each event to represent the " now "; is the event to be regarded as existing all together, in one block, so to speak, or as containing past and future in it ? If it is successive it seems that part of it must be continually past and part future, and then we have the same difficulty as before. Inside the " now " represented by the event there will either be two non-entities, past and future, or three, if you add a second, this time unextended, " now."

To return to the subject of the " specious present," some declare that in this we can see one event, or part of an event, beginning and another ending. But we could not tell which it was that was coming and which was disappearing, unless we also had before us a picture of another " specious present " in which the two events or parts of events were at different stages of their movement. If that other " present " no longer existed we could not see it directly, but could only have an image of it in our minds. But the existence of this image cannot assure us that the time it represents is past rather than future. It exists together with *this* " specious present," and cannot label that other as preceding this.

To escape from the difficulties arising from the idea of time as successive, if you suppose neither past nor future to exist, some might be ready to admit that the past does remain ; that time is not a moving point but a continually lengthening line. They would give two meanings to the term " now," like those we give to a number ; " now," for them, could mean the whole of past time or its limit, the last point or event, just as the number ten may mean either ten units or the last of them. The " present " event would mean the event which is " going on," *i.e.*, extending its length, as opposed to the past, whose length is fixed. Not only every phase of human consciousness would remain, as in the " pure memory " described by Bergson, but every event in the world. Such a view might be supported by several common ideas and expressions about time ; the very word " past " implies something still existing, though behind us. The past is regarded as fixed, the future as indeterminate ; the past as blocked, and the future as empty.

On such a theory time might properly be called successive ; each moment would be, not a unit or zero nor a single event, but the whole amount of past time, and these innumerable amounts, each including, with an infinitesimal addition, the one on this side, and included in the one on that, would form a scale of ascending values, like the series of numbers. The second objection raised above would also be removed; what exists at any time would be an extending line of events and not an unextended present. If time is to be taken as successive, this conception of it would certainly be preferable to the inconsistent ideas generally prevalent on the subject.

But if it were correct, how could we know any better than before which time was the past? As we have seen, it is not necessarily the time of which we possess representations in "memory," since there might just as well be images of the future. For in any case the whole course of the world might have occurred in the opposite direction to that which we suppose it to follow, and what can assure us that we are right? Supposing the past to exist, we cannot see it directly, any more than we can see directly objects outside us in space; in each case it is only an image of the event or object that we have in our minds. If the events are past, we have no means of knowing it.

III. It is always accepted as quite natural that we should have in our minds representations of the past and not of the future. But there is nothing in the mere idea of succession to make it necessary. From this we may infer that we get the idea of a past time not from the existence of any such kind of time, but from the fact that we have representations in our minds of events other than the present. On whichever side of the present these events lay, we should suppose that to be the past. The images in the "memory," differing from sensations in that they are not entering the mind now, and are much fainter, we take to be representations of events more or less distant from us in time, and therefore not existing "now," as the objects of which we have fainter images in sensation do not exist "here." But the fact that they do not exist "now" does not cut these events off altogether from existence, any more than an object is cut off from existence by the fact that it is not "here." They are behind us and not with us, yet still they are; otherwise we could not see them, any more than we can see the future. We even take them as existing "now," in one sense of that word, for, as I said, we sometimes regard the "now" as the whole line of events behind us, instead of applying the term only to the final event. It is in this way that the idea of the past is developed, a strangely confused idea, for we sometimes speak of the past as non-existent, while yet we regard it as full of existence, as distinct from the void future in front. The meaning of it might well puzzle Goethe's Mephistopheles.

> Vorbei! ein dummes Wort. Warum vorbei?
> Vorbei und reines Nichts, vollkommnes Einerlei!
> Was soll uns denn das ew'ge Schaffen,
> Geschaffenes zu nichts hinwegzuraffen?
> " Da ist's vorbei! " Was ist daran zu lesen?
> Es ist so gut, als wär'es nicht gewesen;
> Und treibt sich doch im Kreis, als wenn es wäre.
> Ich liebte mir dafür das Ewig-Leere.

The idea of succession arises from the fact that owing to memory the series of parts of time, for us, are like the series of numbers. Each of the times A and B contains certain impressions of events, or of an event, impressions vivid at one end but fainter and fainter towards the other, and these impressions are the same in both, but B contains an infinitesimal addition, just as each number contains the same as the number preceding it, with a unit added. And the events, or parts of an event, appear more faintly in B than in A, and farther off from that vivid end we call the present sensation. We infer that the whole course of the world is like this, that the past somehow continues to exist behind the present, and is included in the " now." Thus the time order differs for us from the spatial order, for the parts of space do not each contain all the other parts on one side, in different degrees of faintness. Besides, owing to the fact that we have impressions of events only on one side of the " now," we treat that side alone as existing, unlike the future, whereas we do not imagine that space exists only on one side of the " here," for we can have impressions of objects on all sides of it. The idea of the future is derived from the " memory " of a time when the present did not exist; as the present came after that time, so another time, not yet existing, is to come after the present.

Another reason why we make such a difference between time and space is that the states of things at adjoining times are always either the same or bear a definite correspondence with one another, and are continuous, whereas objects adjacent in space appear not to have necessarily any mutual resemblance or correspondence or continuity. If the order of events in the past had been as chaotic as some collections of composite things near to one another in space we could never have formed the idea of things persisting throughout one Time; we should have had to imagine a number of times, or worlds with times of their own; times adjoining one another but having no further connection. We could not talk of motion or succession between these, any more than between the objects adjoining one another in space. For we should have to regard each as a new beginning of time, and therefore not before or after another. There is not, however, so much difference between the states of a thing at different times and what we call the separate things at different places. The further matter is analyzed, the greater the identity found between its elements; the atoms resemble one another so closely that they have been called " manufactured articles." They are different states of one and the same thing scattered through space, corresponding to the different states of one thing in time. But the visible objects composed of these atoms are so various that they appear to stand side by side with one another without any connection between them, and we do not regard the same thing as having a continuous series of existences in space as in time.

In space we can go in any direction we please, or at least imagine such motion as possible, whereas there is one of the two directions in time along which we cannot go or even imagine ourselves as going. For movement seems necessarily to imply an addition to the time already existing, *i.e.*, the past, and therefore we cannot go backwards to past history, which would involve rather a shortening than an extension of the line of events. After drawing a line you cannot make it longer by going over it again backwards. The past, therefore, appears as fixed and unalterable, and the future alone as uncertain and capable of being affected by our action. But in fact the events we call " future " are just as fixed as those we call " past," and once this is recognized we are a long way on towards abolishing the distinction between " past " and " future."

In maintaining that there is no succession in time and that the whole of it might be considered as an eternal " now " we are not, of course, making all time simultaneous, any more than we reduce all space to a point by denying such distinctions as "here" and "there," "above" and "below" to be anything but creations of the human mind. We are not giving the past a longer existence, but declaring that it might equally well be taken as future, *i.e.*, that such distinctions do not exist at all in time. Each part of time exists in its own extent, and is not cancelled or succeeded by another. The present is the only real tense; any limit we fix to the "now" must be more or less arbitrary, like the "here" of space. But if we choose we can, during any thought or other state of consciousness, define the "now" as the time which that thought occupies, or the state of the world at that time; and the things existing at any time may be defined as the things which at that time give us our sensations, as opposed to the fainter images we call memories, and whatever affects those things, or merely stands in a spatial relation to them.

So far as I know, the only writer who has given adequate attention to the problems raised in this chapter is Lotze, who deals with them in his *Metaphysics*, bk. ii., ch. iii. After a long argument he comes to the conclusion that time is real and the parts of it successive. But the reason he gives for this conclusion only proves that time has length, not that it has succession; it would have no force against the theory that time is just like space. His final argument, in a sentence, runs thus: "If one and the same timeless being by its timeless activity of intellectual presentation gives to one constituent of its existence the past character of a recollection, to another the significance of the present, to a third unknown element that of the future, it could never, if it is to be really timeless, change this distribution of characters."[1] But this does not affect the argument against succession. For that it is not necessary to say that the mind, either of the individual or of the world, is timeless; all that it denies is that the times at which it exists come one after another. The individual mind may at one moment regard s^1 and s^2—to give Lotze's own symbols—as past, s^3 as present, s^4 as future, and at another regard s^1, s^2, s^3 as past, s^4 as present, and s^5 as future; but this is no proof that the one moment precedes and the other follows.

[1] Lotze, *Metaphysics*, translation ed. by B. Bosanquet, p. 264.

A man at one place regards the objects a^1 as lying on his left and a^2 as on his right; at another place he regards both a^1 and a^2 as being on his left and a^3 as on his right; but that is no argument that in moving from place to place he has moved from an absolute left to an absolute right. Everyone admits that these terms are relative to each man, that they do not represent any real difference. Why should not the same be true of the distinctions we make in time?

Earlier in the chapter Lotze remarks: " Future and past alike are not; but the manner of their not-being is not the same." [1] But there cannot be two ways of not existing. It is only from the standpoint of the present, in the narrower sense of the word, that the two do not exist, and the present cannot determine either as past or future. It does not, if taken in the narrower sense, contain them, and therefore they do not exist for it; but it cannot give them any other attribute or make any distinction between them. Lotze himself seems to hesitate on the point almost immediately afterwards, and observes that we take the past " as given, and in a certain way belonging to reality." And at the end of the chapter he admits that the ordinary view of time is unintelligible, and asks : " The teeming past, has it really ceased to be at all ? Is it quite broken off from connection with the world and in no way preserved for it ? The history of the world, is it reduced to the infinitely thin, for ever changing strip of light which forms the present, wavering between the darkness of the past, which is done with and no longer anything at all, and a darkness of the future, which is also nothing ? " [2] It must be noticed that " infinitely thin " means nothing, and that the present is thereby reduced to a third non-entity. Finally he relegates the problem to the philosophy of religion. From this he might have learned that the distinctions of past, present, and future do not exist for the mind of God, *i.e.* that they have no genuine reality, are nothing but creations of the human mind, and only exist for that.

[1] *Op. cit.*, p. 246.
[2] *Op. cit.*, p. 268.

CHAPTER VII

RELATIVITY

> How charming is divine Philosophy!
> Not harsh and crabbed, as dull fools suppose,
> But musical as is Apollo's lute.
> MILTON, *Comus*.

EVERYONE who deals with metaphysics—or in fact with almost any other subject—is expected nowadays to say something about the theory of Relativity; on the other hand, we are sometimes told that Relativity has nothing to do with metaphysics, or even that it puts an end to the accursed thing. That is untrue, of course; it is as metaphysical as anything in the philosophy of Spinoza or Hegel. Obviously it goes beyond science, for science would stop at the result of the Michelson-Morley experiment, for instance, without offering any explanation. It is the task of metaphysics, or one of its tasks, to investigate the ideas used by the scientists as by other people. So the advocates and opponents of Relativity examine the idea of motion and, when they are discussing Einstein's theory, the ideas of simultaneity and of length in time and space as well.

I. The doctrine of Relativity in its simplest form is this, that we ought only to speak of a change in the distance between two bodies, without saying that one changes its place rather than the other. The place of a thing can only be defined by its distance from others, but then the places of those others may also be defined by their distance from it, so that when we say that it changes its place we might just as well suppose that it was they that were changing theirs. It sounds absurd, when you walk from one village to another, to say that they may be moving and you yourself standing still. But remembering the motion of the earth round the sun you would admit that they were moving, and if you were walking in the opposite direction to that motion you would have to say that they were travelling faster than you were. They would be moving at the rate of eighteen miles a second—the velocity of the earth—and you would be going—backwards—at a little less. Imagine some object, a bullet, say, which appeared to you to move in the same direction as yourself, opposite to the earth's motion, but at eighteen miles a second; which is really changing its place, the bullet or the villages? When you take into consideration the motion of the earth you must regard the bullet as standing still and one village as coming towards it, the other as moving away. It seems that, like the heroine of *Alice through the Looking Glass*, the bullet would have to go twice as fast in order really to move forwards. This is not all, for the whole solar system is moving relatively to the fixed stars, and the whole array of fixed stars visible to us may be moving relatively to some other system beyond the range of our telescopes. In this complicated mechanism of movement within movement what is to tell which bodies are really changing their place, and what their real velocity is? We might take any one in the universe we please and imagine it as at rest and all the others as moving round it, towards it, or away from it, or else as remaining at the same distance, in the same direction, and therefore also at rest.

This line of argument, however, does not, as is often assumed, actually disprove the existence of absolute motion. It is true that absolute motion would be meaningless if rest and motion were only determined by the relation of one body to another, by the fact that the distance of A from B remained the same or changed. You may say that A has moved, because it is now farther away from B: but what is there to determine whether B has remained at rest all the while? Judged from a third body C, B may have moved and A remained at rest. If we could know that a certain body X was at rest we could judge from it the rest or motion of all the others, but if its state of rest depends upon its relation to some other body, and the rest or motion of that body depends upon its relation to some other, we should obviously have to go on *ad infinitum*. But there seems no reason why motion should not mean that A becomes distant, not

RELATIVITY

from another body, but from itself; that the A of this moment is more or less removed from the A of that. Its existence during the time of its movement would form a line in space, whereas if it were at rest it would not be thus extended. It would be impossible for us to know this, for we cannot directly see the past, or have the whole line of movement before us at once. But it is not inconceivable, for the general idea of change implies that the A of this moment is different from the A of that, and if difference between the two states is possible, why not distance too? There might then have been motion, if there had been only one thing in the world.

It seemed at one time that we might use the velocity of light to decide which bodies were moving, and this idea led to the famous Michelson-Morley experiment. Light, as is well known, travels at a constant velocity of 186,000 miles a second; by "constant" is meant that the rate is the same whether the body that sends out the light is moving or not, relatively to any other body you choose. As the earth moves round the sun at the rate of eighteen miles a second it was thought that if we measured out any distance, say a yard, from a to b in the direction of the earth's motion, and a yard from x to y at right angles to that motion, light should take a longer time to go from a to b and back than from x to y and back again. In the first case the motion of the earth would make the distance longer when the light was proceeding from a to b, for the distance covered by the earth would have to be added to the length $a—b$. On the return journey the motion of the earth would, of course, be in favour of the flash of light and shorten the distance it had to cover. But this shortening would not wholly compensate for the previous lengthening. The time taken in the whole journey would be longer than if the earth were at rest. In the second case, when a flash passes from x to y and back, the motion of the earth would increase the distance both ways, so that the time taken in the journey would again be longer than if the earth were at rest, but not by so much in this instance as in the other.

It is as though a man were to mark out a certain distance a to b along a current at sea and the same distance from x to y across it. He would take longer to row or swim from a to b

and back, with the current first against him and then in his favour, than from x to y and back, though in this latter case the current would lessen his speed both in his going and returning. So a flash of light, it was expected, should take longer to go from a to b, in the direction of the earth's motion, and back again than in the journey to and fro between x and y, an equal distance across that motion. It was found, however, that light took exactly the same time in both cases, so that for all we can tell from this experiment the earth is at rest. It was an astonishing and disconcerting result, and naturally several attempts were made to explain it.

The first was that made by Fitzgerald and Lorentz, who suggested that the size of every body was reduced in the direction of its motion and in proportion to its velocity. Thus when we used a measuring-rod to measure a yard first at right angles to the direction of the earth's motion, and then a yard in that direction, the distance would not really be the same, for the rod would shorten as soon as it was turned round to point in the way the earth was moving. We could not know this, of course, for anything we used to test the measuring-rod would also shorten in the direction of the earth's motion. This theory would explain the result of the Michelson-Morley experiment by assuming that the yard measuring-rod shortened when it was turned from x—y to a—b, so that the latter distance was really less by an amount sufficient to make the time taken by the flash from a to b and back no longer than that of the flash from x to y and back.

This is a strange hypothesis and does not explain why any such contraction should take place. Besides, supposing that the earth were suddenly to begin moving twice as fast relatively to the sun as before, we should on this theory have to assume that the earth and every measuring instrument on it shortened by a certain amount. But both ends of the measuring-rod would increase their velocity to an equal degree at the same time, and how could there then be any contraction? All contractions during motion presuppose that the front moves at first slower than the rear, or starts later. In any case, even if this theory were acceptable, the fact would remain that the attempt to prove absolute motion by means of light failed. Its failure gave rise to another theory,

RELATIVITY

that of Einstein, which has caused a revolution in our ideas of time and space—though we may remind the Relativists that no revolution can be absolute.

It begins with a criticism of the idea of simultaneity. How can we be sure that events at two places occur at the same time? We must be sure of this in measuring a body with the length a to b which is moving relatively to the earth, for to do so we must mark a position on the earth a^1, coinciding with a, one end of the moving body, at the same time as we mark on the earth b^1, coinciding with b, the other end. The answer of most men will be that we can see the two marks being made at the same time. But take an obvious instance, a moving train. Suppose that you stand at the point a^1 and set a mark there when a, the rear end of the train coincides with it; if at the same time you see a man setting a mark at a point b^1 along the line because b, the front end, coincides with it, you will be quite wrong if you imagine that the two of you set down your marks simultaneously, and that a coincided with a^1 at the same time as b coincided with b^1. For the ray of light which brings you the image of the other man marking b^1 takes time to travel from him to you, though the time is only a very small fraction of a second, of course. Therefore if the ray reaches you at the same time as you mark a^1 he must have set down his mark some fraction of a second earlier, and b must have coincided with b^1 so much earlier than a coincided with a^1. So a^1 to b^1 will not represent the length of the moving train a to b, for when the end b was at b^1 the other end a was not yet at a^1 but at a fraction of an inch to the left of it, supposing the train to be travelling to the right.

This answer, then, that we see events occurring at the same time will not help us at all, for what we see is always past. But it seems that one might test simultaneity in this way. Between the two points a^1 and b^1 you might find the middle, c^1; then, at the moment when a, the rear end of the train, coincides with a^1 you might signal by a flash of light to c^1, and the other man might do the same when b^1, the front of the train, coincides with b. If the two flashes reach c at the same time it might seem that they must have been sent out at the same time, too, since they had the same distance to travel, so that a must have coincided with a^1 at the moment when b coincided with b^1. The middle point, c, of the train must also have coincided with c^1 at that moment.

Unfortunately the passengers in the train, if they were Relativists, would dispute all this, and have equal right on their side. During the movement of the two flashes of light from the ends to the middle, the middle point of the train, c, will have moved away from c^1 towards the light coming from b, the front of the train, and away from the light coming from the rear end. The light from b will reach it earlier, and therefore a man standing on the train at c may conclude that it must have been sent out earlier. For though, so far, we have been taking your point of view, that the line is at rest and the train moving, on the theory that motion is relative, he has just as much right to assume that the train is standing still and the earth moving past it; that the train's energy is employed in counteracting the line's motion so as to keep itself still. He may say, then, that it is c^1, the middle point on the embankment between a^1 and b^1, that has moved away from c, the middle of the train; that c has stood still, and that as the flash from b reached it first, it must have been sent out before that from a. And as one flash was sent out when a coincided with a^1 and the other when b coincided with b^1, he may conclude that b and b^1 coincided earlier than a and a^1. For him, then, when the front of the train was at b^1 the other end must have been, not at a^1, but at a point slightly to the left of it, and the length of the train a to b must be slightly longer than a^1 to b^1, which you suppose it to equal. You will thus differ from him not only about the simultaneity of events but about the length of the train, which you will suppose him to be exaggerating. It must be remembered, however, that you will not differ about its breadth; you may send out a flash from each of the rails, and at the moment of sending them mark on the rails the points x^1 and y^1, coinciding with x and y, the two sides of the train; and as the train is not travelling towards either flash, if the two meet in the middle for you they will meet in the middle for the man on the train too, so that neither of you will deny that they were sent out at the same time. It is only in the direction of the train's motion that difficulties arise.

Suppose, now, that you mark out a line x^1—y^1 across the rails and a^1—b^1 along them, and that the two lines as measured by you are equal in length. Suppose, too, that the traveller marks the line x—y, equal to x^1—y^1, across the train and a—b along it, and that these two lines on the train, as measured by him, are equal. If you then compare the lengths a—b on the train and a^1—b^1 on the rails in the manner described above, and find them to be the same, the traveller will not; he will take a—b to be longer than a^1—b^1, for while you think that a coincides with a^1 at the same time as b with b^1, he will think that a is a little to the left of a^1 when b is at b^1. As he thus finds the line on the rails a^1—b^1 to be shorter than a—b, he will suppose it to be shorter than either of the two lines from side to side, x^1—y^1 and x—y, since each of these, for him, is equal to a—b. He will think you are wrong in supposing that a^1—b^1 is as long as x^1—y^1. On the other hand, if it is he who finds a—b and a^1—b^1 to be equal, you will think, for the same reason as before, that he exaggerates the length of the train; that a—b is really shorter than a^1—b^1, and consequently that it is also shorter than either x^1—y^1 or x—y, each of which, for you, is equal to a^1—b^1. You will think him wrong in believing that a—b is as long as x—y.

It follows from all this that whenever an observer A on any body marks on its breadth and length what he supposes to be equal distances, another observer B for whom that body is in motion will take the lengthways distance, *i.e.*, that in the direction of motion, to be shorter than the other, at right angles to that direction. Even if the same measuring-rod be used by A, it will, as judged by B, contract when it is turned in the direction of motion; and so, too, as judged by A, would any measuring-rod used by B. For either of them may equally well suppose himself to be at rest and the other in motion. This explains the result of the Michelson-Morley experiment. An inhabitant of the sun, for whom the earth is moving at the rate of eighteen miles a second, would find that the yard measure on the earth, as judged by his standards of length, was shorter when lying in the direction of the earth's motion, from a to b, than when it lay at right angles to that direction, from x to y. He would not be surprised, then, that light took no longer to pass from a to b and back than from x to y and back, although the earth is moving, from his standpoint, in the direction a—b, and one would therefore expect light to take a longer time over the journey to and fro in that direction than in the other, if the two distances were equal. For he would assume that the measuring-rod marked a shorter distance when turned in the direction a—b than when it lay from x to y, crosswise to the line of the earth's motion. This explanation looks as though it were the same as the Lorentz theory, but it must be remembered that we are not now talking of a real contraction of the measuring-rod, but only of a contraction relative to the measurer on the sun. On the theory of relativity we on the earth have just as much right to assume that the earth is at rest and that our measuring-rod marks the same distance in each direction, so that light naturally takes the same distance each way : that the sun is moving, and that it is the measuring-rods on the sun which shorten when turned in the direction of the sun's motion. The solar surveyors are right from their standpoint, or moving point, and we are equally right from ours.

But to return to Einstein's famous " train and embankment " illustration of his theory, there is one point which I have not yet seen noticed, though it is fairly obvious and is at least as worth consideration as some others that have been raised. It does not properly belong to the special form of Relativity, which concerns only bodies moving with uniform velocity relatively to one another, but as far as I know it has not been mentioned in any account of the general form of the theory. It is worth while noticing, because it shows that on this theory an observer will not only differ from other observers on bodies moving relatively to him, but also from himself, whenever his own standing ground comes into contact with one of those bodies and is " set in motion " or " increases its rate of motion."

Suppose that the train is first at rest—relatively to the earth—and that flashes of light are sent out from c, the middle, to the two ends, a and b, and reflected back from them to c; they will, of course, arrive back at c together. And both the man on the train and the man on the embankment will agree that the flashes from c reached a and b simultaneously.

RELATIVITY

After this has been done once or twice, suppose that two flashes are again sent out from c and that the moment they reach a and b the train—or the earth, as the passenger might say—begins to move. One could conceivably arrange that the two ends at least should begin to move when the flashes reach them, and that the middle point c, after sending out the flashes, should also begin to move at the end of half the time taken by the previous flashes in going and returning. This would ensure that the three points on the train—or, for the passenger, the three corresponding points on the earth—begin to move simultaneously for both observers. But this time the reflected flashes would not arrive back at c together, though they would at c^1, the middle point on the embankment. That from a, the end of the train, would reach c a little later than that from b, the front, since c would be moving away from the one and towards the other. But from the standpoint of Relativity the man on the train cannot be forced to admit that the train is moving; he may assume that it is still at rest, and that it is the earth that has begun to move. Yet the two flashes, which he admits to have reached a and b simultaneously and been reflected at once, do not reach the middle of the train together. If he is not to allow that the train has moved, he must suppose that the flash from a this time travelled slowlier than that from b, though the previous flashes from the two ends travelled at the same speed.

He has indeed another alternative; he may suppose that light now travels at equal speed in both directions, but that formerly, when the train was at rest relatively to the earth, the flash sent out from c to a travelled slowlier than that from c to b, and therefore reached its end and set out on the return journey later than the other. This would equally well explain why the two flashes did not now reach the middle point c again simultaneously, though both on the return journey travelled with the same speed. If he adopts this explanation he must assume that he was wrong in his ideas of simultaneity before, since he then believed that the two flashes from c reached a and b at the same time, and now has to believe that the flash to a, the end of the train, arrived later.

But to return to the first of the two assumptions open to

the observer on the train, when this " begins to move," the assumption that the flash from a to c travels slowlier than that from b, the front. This slower speed certainly calls for explanation, and would, I take it, be explained by the Relativists in the same way as the jerk backwards a man feels when his train starts, and the jerk forwards when it stops. In the latter case, we are told, the man in the train may assume that " there exists, during the period of application of the brakes, a gravitational field which is directed forwards, and which is variable with respect to time." [1] Its action, he may suppose, causes the jerk forwards, and reduces the movement of the embankment, as of the whole earth, till it is at rest, but its effect on the train is neutralized by the application of the brakes, which, in his view, do not bring the train from motion to rest, but prevent it from changing a state of rest for motion forwards. In the same way, I infer, the man on the train is to explain the change in the velocity of light when the train starts. He must assume that a gravitational field then comes into existence which not only causes the motion of the railway embankment in the direction from b to a, but also affects the flashes of light, which is subject to gravitation; that it lessens the speed of the flash from the rear end of the train and accelerates that from the front.

But this gravitational pull cannot be confined merely to the moment when the train starts, as is the jerk backwards felt by the passenger. Suppose that at the moment of starting, at each end of the train, a man sends a flash of light across the train and back, and that at the end of the journey to and fro of the flash at each end, $i.e.$, some fraction of a second after the train starts, each of the men sends another flash to the middle of the train. These flashes must have been sent out simultaneously for the men on the train as well as for the man on the embankment, since they will agree that both were sent out at the same time after the start, the journey across the train at each end being equal. But these new flashes towards the middle of the train, like those sent out at the moment when the train started, will meet, not at c, but at d, a point a little to the left of c, supposing that the train is moving towards the right. However often

---

[1] A. Einstein, *The Theory of Relativity*, tr. by R. W. Lawson, p. 70.

the two passengers repeat this, using the flashes sent across the train at each end as their clock, they will find the same result in the case of those sent along the train; they must, therefore, assume that the gravitational pull, which causes these latter flashes to meet at d, and not at c, the middle, is continued as long as the train moves, or rather the embankment, from their point of view.

But if they are to assume the existence of this gravitational pull they will find it difficult to explain the relation between the width and length of the train. To simplify matters, suppose we take a single compartment and imagine it as exactly square; then while the train is at rest a flash of light will take just as long to travel from side to side—from x to y—and back as from one end of the compartment to the other—from a to b—and back. But when the train has started and gravitation comes into play this ought to be so no longer. The flash from a to b ought to return later than that from x to y, for just the same reason as, in the Michelson-Morley experiment, it was expected that a flash in the direction of the earth's motion would return later than one sent at right angles to that direction. Gravitation might be regarded as a current in the ether, and it takes a longer time to go a certain distance against a current and then back than to go an equal distance and back across the current. Yet, just as in the Michelson-Morley experiment, it would be found that the two flashes in the train took exactly the same time in their journeys. The man standing on the embankment will explain this, as we saw, by saying that the compartment of the train became shorter in the direction of motion when it began to move, or that at least light travelled as though the distance were shorter; it seems that the passengers must also assume that the compartment shortens, but since, as good Relativists, they are always to suppose themselves at rest, they must assume that the shortening is due to the same gravitational force which has changed the velocity of light. From this they will infer that under the influence of gravitation every body which resists it and remains at rest, and even the space between any two bodies which remain at rest, become shorter in the direction of the gravitational pull. So too, of course, would all the measuring rods on the train, since they share its motion. This, as we shall see later on, helps to explain the "curved space" of Einstein's theory, and why the curve in the path of light near the sun is greater than would be expected from Newton's theory of gravitation.

But this idea of a gravitational pull coming into force as soon as the train "begins to move," and in fact the Relativists' account of "beginning to move" as well, seem to require more explanation than is usually given. As long as we are considering uniform motion or rest we find it easy to admit the Relativists' theory that every body has equal right to suppose itself at rest. But when there is a change, when the engine sets a train in motion relatively to the earth, it seems absurd to say that a man on the train may equally well suppose the earth to be set in motion by the engine. He certainly might suppose that the earth, and the train with it, had been moving before, and that the engine was now counteracting that movement for the train while the earth continued to move. But then he will be admitting that the state of the train has changed, not the state of the earth. It would be better if the Relativist could avoid the words "movement" and "rest" altogether, and substitute for them "continuous change of the distance between one body and others," and "maintenance of that distance." Such phraseology would be cumbrous, but if we continue to use the words "motion" and "rest" we must at least mentally substitute for them the definitions just given. When we say that a body begins to move on contact with some other we must think that its distances from all other bodies which do not come into contact with any other change at the same rate. This would have to be amplified, of course, to take gravitation as well as contact into account as a cause of "movement."

And yet, after all, when any body is "set in motion" by an impulse from another it might be supposed to be pulling the whole universe in the opposite direction while remaining at rest itself. One could not well prove that it was not so, and that account of the matter might be more intelligible to the average man who cannot rid himself of the ordinary idea of motion. We say that every atom attracts every other, which implies that each for itself is the centre of the universe, and this assumption is not so much stranger than the other.

The meaning of Relativity is that every atom is entitled to its own theory of the world, so long as that theory explains the facts. But as the world is a cosmos and not a chaos the apparently different theories will really be the same and include the same laws. Whenever one body comes into contact with another it might suppose, as I said, that it pulls the whole universe, including light and, at first, the objects on itself, in one direction, setting in motion those previously at rest relatively to itself, and accelerating or retarding the motions of others. It will have to assume, though, that it is itself shortened in the direction of that universal impulse, for otherwise it could not explain the motion of the flashes of light sent in that direction as compared with that of the flashes sent athwart it. It may seem that in attributing to itself this power of pulling the world to and fro it is supposing itself to produce enormous changes in the world. But in fact it is not supposing itself to produce any change except in the distance of other bodies from itself and their motions relative to itself. Since the impulse is to be exactly alike everywhere, all the other bodies would remain in precisely the same relations to one another as before, and the laws of mechanics would remain the same, so that the change produced would be nothing wonderful.

To return to the case of the train; as soon as it is set in motion every body upon it will behave as if it had received a sudden pull backwards, *i.e.*, just as if a gravitational force had been exerted at that moment. Every body, it might be assumed, follows this pull until a force from the engines in the opposite direction restores it to a state of rest; a force which does not affect light, for that still remains subject to the pull. The usual explanation of general movement backwards relatively to the train is, of course, that the train begins to move and that their inertia maintains at rest the bodies upon it until the force from the engines is communicated to them; but the other theory explains the facts just as well. This equivalence of the two accounts becomes clearer from another illustration given by Einstein. Suppose that in empty space, far away from any other body, and therefore from any considerable force of gravitation, there were a large chest like a lift, with one or two men in it and objects of various materials. As there would be practically no gravitation, nothing there would have any weight worth mention; a lump of iron might be held up by a man in the lift without any effort, and if he removed his hands it would not fall to the floor but remain suspended where it was. Suppose then that some being like the Jinnee in Arabian tales fastened a rope to the lift and began to pull it upwards as the eagle carried off Gulliver's chest. All the objects in it would appear to fall to the floor at the same rate, and the more massive ones, if held by any of the men, would press down their hands, or, as you may prefer to put it, the hands will press the objects upwards with them; it comes to the same thing. That is to say, everything will happen just as though gravitation had come into play and were pulling the objects downwards. The men in the lift could not tell whether it was being pulled upwards or gravitation was pulling everything in it downwards, while the rope was counteracting the gravitation in the case of the lift itself. Or they might suppose that the floor of the lift itself was exerting the gravitational force. All the objects, as I said, except those held up, would come to the floor at the same rate, and this too would be a natural consequence of gravitation, for all bodies fall at the same rate in a vacuum; it is only the resistance of the air that makes some fall more slowly than others, and we may suppose that there is no air in the lift, however unfortunate this might be for the men. If the mysterious being who pulls the lift upwards continues to do so at a continually increasing rate, every object in it will fall as often as it is lifted up and let go again, so that the men might suppose the gravitational force to continue.

But it seems at first that there might be one exception to the rule that when the lift is pulled upwards everything will happen in just the same way as though the lift were at rest and gravitation were pulling the objects in it downwards. In the former case a ray of light passing in a straight line from one side of the lift to the other would appear to depart from that straight line and be inclined down towards the floor when the lift was pulled upwards, just like any more concrete object that had moved previously in a straight line. But would gravitation have the same effect on light? Does it deflect light from a straight line as it deflects every moving body?

The photographs taken of the stars whose light passed near the sun during an eclipse proved that the gravitational force of the sun did turn that light from the course it would have followed had there been no such force to affect it. What is equally important, the deflection was twice as great as that deduced from Newton's theory of gravitation, as Einstein had predicted it would be. The reason for his prediction was the famous " curvature of space " which has exercised so many minds since the eclipse photographs confirmed his theory.

It has been shown in the case of the train beginning to move, that any man in the train who assumes it to be still at rest must assume not only that gravitation is affecting the velocity of light from one end to the other and pulling backwards at a slight angle any flash sent from side to side, but also that the train is shortened. For in a compartment which was an exact square before the train started, light, even when the train starts or gravitation comes into play, takes no longer to go and return in the direction of the gravitational pull, *i.e.*, along the train, than from side to side. Like the passenger in the train, the man in the lift, which we may suppose square before it is pulled upwards, will find that even after the light begins to be deflected downwards, a deflection which he may attribute to gravitation, in spite of that a flash sent from roof to floor and back returns in as short a time as a flash sent from side to side. For the reason already given in the instance of the train, this would be impossible if the lift had remained square; he will infer, then, that the distance from roof to floor is now less than that from one side to the other. But as all his instruments of measurement will shorten too, when changed from a horizontal to a vertical position, he will be unable to confirm this by measuring the distances. If he attributes the deflection of light to gravitation, then he must infer that gravitation affects the dimensions of a body at rest in precisely the same way as motion affects a moving body according to the Lorentz theory. As there every moving body shortened in the direction of motion, so here every body at rest relatively to a gravitational centre will shorten in the direction of the gravitation. Even if he will not admit this to be true, he must admit that light behaves as though it were.

The stronger the gravitation the greater will be the shortening, just as in the Lorentz theory the contraction increased with the velocity of the moving body. For if the lift comes to rest again and then is pulled faster upwards than before, the men in the lift will assume that there is a greater force of gravitation, since all the objects in it, and light too, fall downwards faster, or, if in movement, take a steeper incline downwards. But as light will still take no longer time to go from roof to floor of the lift and back again than from side to side and back, he must infer that the distance from roof to floor has lessened more than it did before. The being whom we supposed to be pulling the lift upwards would explain this second shortening as due to the greater motion of the lift, just as an observer on the sun would explain the result of the Michelson-Morley experiment by assuming that the earth and all the measuring instruments upon it shortened in the direction of motion, and would infer that they would grow still shorter if the motion increased. But the man in the lift, if he is to regard the lift as at rest, must explain the greater shortening as due to the greater force of gravitation. And if gravitation produces exactly the same result on a body at rest relatively to the attracting mass, and on all the objects in it, as the motion of that body upwards would produce if there were no gravitation, then the nearer the body at rest to the gravitational centre, the more it will contract in the vertical direction, the gravitational force being stronger. Hence it may be inferred as a general rule that everything that comes to rest relatively to an attracting body shortens in the vertical direction according to the nearness and size of that body.

This shortening will lead to some strange results in the geometry of a gravitational " field." Suppose a great circle could be drawn round the sun with a compass, and a rod were then used to measure first the circumference of the circle and then the radius. Being straight, the rod could not of course give the length of the circumference exactly, but if it were short it could give it approximately enough. When it was turned in the vertical direction and began to measure the radius it would contract, though by a very small degree, and would continue to shorten more and more as it was taken along the radius nearer and nearer to the sun. This, of course, would affect the estimated length of the radius as compared with that of the circumference, for owing to its contraction, the rod will have to be laid down oftener than it otherwise would be, and so would find the length greater than if there were no attracting body near. So, too, in measuring the whole diameter. The normal relation between the length of the circumference and that of the diameter is indicated by the number 3·14159 . . ., usually nicknamed π. But as the measuring-rod owing to its contraction exaggerates the length of the diameter, anyone who measured a circle in a gravitational field, *e.g.* in an area round the sun, and did not account for the contraction, would estimate that the circumference was less than 3·14159 . . . times the length of the diameter. It would appear as the circumference of a smaller circle than that indicated by the length of the radius. This, as far as I understand the theory, is the explanation why the path of light near the sun appears as an arc of a smaller circle, *i.e.*, as deflected to a greater degree, than would be expected from Newton's theory of gravitation. A more obvious consequence is that though light is subject to gravitation, if one measured out a certain distance in a horizontal and then in a vertical direction from the earth or any other body, and then sent a flash of light along each line and back again, the two flashes would take the same time over the journey there and back, though, for the same reason as that given in the case of the Michelson-Morley experiment, one would expect the flash up and down to take the longer time. For the gravitational force of the earth, it would seem, ought to produce the same result on this flash as was expected from the motion of the earth in the experiment just mentioned. Yet no such result would be found in this case either.

The curvature of space due to gravitation is just that divergence from the normal proportion, mentioned above, between the diameter and the circumference which would be found on measuring a circle round any body; a divergence which is the greater in proportion to the gravitational force of that body, and the nearness of the circle to the gravitational centre. It might also be illustrated in the following way. Imagine a line *a* drawn upwards from a gravitational centre, and on top of this a horizontal line *b*, so as to form a large T. Suppose that points are marked at equal distances—equal as judged with a measuring-rod unaffected by gravitation—from the join of the T all down a, that the same distances are marked out along b, and that each point on a is joined to a point on one half of b, in such a way as to form a set of parallel lines. If we measure the length from the top of a to any point down it we shall exaggerate the distance owing to the contraction of the measuring-rod in the vertical direction under the influence of gravitation; and the farther we go down, the greater we shall find the length from the top to the point reached as compared with that of the line extending from the point reached to the corresponding point on b. For the measuring-rod, though it will contract to some extent when turned from a horizontal to a slanting line, *i.e.*, a line from a point in a to a point in b, will not contract so much as when turned directly downwards. It will seem, then, that the line from a point in a to a point in b is shorter than it should be as compared with the distance from the top of a to a point down its length, and that this shortening increases the farther we measure down a. If so, we should have to account for it by assuming that b is not in a straight line but is gradually inclined more and more downwards.

Again, if we marked at equal distances the points a^1, a^2, a^3 . . . along the ground, and then from these points drew upwards the lines b^1, b^2, b^3 . . ., each line in turn being an apparently equal degree higher than the one to the left; and if we drew a line connecting the tops of those lines together, we ought of course to have a straight line slanting downwards. But in measuring the upward lines the rod used is contracted owing to gravitation, and the contraction will be the greater the nearer the rod is to the ground. The difference, too, between the contractions of the rod in marking out lines rising 5 and 10 yards from the ground will be greater than that between its contractions at 1000 and 1005 yards above the ground. Therefore b^2 will be taller than b^1, the shortest line, by a greater amount than that by which b^3 overtops b^2, and so on, the difference in the heights of that of any two that stand side by side becoming less as we take taller and taller lines. The line connecting the tops of b^1, b^2, b^3 will therefore not be a straight line but will form a steeper and steeper curve as it approaches the ground.

RELATIVITY

The vertical contraction must in most cases be exceedingly small, for it is only assumed in order to explain why, if a certain distance were measured straight upwards from a gravitational centre and an equal distance at right angles to it, light would take no longer to go and return in the one case than in the other. It should take longer to do the former, owing to gravitation, but only an infinitesimal fraction of a second longer, unless the gravitational force is exceedingly strong, for light travels with such a velocity that it could only be affected to any considerable degree by such a force. Therefore we need only assume a correspondingly small contraction in order to explain why the two flashes of light in fact take an equal time to go and return.

It is only in objects at rest relatively to the gravitational centre that we need assume a shortening of their vertical length. In a lift that fell through a vacuum towards that centre no effect of gravitation would be observed at all, supposing there could be any observers. For as all things in a vacuum fall with equal velocity, a bar of iron or a feather would remain in just the same position relatively to the floor of the lift or any other object there; if it was half-way between roof and floor when the lift began to move downwards, it would remain suspended so without being held upwards. Neither bar nor feather would appear to have any weight at all, for no force would be required to keep them in that position. A body moving across the lift, which appeared, if viewed from another body at rest relatively to the gravitational centre, to be travelling in a curve downwards owing to gravitation, would appear to a man in the lift to be travelling in a straight line, just as an object falling in or from a moving train falls in a curve for a man standing on the embankment, but in a straight line for anyone on the train. This would apply to a ray of light in the lift as well, since light is subject to gravitation; it would move in a slight curve downwards as viewed from the gravitational centre or any body at rest relatively to that centre, but would be quite straight for anyone in the lift. That is to say, everything in a falling body happens exactly as if that body were at rest and there were no such thing as gravitation at all. Viewed from the earth, or whatever the attracting body might be, the lift would appear to be falling with a continuous increase in speed, and therefore it would seem as though, for the reason given when we were considering the instance of a train first at rest and then in motion, a man in the lift would have to assume a shortening of its height in order to account for the fact that at no moment of the fall would light take any longer to go and return from roof to floor than from side to side. But according to the theory of Relativity, it is in the bodies that do not fall that the contraction has to be assumed by anyone on them. It is in the falling lift that everything happens as though it were at rest; no alteration has to be assumed in its shape, nor do the relative positions of the things in it change, and, as judged by an observer in it, light travels across it in a straight line. The only change that gravitation produces is in the distance of the lift itself and all the things in it, including light, from the gravitational centre.

Light appears to travel across it in a straight line, and so does every object moving from side to side, though as judged from a body " at rest " it is describing a more or less accentuated curve downwards, owing to the continuously increasing pull of the earth. Suppose, now, that the earth were enclosed like a small globe in a box falling directly towards the sun. Everything in that box would happen as though it were at rest; as judged by an observer in it there would be no deflection of light downwards, and the earth itself, which we suppose to travel in a curve round the sun, would move in a straight line. According to the theory of Relativity one might just as well suppose that the box is at rest and the sun moving towards it, and therefore that the path of the earth is straight. All that we should properly assume as a result of gravitation is a change in the position of the earth, the planets, and the sun relatively to one another.

It is only when one object comes into contact with another that any alteration of its size and shape has to be assumed. On a body moving through empty space there can be no change, none even from gravitation, for as gravitation acts equally on that body and on everything in it, including light, its influence may be cancelled out. Any observer on such a body A moving under the influence of gravitation will agree in his measurements with another on a body B moving relatively to A but not subject to any attracting force. Suppose that a flash of light were sent out from a^1, the rear end of A, when it coincided with b^1, the rear of B, and another from a^3, the front of A, when it coincided with b^3, the front of B, and that these two flashes met at b^2, the middle. Then an observer on B as well as the observer on A would conclude that the flashes were sent out simultaneously, although A is moving relatively to B, and therefore one might expect them to differ like the men on the moving train and the embankment. For here the observer B must allow for the influence of gravitation in accelerating the light from the rear end to the middle and retarding it from the front, an influence which counteracts that of the motion of A. He would find, too, that if flashes were sent out from b^1 and b^3 when they coincided with a^1 and a^3 these flashes would meet at b^2, the middle of B, as the other two met at the middle of A. For the flashes from b^1 and b^3 would not be accelerated or retarded by gravitation, since we have supposed B to be outside any such influence.

Any body, therefore, which does not come into contact with another—whether to be " set in motion " by that contact or upheld by it " at rest " in a gravitational field, *e.g.* above the earth—will act as a convenient standard from which the relative speeds and magnitudes of everything else in the universe can be measured and the laws of nature established. It is true that for another moving at a different velocity, but not coming into contact with any other, the measures thus made will appear to be wrong, but as they will be uniformly wrong that will not make much difference. If a man estimated the comparative size of a number of objects with a measuring-rod assumed to be a yard long but really a little shorter, he will certainly give the length of these objects wrongly, but not the relations between them. The earth itself or the sun generally acts as our standard for the establishing of the laws of nature, for they are not, like the objects on the earth, continually coming into contact with other bodies; and though measurements made from the standpoint of the earth would be slightly wrong for an observer on the sun, they would be uniformly wrong, and therefore as valid for establishing the relation between objects and their movements as though they were correct.

To put the laws of nature in a form valid for arbitrarily moving bodies or " reference systems," as in the general theory of Relativity, seems a work of supererogation. If there were such things as bodies that moved with arbitrary changes of speed there would obviously be no laws of nature at all but a general chaos. As we saw, on an object that comes into contact with another and thereupon suffers a change relatively to all surrounding objects, even if we suppose it to remain at rest, we must assume a shortening of its length. The man on the train when it started to move had to assume it in order to account for the fact that light, in spite of the gravitational force he supposed to come into play, took no longer to go and return along a line down the train than along a line across it which was marked as equal to the other before the start. So, too, a vertical contraction must be assumed on a body which is at rest relatively to a gravitational centre and therefore must also be in contact with some other to maintain itself in the same position relatively to that centre. It must be unnecessary to attempt to establish the laws of nature in a form valid for observers on a system which those observers themselves admit to vary in its dimensions and measurements of time ; in a form that is to be valid for them on the supposition that the dimensions of their system and its measuring instruments do not change. To return to the instance of the train, the passenger must admit that when the train starts there is an alteration in the length of the train and, for him, in the velocity of light, and that it is the man on the embankment who is consistent in his measurements ; he cannot expect, then, that the laws of the universe should be so formulated as to agree with his own measurements as though these were unaltered.

II. There is one form of motion which for a long time troubled the Relativists considerably, *i.e.*, rotatory motion. The centrifugal force on a rotating body A would, it was thought, be inexplicable if we supposed that this body might equally well be regarded as at rest, and the universe as rotating around it. But the Relativists have suggested that this force does not, after all, prove A to be moving, for it might be explained as a gravitational pull outward exerted by the rest of the universe in its revolution round A, which we may take to be motionless. This outward pull corresponds, of course, to the backward pull assumed in the instance of the train changing from relative rest to motion. But the problem of rotatory motion leads to greater difficulties than that of acceleration in a straight line, like the starting of a train.

In the first place it is worth while noting that a round body which was perfectly homogeneous and therefore without parts, like the traditional atom, could not be said to revolve at all. As a whole it would of course remain at the same distance from other bodies as before, except for any motion we attribute to them; and since one point or side of it could not be distinguished from another, since, in fact, there could be no points in it at all, the whole body being continuous and homogeneous, we could not have any reason for saying that any point or side was now nearer to the objects on the right and now to those on the left. The assertion that such a body was rotating would be meaningless, for there would be no change in the aspect of the world. If a "sleeping" top were absolutely homogeneous there would be no justification for saying that it was in movement. Centrifugal force on such a body would therefore be inexplicable whether you believe in absolute or only in relative motion. This would be true of a disc or sphere consisting of concentric rings or spheres differing in quality from one another but each completely homogeneous in itself. The aspect of the world would be just the same whether the disc were "rotating" or at rest, so that it is absurd to make any distinction between the supposed two conditions.

No visible object is entirely homogeneous, but it seems that the ultimate particles of matter must be so, and consequently no such particle could be said to rotate. This disposes of the idea of an atom as a vortex ring of ether. Nor could one spherical particle revolve round another, except relatively to the rest of the universe; if only two particles A and B existed, B could not be said to go round A, since one side of A would be indistinguishable from another, and all that would happen would be that B preserved its distance from A. It could not even be proved to move in an ellipse; the supposed elliptical movement would only be a varying of the distance between A and B, a varying which might be simply due to alternate movements of B towards and away from A along a straight line joining the two.

But we must not treat composite bodies as though they were homogeneous throughout. In the well-known problem of the revolving bucket full of water, the instance from which he attempted to prove the existence of absolute motion, Newton regarded both the bucket and the water in it merely as whole bodies without considering the particles of which they consist. He pointed out that at first, while the water was still and the bucket revolved, the surface of the former remained level; but when the water began to share the motion of the bucket it sank in the centre and rose all round the side. At first it was in motion relatively to the bucket, for though, of course, we say that it was at rest and the bucket revolving, from the latter's point of view the water was whirling round. But this relative motion of the water produced no change in it. Later on, when the water was whirling round with the bucket, and was therefore at rest relatively to this, as it was before either began to move, a change occurred in it, for its surface began to sink in the centre. In Newton's opinion this could only be explained as due to an absolute motion of the water, since its relative motion had produced no change.

This argument has been met by the objection that, though in the later stage the water is not moving relatively to the bucket, it is moving relatively to the earth and stars, and that the depression in its surface at the centre may be attributed to this relative motion. But it must be remembered that motion relative to the bucket apparently made no change, and there is no obvious reason why the earth and stars should produce any effect by their revolution. Suppose that no earth and stars existed and there was nothing but the bucket, the water it contained, something to turn it round, and some quite small body relatively to which it rotated all the time; is it conceivable that the result of the experiment would be different and that the water would remain flat all the time?

The mistake lies in treating the water as a homogeneous body without parts. Of course there is a change in the water from the moment when the rotation of the bucket begins, but it is a change in the relative position of the molecules and not in the water as a whole. Later, when the water appears to be revolving with the bucket and therefore at rest relatively to it, it is by no means so in reality, nor is it at rest in itself. The rising of its surface near the side of the bucket is due to the impact of its molecules upon the side, and this would be impossible if those molecules were really describing the same circle as the bucket. But not a single particle of the water really describes a circle; every one moves along a polygon, *i.e.*, a series of straight lines at right angles to one another, an effect which would generally be attributed to centrifugal force.

This brings us to the wider question what is meant by this mysterious force. It is believed to exist in all rotating bodies and to drive outward the objects upon them. But it is also believed to affect the particles of the rotating bodies themselves, with the result that each of these particles really moves along a polygon, not in a circle. That is to say, the body described as rotating is not in fact rotating at all, for the movement of no part of it is circular. Thus we begin by saying that there is a centrifugal force due to rotation, and then add that this rotation does not in fact exist owing to centrifugal force. It would be more natural to describe all the particles of the rotating body and everything on it as striving to move in a straight line, and to add that the former continually shift the direction of their lines owing to the attraction of each by the rest.

According to the Relativist any observer on a body usually supposed to be rotating, for instance the earth, might equally well suppose it to be at rest and explain the "centrifugal force" as a gravitational pull exerted on that body by the rest of the universe, which he might assume to be revolving round it. If so, he would have to suppose that if the rest of the universe were annihilated there would be no effects of "centrifugal force" upon the earth. Nothing would be left relatively to which the earth could rotate, or which could rotate relatively to the earth, and therefore, if there is no such thing as absolute rotation, it might seem that there would be no reason why the effects should continue.

But properly an observer on a rotating body ought not to be able to discover any effects in that body itself, for his instruments of measurement would be affected by the rotation. In a revolving disc the most noticeable effect, for an observer at rest, would be the loosening of the molecules in proportion to their nearness to the rim, and the slight expansion of the circle; but as a measuring-rod would also expand in the same direction, in proportion as it was taken farther from the centre, this result could not be noticed. Similarly the change in the shape of a revolving sphere would either not be observable at all, as a measuring-rod would lengthen when turned from the direction of the axis to a line at right-angles with it, and so would find the same diameter both ways; or if a difference were found it might be assumed that the rod always shortened when turned in that direction, which would explain why the diameter that way was apparently greater than along the axis. Again, a ball placed on a rotating disc would fly off at a tangent; but for anyone who regarded the disc as at rest it would appear as though the ball had been flung upon the disc at a tangent and consequently had bounced off again.

It must be admitted that the results of some hypothetical cases that might be put forward are puzzling questions and almost beyond conjecture. Suppose that nothing existed but the earth and a companion body of the same size rotating relatively to the earth; if Foucault's well-known experiment were tried on both, would the result be a change on both in the apparent direction of the pendulum's movement, or would there be a change on one only, or on neither? If it were found on one only this would be a difficult problem for the Relativist, since both the bodies are in the same position with regard to one another. If it were found on neither, an observer on the earth would be puzzled to explain why it did not occur on the other body, and of course an observer on that other would have the same difficulty with the result on the earth. If it occurred on each the change might be attributed to the influence of the other, though as the change would presumably be the same however far the two bodies were apart, the explanation would not seem of any great value.

The Relativists, as I said, consider that the effects of "centrifugal force" on a disc supposed to be rotating might be ascribed to a gravitational force exerted by the rest of the universe, regarded as rotating round the disc. But are we to suppose that this force is exerted outwards in a radial or in a tangential line? When we were considering the case of the train we assumed that the backward motion of all the things on it when it started might be due to a gravitational pull exerted backwards, *i.e.*, in the same direction as the earth begins to move, for anyone who supposes the train to be at rest. It might be due to the general movement of the universe in that direction. On the same principle it seems that the pull of a " rotating " universe should be in the direction of its motion and opposite to that we attribute to the rotating disc; that it should draw any loose object on the disc in a circle round the centre of that body, and not along a line outwards. Strictly speaking, since every particle of the disc owing to " centrifugal force " is moving along a polygon or series of tangents, and consequently from its standpoint the universe is doing so, the gravitational force should be exercised along a series of straight lines at slight angles to one another.

That this pull cannot be along a radial line outwards, as the exponents of Relativity seem to maintain, is obvious from the fact that when a disc begins to rotate no loose object on its surface proceeds along such a line; rather it moves outwards at a tangent. It would be equally evident if Foucault's experiment were tried on the disc. It must be assumed that the force exerted by the rest of the universe acts in the direction along which an object hanging just above the disc appears to move from the standpoint of the disc; that is, in a circle around its centre, in the opposite direction to that in which the disc appears to be revolving. The reason why an object on the disc does not actually move in such a way, but flies outward at a tangent, must be attributed to the action of the disc itself, which prevents it from continually swerving and keeps it along one straight tangential line, different from that of a body just over the disc and therefore unaffected by its action. Though one may suppose the disc to be at rest as a whole, on no theory can it be so in all its parts, for the molecules nearest the loose body on its surface, being driven backwards by it, will move relatively to the others, and therefore must be exerting some influence on the motion of that body. This influence can only be a straightening of its motion, which would otherwise be circular, like that of an object hanging just above the surface.

If, then, on the theory of Relativity we may assume the "rotating" disc to be at rest and the "centrifugal force" to be really a gravitational force exerted by the rotating universe, it is important that we should not suppose this to be exerted along a radial line outwards. If we did, it would lead to some confusion in an illustration given by Einstein himself to explain the idea of the "curvature of space." Suppose that we have two enormous discs before us, one above the other, and that A, the lower, is at rest, and B, the upper, rotating relatively to surrounding objects. On B "centrifugal force" will exist, which may be ascribed to its motion; but if B may just as well be assumed to be at rest, on this assumption the effects must be attributed to the gravitational pull of the rest of the world. If a man on B measures first the radius and then the circumference of his disc, his measuring-rod, when set along the circumference, *i.e.*, at a tangent, will become shorter, from the standpoint of a man on A, than when set along the radius, since for the second man B, with everything on it, is moving in the tangential but not in the radial direction. Any small part of the circumference may be treated as straight, and from the standpoint of A moves for a moment in a practically straight line along a corresponding part of A, whereas no part of B's radius has any motion relatively to A's, either towards or away from the centre. When taken from the radius to the circumference, then, the measuring-rod on B will appear to the man on A to shorten, just as, in the case of the moving train, the measuring-rod on it appears to the man on the embankment to shorten when laid along the train, as compared with its length when laid across it. Owing to the shortening of the rod when laid along the circumference the measurer will overestimate its length as compared with that of the radius or the diameter. He will find, therefore, that the length of the circumference is more than π (*i.e.*, 3·14159 . . .) times the length of the diameter. But suppose his disc had been before at rest relatively to A, he must then have found that the figure π did at that time express the ratio between circumference and diameter, and since he estimates this at a greater number now, he must conclude, if he is a thorough Relativist and suppose his disc to be still at rest, that this comparative increase in the length of the circumference is, like the "centrifugal force" on the disc, one of the phenomena due to the gravitational influence of the rest of the universe, which he will now suppose to be rotating round B. There follows from this the general rule that gravitation affects the geometry of the body on which it is acting.

But in this explanation of the curvature of space it should not be forgotten, as it has been in some books on the subject, that the measurer on B, the rotating disc, will have to take into account the effect on light of that gravitational force by which he explains the phenomena usually attributed to "centrifugal force." In comparing his measuring-rod with that on A he will have to use the velocity of light in order to determine whether the two ends of his rod coincide simultaneously with those of the other, so that the two rods are to be considered equal in length. If he allows for the influence of gravitation on that velocity and takes it to be exerted along the circumference—not along the radius—in the opposite direction to that in which his disc is supposed by the observer on A to be rotating, he will agree with this latter as to the coincidence of the ends of his rod with the ends of the one on A, and consequently agree with him as to its length. And for just the same reason as that given in the instance of the train starting, it must be concluded that his measuring-rod shortens when turned along the line of the gravitational pull, *i.e.*, the circumference, as compared with its length when laid along the radius; the circumference of the disc corresponds to the length of the train, and the radius to its width. Even the man on the rotating disc, who supposes it to be at rest, will agree with this conclusion. For in spite of the gravitational pull he supposes to exist, a ray of light sent along the measuring-rod when laid at a tangent will take no longer to go and return than a ray sent down the rod when it lies along the radius. Since the rod, then, shortens when laid along the circumference, the length of this latter will be found, as was shown, to be more than π times the length of the diameter.

III. One of the facts upon which the Relativists lay considerable stress, the identity of inertial and gravitational mass, does not seem to deserve so much attention as it has received. If there are ultimate elements of matter identical in size and character, every body must be regarded as an aggregate of these in more or less dense formation. It is for this reason that all objects in a vacuum fall with the same speed; the earth exerts the same attracting force upon every particle of matter at a certain distance, and it makes no difference whether they are grouped together closely and in large numbers, forming a bar of iron, for instance, or comparatively few of them are joined at wider intervals to form a feather; where there is no resistance, as in a vacuum, they will all come to earth with the same speed, whatever their formation. So in a vacuum a number of grains would fall no more quickly if held in a heap and dropped from one hand than if each were dropped from a different hand. But where there is resistance, as in the air, this will obviously be overcome most easily by the energy of motion in these particles when they are most closely massed together. This explains the differences between the weights or "gravitational masses" of various bodies; each particle owing to gravitation has a certain downward energy, and when many are closely united, their combined energies concentrated upon a small area, *e.g.* one of the scales of a weighing-machine, will naturally produce more effect in pushing this downwards. The gravitational mass of a body is thus proportionate to its size and density, and so too will be its inertial mass; the greater the aggregate of particles grouped within a certain space to form one body, the greater will be the force needed to set them in motion or bring them to rest. The motion has to be communicated to every particle of the body propelled, and this cannot be done, or at least will not be visible, if the propelling body be small, or consist of few particles at comparatively wide intervals, and the body propelled, whose inertial mass we are estimating, consist of many particles, to each of which the motion has to be imparted. It is no wonder, then, that inertial mass and gravitational mass are the same, since they both depend on the same conditions, the size and density of the body to which they belong. Their identity depends mainly on the fact that gravitation acts on every particle alike, and that can only be surprising to one who is surprised that there is any uniformity in the world at all.

If a body A is practically outside the gravitational influence of B, but is moving parallel to, and with the same continuous acceleration as, a third body C falling towards B, it is commonly said that this last, as viewed from A, will appear to have no gravitational force at all, since C, for A, will be at rest, not falling. But A could not move with the same continuous acceleration as C unless, like C, it were within some gravitational field, for nothing can accelerate an object continuously except gravitation. It is true that according to the theory of Relativity, A, while falling towards an attracting body D, may consider itself to be at rest, but it cannot be denied that the distance between A and D decreases at an ever faster rate, and this must be explained somehow. If A does not suppose itself to be attracted by D it might instead suppose itself to be exerting the attraction. You can, of course, avoid the word "attraction" with its implication that one body exerts a force on the other, by saying merely that when two objects are at a certain distance from one another the interval between them diminishes at a continually increasing rate. But then you must add that the relations of the smaller body with the rest of the universe are changed to a greater degree than those of the larger. When, for instance, a stone falls down a precipice its distance from the centre of the earth diminishes and its distance from the sun above it increases, but there is no change in the relation between the centre of the earth and the sun.

From some accounts of Einstein's theory of gravitation one would gather that the main difference between Newton's doctrine and Einstein's was this : according to Newton every body moves in a straight line except when it is near some other body, in which case it moves in a curve ; whereas, according to Einstein, every body moves in a curve except when it is far distant from every other, in which case it moves in a straight line. The distinction is certainly subtle. Some of the Relativists are not clear enough on the subject of the curvature of space ; they leave it doubtful whether this curvature accounts for what we call gravitation, or whether it is an additional effect of the presence of matter. Einstein himself speaks of it as explaining why the deflection of light near the sun is greater than would be expected from Newton's law of gravitation;[1] one would infer, therefore, that it is to be taken as something additional to gravitation itself. It makes no observable difference except where the gravitational force is very strong, like that of the sun, and the object affected by it is a ray of light or is travelling with a velocity not too far below that of light. The curvature of space in the neighbourhood of matter, or the shortening of measuring rods in a vertical direction, exists only for a body at rest in that neighbourhood, not for one that is falling; whereas the effect of gravitation in reducing the distance between the attracting and the falling body exists clearly enough for the latter, even if there is a Relativist upon it who supposes it to be at rest.

IV. Relativity deals only with quantities, neglecting qualities altogether, although the two are inseparably connected. This is quite in accordance with the customary disregard shown by modern science towards the "secondary," *i.e.*, the real qualities as existing in the objects themselves. It is even doubted whether they exist outside the mind at all. But to deny their presence in the external world is to reduce that world to a blank void, where there could not even be any shapes or sizes, since there would be nothing to distinguish one figure from another. Every body, even every wave in the ether or field of force, must have or rather be some quality if it is to be distinguished from empty space. It is obvious, too, that these qualities change from time to time, for those bodies of which we are immediately aware, whether you suppose them to be parts of the brain or objects more or less distant from us, certainly vary their colours, sounds, and temperatures, and it is not to be supposed that they are different from the rest of the world in this respect. There must be changes of these or similar qualities everywhere.

But what is it that determines these changes? If each quality depends on, or at least corresponds to, some quantitative property of the atom, this fact must effect the problem of Relativity. If, for instance, we supposed that a body

[1] *The Theory of Relativity*, p. 127.

possessed, or rather became, a certain quality whenever it moved with a certain velocity, we should evidently have to infer that motion was absolute. No atom could be supposed to be at rest, for then it would be devoid of any quality, and therefore would be nothing. Whenever there was any change of quality it would not be open to the Relativist to say that the motion of the body in which the change took place might still be regarded as the same. He would be forced to admit that it had become faster or slower. From the standpoint of Relativity whenever we say that a body has been set in motion, accelerated, or retarded, we might just as well maintain that it is standing still while the rest of the universe is undergoing the change. This would be no longer possible, of course, if quality corresponded to motion, for a change in quality cannot be denied.

It seems that in some cases at least, as in that of warmth, the quality corresponds to a certain state of motion; but whatever may be the quantitative element with which quality agrees, whether it be extension, mass, time, or some other, it must be subject to the principle of Relativity, if Einstein and his followers are right. Quality, on the other hand, is certainly absolute, for a change in it, as I said, is undeniable. Unfortunately the relation between quantity and quality is not so clear that it can throw much light on the mysteries of Relativity. There seems to be no more natural connection between the colour red and a wave-length of $\frac{1}{10000}$th of a millimetre than between first love and an isosceles triangle. It is true that the colour exists in the retina or in the brain as affected by the ether-waves and not in the ether-waves themselves, though these too must have some distinguishing quality if they exist; but it would be just as hard to explain why the colour should come into existence within the brain when an ether-wave of a certain length acts upon the retina. Yet it is certain that there is a correspondence between the qualities and quantities of the world, and this must affect the theory of Relativity, which so far has only considered the latter. Suppose again that the quality of each atom depended on its rate of motion; then if A at one time is of the same quality as B has been at another, it must be presumed that the motion of A is the same as that of B before, though relatively to a third body C, which has changed its own rate of motion, the velocity of the two is different. Quality would thus give us an absolute standard of motion.

V. The idea of a curved or spherical space, finite but unbounded, which has lately been brought into prominence by Einstein and outlined in several works on his theory, was put forward by Riemann and Zöllner a long time before public interest was drawn to the subject of Relativity. There is even something superficially like it in the philosophy of Parmenides. Its latest advocates offer it as a way of escape from the antinomies into which the conception of a finite or of an infinite space seems to lead us. Our natural inclination is to regard space as infinite; even if we suppose the amount of matter in the world to be limited, we believe that beyond the farthest stars there must be an endless void into which a body or a ray of light starting from one of those stars or a star itself might go on moving for ever. It seems impossible that such a body should be brought to a stop at any point where there is nothing material to stop it. If its outward motion through the void did come to an end we should for that very reason suppose that it had come into contact with something material, perhaps an endless and continuous extent of matter lying round the void encompassing the mass of stars.

On the other hand, objections are brought against the idea of an infinite space whether we assume the amount of matter to be finite or infinite. In the first case, it is said, the stars would gradually have dispersed into the surrounding void during the infinite past, and so, too, would their energy. Rays of light and heat would continually have been cast forth into the outer darkness and thus have been lost to the material world, which by this time would have become cold and dead. On the other hand, if the amount of matter were infinite and it were everywhere of mean density, it would follow that the force of gravitation acting on any particle from every direction would be infinite too.

These and other difficulties of a similar nature have often been discussed, especially since the time of Kant, and are very fully set forth and examined in an essay by Wundt, *Über das kosmologische Problem*,[1] which includes a criticism

[1] *Kleine Schriften*, Bd. 1.

of Zöllner's theory of a spherical space, finite but unbounded. His objections are not based on geometrical but on cosmological grounds, on the effects which such a space must produce in the material world. But before coming to these we must answer the very natural question how such an entity is geometrically possible. The spherical, three-dimensional space of which we hear so much nowadays is usually compared to the surface of a globe or to a circle, the former representing a finite but unbounded area in two dimensions and the latter in one. A being who could only move on the surface of the globe, who was, in fact, part of the surface himself, as the human body is part of the three-dimensional world, might go on for ever without finding a boundary anywhere, but as in the end he would return to the place from which he had started, he could not call his world infinite. If a number of such beings all set out from the same place and walked in a straight line—straight to them, as the shortest possible for them, but more or less curved, of course, from our three-dimensional point of view—and if A kept at the same distance from B as B from C and so on, then they would in the end meet again at their Antipodes. Imagine that the surface of the globe were the only thing that existed, and you have an idea of a spherical two-dimensional world.

The same things, it is supposed, would happen in our three-dimensional space, if one could go far enough; a voyage through the universe would end where it began. If it were possible for six men from the same point to set out along straight lines due east, west, north, south, up and down, and for each to continue his journey long enough at the same rate as the others, they would meet again at a point in the universe which may be called the Antipodes of the earth, or, to be exact, of the point from which they started. For a time they would of course increase their distance from one another, as the longitudinal lines on the surface of a globe spread farther and farther apart between the North Pole and the Equator; after that they would draw together again, and if one of them, A, tried to keep or increase his distance from B he would find himself rapidly approaching C on his other side.

Again, on the surface of a globe the ratio between the length of the circumference of a circle and that of its radius or diameter varies according to the size of the circle. Take each latitudinal line as the circumference of a circle and the longitudinal line from the North Pole down to each latitudinal in turn as the radius. A being who could only move on the surface of the globe and knew nothing of "up" and "down" would take each longitudinal line to be absolutely straight; but he would find that as he approached the Equator, and his circles, formed by the latitudinal lines, grew wider, the length of their circumferences became smaller in proportion to their radii. Near the North Pole the ratio between latitudinal and longitudinal, circumference and radius, would be nearly expressed by double the number π, which expresses the normal ratio between circumference and diameter. But at the Equator it would be much less; instead of being 6·2831 . . . it would be only 4. Farther south it would continue to decrease until the circumference was shorter than the radius, and finally the radii met at the South Pole. So those who believe our space to be spherical in three dimensions, as the surface of the globe is in two, suppose that the number π only expresses closely the ratio between the circumference and diameter of a circle small in size compared with the whole universe. If we took an enormous circle having as its radius the distance between the earth and one of the fixed stars we should find a different ratio; the length of the circumference would be less than π times that of the diameter. The number expressing the proportion would continue to grow less as the diameter increased, until at last the radii met at the point which was the Antipodes of that from which they started.

In this way, it is held, our three-dimensional space is spherical, and finite yet unbounded, like the surface of a globe. But the comparison with such a surface or with a circle is not free from objection. Is the former of these possible except as part of a world with three dimensions, or the latter except as part of a world with at least two? In considering the geometrical properties of a spherical surface you may ignore the third dimension, depth or height, but it does not follow that without it such a surface or any of its properties is possible; that there could be another space, of only two dimensions, possessing all these properties.

RELATIVITY

Granted that a two-dimensional space is possible, it might be a necessary condition of its existence that it should be infinite, that lines branching out from any point in it should never meet. Such a geometrical figure as the surface of a globe, finite but unbounded, might only be possible in an infinite space of three dimensions. Similarly a spherical three-dimensional space, finite but unbounded, might require as a condition of its existence enclosure in an infinite fourfold space.

If the idea of such a spherical space were free from objection on other grounds, and the arguments against the ordinary conception of space were conclusive, we should be forced to accept the former. But the criticisms of Zöllner's theory contained in Wundt's essay have at least as much weight as those directed by Einstein and others against the traditional theory. In the first place Wundt observes that in a spherical space every body must exert a gravitational force upon itself, for according to the theory every straight line must return to the point from which it started, and this must be true of the lines of force setting out from any gravitational centre. Every body must attract itself with equal force on all sides, and therefore in different directions, for two lines setting out to left and right, or up and down, will in the end return to their common starting-point. For the same reason it must attract every other thing throughout the world in two opposite directions. To make this clearer, take any point on the surface of a globe and imagine rays spreading out from it to all quarters; a neighbouring point will be reached not only by the short ray travelling by the direct route, but by another which goes right round the surface of the globe and comes up on the other side. So with the lines of gravitational force; there must be two of them from any particle to another. This would be a necessary consequence of a spherical space, whether with two or three dimensions, but it is not easy to accept.

It might even be argued that as a line may be drawn round and round the surface of a globe from one point to another any number of times, the length of the line of course increasing each time by the whole circumference of the globe, so the line of gravitational force from A to B in a spherical Space must reach

B over and over again, though the force will be less each time in proportion to the whole extent of Space. It will be as though in an infinite, non-spherical or Euclidean Space there were an infinite number of bodies A^1, A^2, A^3, ... set along a straight line from B and each of them distant from its two nearest neighbours by an interval equal to the diameter of the spherical world, whatever that may be. They would all act upon B, though of course A^2 would exert a far smaller attraction upon A^1, and the force of the others would decrease in proportion. In a spherical Space A would exert upon B an infinite series of gravitational forces corresponding to those of A^1, A^2, A^3 ... in an Euclidean Space, and as every other body would do the same, the force exerted upon B from every direction would be infinite. The theory of a finite unbounded Space would therefore be open to the same objection as that raised by Einstein and others to the belief in an infinite Space everywhere filled with matter of a mean density. Certainly we may regard as strange the idea that A can stand at a number of distances from B and so exert a number of gravitational forces upon it; but if a straight line in spherical Space continually returns to the same point a line of force must do the same. This is especially obvious if we assume that gravitational force takes time to travel from A to B, for then we can more easily imagine it as continually traversing the whole extent of Space and returning to B again and again.

The objection on which Wundt lays most stress is derived from the principle of entropy, or dissipation of energy. According to this principle all energy tends to take the form of warmth, and warmth tends to become evenly distributed, so that in the infinite past a finite world must have reached one uniform level of temperature. This objection is not decisive, for there may be or may have been processes in the world working counter to the dissipation of energy. Still, it makes the theory of an infinite world more probable, for in such a world new stores of energy might reach our system from others infinitely remote.

The theory of a spherical Space is also open to one of the criticisms advanced against the theory of an infinite Space containing an infinite number of stars so distributed that the mean density of the whole universe is equal to that of the domain revealed by our telescopes. It is urged that if this latter supposition were correct the sky would have a background as bright as the average brightness of the space visible to us, stars and void together, whereas in fact its background is perfectly dark. But here too, as in the case of gravitation, a spherical Space where matter everywhere maintains a certain average of density is equivalent to an infinite Euclidean Space in which matter is similarly distributed. If light can go round and round the world like a ship continually circumnavigating the globe, we must see not only the rays sent out direct to us from a star, perhaps some twenty years ago, but also the rays from that same star which have travelled round the entire universe. It will be as though beyond the stars which we took to be farthest from us in the spherical Space there were a second series of stars which had sent out light to us millions of years ago, and then again a third series, and so on *ad infinitum*. The members of these series would, of course, be really the same stars in the positions they occupied farther and farther back in time, and their light would reach us after one, two, three, or more journeys round the universe. But the result would be the same as though they were different stars farther and farther away from us in infinite Space. If the background would not be perfectly dark in the one case, it would not be so in the other.

As a solution of the cosmological problem, Wundt prefers the theory that Space and Time are infinite but the amount of matter finite, for though he supposes matter to be distributed throughout Space, he suggests that its density may decrease in all directions from a certain point, which may be called the centre of the universe, so that the sum of it is limited, like the sum of the fractions $\frac{1}{2}, \frac{1}{4}, \frac{1}{8}, \ldots$ Against this theory it might be argued that in the infinite past the denser masses of matter would have been dissolved and dispersed into areas of less density, so that by this time matter would be evenly distributed throughout Space. His answer to this objection is that in the parts of the world far distant from the centre the temperature of bodies must be very little, if at all, above the absolute zero point,—273° Centigrade, and consequently there will be no dispersal of matter in these regions. The loss due to such dispersal in the denser areas may be compensated by gravitation, attracting to those areas such scattered bodies as the meteorites from the rest of the universe. Larger bodies, too, like the planets round the sun, if they move through a resisting medium, must gradually reduce their speed and in the end unite with the mass forming the centre of their system. Thus the aggregation of matter makes up for its dispersal; to some extent it is continually doing so, but there is also an alternation of the two processes, now one prevailing and now the other, as Empedocles held long ago, with periods of relative stability in the interval.

But our knowledge is too narrowly limited to enable us to decide between the three hypotheses of a finite, spherical Space, an infinite Space with an infinite sum of matter, and an infinite Space with finite matter. The last seems the most plausible, but no objection could be brought against the second, if we suppose that the extent of gravitational force is limited, so that each body attracts only those within a certain area. It is the first theory, favoured by the Relativists, which involves the strangest consequences, and though it has the charm of comparative novelty it seems to me the least acceptable on other grounds.

CHAPTER VIII

MECHANISM v. VITALISM

In declaring consciousness to be universal we may seem already to have taken our sides in a controversy which has long divided the philosophical world and is particularly violent to-day. At the close of the nineteenth century the belief had prevailed that the universe could be, and some day would be, explained on mechanical principles; that even the movements of the mind would be found to be governed by laws essentially akin to those which govern the movements of material bodies. But since then there has been a strong reaction, and the mechanical philosophy has been pronounced inadequate to account even for all the events in the material world. Vitalism has been brought to life again in biology by the works of Professor Driesch, and Dr Haldane has gone still farther by suggesting that " inorganic can ultimately be resolved into organic phenomena," thus completely reversing the old ideas on the subject. But the writer who has done most to bring about this revolution in thought is undoubtedly Professor Bergson, who in order to rid life and mind of determinism has thrown doubt on the intellect itself as being too much of a machine to grasp the reality.

At the present time consciousness and mechanical laws are generally thought to be so much opposed that anyone who affirms the whole world to be conscious will be taken to deny the supremacy of those laws anywhere. And certainly if we suppose that the human mind is not subject to them we are bound to admit that the lower forms of existence are similarly exempt; the continuity of the world, which makes us believe consciousness to be universal, will also suggest to us that freedom from determinism cannot be limited to human minds. For if the reign of law prevailed throughout those æons of time, in which there was no life on earth, it is inconceivable that there should have arisen out of the law-abiding elements a race of beings able to break through the hitherto invariable course of things. Freedom, or anarchy, must either have existed from the beginning, even in the inorganic realm, or else can have no existence now, even in the human mind. The life of mankind is ultimately derived, maintained, and multiplied from the " inorganic," and whatever conclusion we reach on this subject about the one must be equally true of the other.

Everyone who has considered such matters at all has some notion what is meant by the mechanical theory of the universe, though an exact definition might be hard to find. Perhaps we might describe it as the theory that each of the ultimate elements of the world always follows a course of action mathematically proportionate to that which it has followed before; in other words, that given a complete knowledge of the past one could predict the future. To put it in a negative and more graphic form, no atom ever goes out of its way to do a good and useful act. It is sometimes applied only to the spatial world, as distinct from our consciousness, which is not generally believed to exist in Space; but since all our actions take place in that world, they too must on this theory be determined in the same way as the movements of " unconscious " bodies, and therefore cannot be affected by our thoughts and emotions, unless these too are spatial. And even if Space were only an appearance, then the reality which is presented to us under the form of Space must be determined by laws exactly parallel to those of spatial phenomena.

The ideal of this theory would be to discover that the ultimate elements of the world are all exactly identical in nature and act in the same way upon all others, without preference. The more we analyze, the more homogeneous do we find the component parts of matter, and the scientist lives in hopes of reducing the ninety-two chemical elements to one, and explaining the various affinities between them as due to the various ways in which they are compounded of identical parts having no such preferences. But even supposing that there were affinities which could not be so reduced existing between the real *primordia* of the world, so that the action of A upon B would be different from its action upon C, even when circumstances were the same in the two cases, this would not overthrow the mechanical theory, provided that A always acted upon B in a uniform manner, and was equally consistent in its relations with each of the others. The only thing fatal to the theory would be the discovery that A acted upon B or any other with a force that bore no proportion to the force exerted upon a previous occasion, taking into consideration any changes in their velocity, the distance between them, and their relations with the rest of the universe.

This last clause may suggest an objection to the mechanical philosophy in general which Professor Bergson has brought against one part of it, the doctrine of determinism in psychology. Since we have to take into consideration the relations of A and B with all the other elements in the world, it may be thought impossible that the same situation in all its details should ever recur for the two bodies in question; impossible, therefore, to tell whether their action is consistent with their action on a previous occasion. But it is not inconceivable, after all, that one state of the world might be exactly the same as another that had occurred countless ages before: in fact, Nietzsche held that since the world is finite it must repeat itself in this way, and that, since the same cause always produces the same effect, not only one of its momentary states but the whole course of its history must be repeated again and again, like a series of recurring decimals. This supposition, however, is not needed to save the mechanical theory; all that we need to show is that when two bodies act upon one another from the same distance or with the same velocity as before, any change in the result is proportionate to the change in the surroundings. Causes that are almost the same produce almost the same results; the differences due to changes in the more remote influences are too small for our calculations and may be neglected. But we may be sure that if we could calculate the almost infinitesimal differences in the result and the almost infinitesimal changes in these influences we should find that the two correspond exactly. Gravitation being universal, the position of the fixed stars relative to the earth must affect the velocity of an apple falling from a tree in a Devonshire orchard, and contribute towards making it faster or slower than that of a precisely similar apple which fell from the same height when the relative position of those stars was different. The increase or diminution of velocity is far too small for us to calculate, but a superhuman mind, we may suppose, would find it to be exactly proportionate to the change in the distance of the stars from that particular spot on earth, added to the differences in all the other conditions, near or remote. Even for human minds, the farther they go in calculating the conditions, the more consistent are the movements of any body found to be; we cannot well resist the conclusion that if all the circumstances were known this consistency of action would prove to be complete.

Another objection raised against the mechanical theory is that the uniformity of the elements of matter may be not absolute, but like the uniformity observed among men. For instance, we may fix on a certain age as the average number of years for which a man lives; but we cannot be certain that the life of any particular man will end at that age; and so, it is argued, we may be able to fix on the average forces or qualities of different kinds of elements without being able to tell whether any particular atom will conform exactly to that standard. To quote from Professor Ward: "The most the physicist is entitled to assert is that if there are molecules, the mass of the mean oxygen 'atom' is sixteen, that of the mean hydrogen 'atom' being taken as unity; and so on for the rest of his table of masses. He is not entitled to say that if there are molecules the mass of every oxygen atom is precisely sixteen times the mass of any hydrogen atom."[1] But he would be justified in saying that it was very nearly so, if not exactly: or at any rate that far the greater number of oxygen atoms were very nearly so. Otherwise we might come upon a number of them with an average mass only four times that of the hydrogen atom, just as we might take the cases of a number of children who have died early in a certain town and find that the average length of human life in that town was only twenty years.

The opponents of the mechanical theory sometimes compare the laws of Nature to habit in men, and argue that while

[1] *Naturalism and Agnosticism*, 4th ed., p. 107.

material bodies generally act in a regular way, they may sometimes depart from their usual procedure as men sometimes depart from the daily routine. But interruptions in our habits are not miracles; we have to look beneath the interruption and the habit for a deeper uniformity which will explain both, just as the same laws explain the course which a river has taken up to a certain time and the earthquake which then turns it into another channel. The mechanical theory does not pretend to set before us a world that is constantly repeating itself, but one in which the same mathematical proportion between cause and effect is always observed. Besides, it would evidently be ludicrous to compare such a thing as the constant velocity of light, for instance, to a habit; when and by what process could we suppose it to have been formed?

It must be admitted that the ultimate elements of matter and their forces are approximately uniform, and after this admission we cannot be content until we find them to be absolutely so. They must either be supposed absolutely alike, or else different to an unlimited extent. For if they may vary, what limit can you set to their variations? Why should any two of them be even nearly alike? One can explain the likeness of men or of other living species by the fact that they are derived from a common origin; but the ultimate elements, which must be simple—otherwise not they but their parts would be the ultimates—cannot be produced as are the complex, visible objects which they form. If these were not all exactly alike it could only be a happy coincidence if any two possessed even the smallest resemblance, since the possibilities of difference are infinite. B might attract others with a force a million times greater than that of A, C might attract with a force a million times that of B, and so on *ad infinitum*; yet even this gives only a faint suggestion of the differences that might have existed.

The uniformity which must exist in the ultimate elements of the world cannot be due to interaction between them, for if the forces they possessed could differ to an unlimited degree, the action of one upon another could not make the two alike. It is true that the motion of a faster body may be reduced to the level of others that are slower by contact with these, and a certain uniformity is the result. But other properties of bodies—gravitational force, for instance—would not be changed in this way. A will always attract B with the same force in inverse ratio to the square of its distance; the influence of another body C could not change this and make A attract B with the same force when a million miles away as when there was only a mile between them. The gravitational force, therefore, has not been levelled down in the past, and unless we admit that it is exactly equal in all atoms we cannot understand why there is so much uniformity as we undoubtedly do find in this respect. It seems futile to suggest that here and there atoms may exist with slightly less power of attraction. If you do not admit absolute equality, the approximation to it, which you cannot help admitting, must be supposed due to chance. But in a world of chance the slightest degree of uniformity, even between any two bodies only, would be a miracle.

As I said in an earlier chapter, the chief reason why each man believes in a world outside his own sensations is that the mixture of order and disorder in those sensations forces him to look beyond them for an absolutely self-consistent order of things. If he could be satisfied with partial uniformity he would not need to go beyond his own consciousness. The sensations he experiences every day are very much the same, and occur in nearly the same order; it is true that one sight or feeling is not always followed by the same one as on the day before, but he need not seek any explanation of this outside himself, if similar variations in the universe require no explantion. Thus there would be no argument against the Solipsist, if the non-mechanical theory of the world were accepted. According to that, no state of the world or of any part of it is exactly deducible from the previous state; new, uncaused motions may begin at any moment, and the direction of an existing motion may change spontaneously. Nature, therefore, is not absolutely self-consistent and regular but only somewhat more so than the sensations of the individual mind; it is merely a question of degree. If, then, the individual mind has in any case to content itself with an order of things which is not rigidly consistent, why should it not rest content with its own experience? Why should it suppose the mingled harmony and discord of its experience to prove that it is only a part, not the whole of existence?

The question may be addressed especially to those who, like Professor Bergson, lay stress on the alleged " spontaneity" of consciousness. I cannot find any meaning for this " spontaneity " beyond the purely negative idea that one state of consciousness is not caused by another; for obviously the term cannot mean that our free will produces our sensations, thoughts, and emotions. We cannot will a thought before we have it. It seems, then, that " spontaneity " = chance; our thoughts just happen to be what they are. At any rate they are not wholly determined by previous thoughts, by memories and sensations. And this, of course, is supposed to be equally true of our will. Why, then, should any man believe his sensations to be determined by any cause, except in some degree by previous sensations, by memories and thoughts? They follow a fairly logical order, like his thoughts, and like them are continually subject to abrupt changes; is there any need to assume an external cause in the one case more than in the other? To this question no answer can be given except by the advocates of the mechanical theory, who believe that our thoughts, too, as well as our sensations, are rigidly determined, partly by previous thoughts, by memories and sensations, and partly by causes outside the area of what we call *our* consciousness.

No progress can be made, or has been made, in science without the mechanical theory, unless you give the name of science to a mere list of isolated facts. If you are satisfied with such a list you must wonder why men have ever troubled to " save phenomena," to reconcile facts which appear to contradict one another, or rather to contradict a general law. While admitting that there are fairly regular sequences of events in Nature you will not be disturbed by any exceptions or attempt to explain them. But this has never been the attitude of the great scientists. If they had not accepted the laws of motion as invariable, Adams and Leverrier would not have felt that there was any need to account for the irregularities in the movement of Uranus by assuming the existence of a still unknown planet; Neptune would only have been discovered by chance, if at all. Again, if the velocity of light had not been regarded as absolutely constant the result of the Michelson–Morley experiment would have been noted down and left there; it would not have led in turn to the Lorentz theory and the revolutionary explanation offered by Einstein. In the presence of the facts that disturb the scientist the opponent of the mechanical theory should logically imitate "the old hermit of Prague" and content himself with saying "that that is, is."

The mechanical theory holds the field in science; the theological view I have examined in another chapter. It is true that Vitalism has always found, and still finds, more or less energetic supporters, but whereas it used to be a positive philosophy, it is now almost entirely confined to criticism of its opponent. In the days of Aristotle life was taken to be something eternal, existing alongside the eternal lifeless matter. The Greek philosopher did not consider the questions which trouble us now; how the inorganic elements are converted into organic, and how the individual soul begins to exist. One cannot say that for him there are souls, in the modern sense, at all; there are only bodies possessing the quality of life, which includes mind and is inherited. Modern philosophy began when it was recognized that the presence of a vital principle or quality does not explain life any better than the presence of a "dormitive virtue" explains why opium sends a man to sleep. If there were certain parts of matter which always had been living and always would be living throughout eternity, parts always the same and never increasing in number, we might perhaps have to accept the older explanation, declare that life is a property of these particular elements, and leave it at that. But we know that for millions of years there was no life upon earth, and that inorganic elements are continually passing into organisms, so that the number of these is continually increasing. Vitalism offers us no explanation either of the origin of life or of its extension; what is worse, it even makes an explanation impossible by setting an insurmountable barrier between the organic and the inorganic.

To avoid the difficulty it has been suggested, as by Dr. Haldane in his *Mechanism, Life, and Personality*, that the whole world is organic. Even the movements of the atoms in a molecule would be then not wholly directed by mechanical laws, but every molecule, even every atom, if the atoms are subdivided, would be a small living body, the parts working together for the preservation of the whole. But the suggestion is left in too vague a form, and does not help to explain how the larger living bodies were developed. Granted that the movements of the atoms or parts of the atoms are directed towards the good of their little system, I see no reason why they should also be affected by the good of any larger body of which the molecule itself might form part. One cannot conceive the atom as divided between consideration for the family, the molecule or cell, and loyalty towards the State, the whole organism. What would happen if the interests of the two clashed? And if the meaning of life is that the parts exist for the whole, why are not the movements of all atoms governed by the interests of the greatest whole, the universe? It seems to me that the vitalists only escape from questions of this kind by refusing to work out their own theory.

They are obliged to admit that mechanical laws do play a large part in the world, for if life, or teleology, were the only power, there could be no death or evil. Whatever force were brought to bear upon the body its atoms would continue to move as before, influenced solely by care for the preservation of the whole; alien and dangerous elements would never be admitted; and the movements of every body would be directed towards the good of the greatest organism, the universe. But as things are we must suppose that while the movements within any body are organic, its relations with other bodies are determined by mechanical principles. There are then two laws, the law of life and the law of mechanics, which govern matter and conflict with each other. What decides the victory in each case? A number of atoms in a living body receive an impulse from without which, according to mechanics, should drive them in a certain direction harmful to the life of the whole; does their movement thereafter depend on this impulse, or on regard for the general good, or is there a compromise between the two influences? And as they communicate the impulse to other atoms in the same body, is the spreading of the shock governed by mechanical principles? If so, we have these principles established *within* the living body, and it must be difficult for the inner atoms to know whether the impulses they receive from the outer atoms of the body are due to a force outside it, and so to be obeyed mechanically, or to be received with due regard to the body's welfare. This sounds grotesque, no doubt, but it seems to me that Vitalism inevitably forces upon us such absurdities as these.

Every living body is composed of elements that were once inorganic; at what point do these abandon the principles governing lifeless matter for those that govern life? One cannot suppose them to become aware at a certain moment of their inclusion within an organism and from that time onwards to behave in a different manner. Why should mere proximity in space to organic atoms compel them to abandon their previous modes of action? What influence can the organic atoms have upon the newcomers, except a mechanical force? Supposing that such organic atoms existed, and that they had special powers over others, so as to make them conform to the laws of life, they could not impart these powers to the others, and when they were removed by the process of metabolism the body would be governed wholly by mechanical laws, for without their presence there is no reason why its elements should continue to act organically.

It is difficult to get from the Vitalists a definition of Vitalism; as Lotze said, if for every idle word men have to give account, those who are responsible for " organism " will find themselves in trouble. Apparently the chief distinguishing mark of an organism is that the parts work first for the development of the whole into a certain complex form and then for the preservation of this form. This leads to the question whether the form exists in miniature from the beginning in the germ-plasm; a theory which the Vitalists reject. There seems, then, no reason why the germ should develop into this form rather than that, unless you suppose, with Butler and Hering, that it retains the memory of the body from which it was derived, and for that reason evolves on similar lines. But if memory is something transcendent and non-spatial, I do not see how it can affect the movements of things in space, *i.e.*, the parts of the body; and if it is a spatial image of the past, there is after all in the germ a model of the form into which it is to develop. Without that why should the atoms of the germ-plasm, an aggregate of elements derived ultimately from many distant sources, combine to evolve a certain living body, more than any other aggregate of atoms in the world? Before they came together to form the germ, the relation between them must have been mechanical, of the same kind as the relation between any other two atoms in the universe; why should their proximity now do anything but increase in proportion the mechanical forces they exert upon one another?

The opponents of the mechanistic theory have brought forward arguments which are certainly difficult to answer in the present state of biological knowledge. There are the facts discovered by Professor Driesch, that the cells of the embryo in the two-cell or four-cell stage, if separated, may develop into complete embryos themselves; and that after the "cleavage" of the egg the blastula may be cut into halves or quarters in any direction, and each part will form a complete larva. Such adaptation to circumstances on the part of the cells would not, he argues, be possible in a mechanism. Dr. Haldane, again, speaks of the "astounding fineness" with which the composition of the blood is regulated by the kidneys, which excrete a liquid always so constituted as to maintain the hydrogen ion concentration of the blood at a constant level. It is difficult, certainly, for the mechanistic theory to explain such facts as these, but what of the explanation given by Vitalism? Can anyone imagine a molecule going forward or turning back simply because without it, or with it, the normal composition of the blood would be disturbed? One might bring against Vitalism the same sort of objection as that brought by Galileo against the introduction of "the will of God" as an explanation of phenomena; it does not satisfy us because it would explain any number of things equally well, including many that do not exist. Certainly it could account for the action of the kidneys in standardizing the constituents of the blood by showing that this was necessary for life; but the same reason would account for any number of miracles which do not happen, such as the ejecting of poison admitted into the body, or the immediate closing of wounds, however deep.

What we want from Vitalism is an explanation why some things necessary for life actually happen and others equally necessary do not. But this it cannot give.

Another objection to Vitalism is that the principles on which it supposes Nature to work are not exact and definite enough. According to the mechanistic theory the path of every atom is mathematically determined by its previous movement and the movements of the bodies around it: there is for it only one course possible. But the Vitalist cannot give any reason why this particular atom, rather than another of the same kind, should enter the blood, for instance. There are always many ways in which the same biological purpose could be fulfilled; what is to decide between them?

Those who condemn the view that the living body is a machine try to overwhelm their opponents by talking of the enormous complexity of the organism. But they themselves do not seem to realize the enormous possibilities of mechanical organization; one would think they regarded the cell as a small and simple thing, for they express astonishment that the whole body should be developed from one germ-cell. But it is in fact an entire universe in itself, composed of millions of molecules, each of them perhaps a world in miniature, so that it is quite possible that the whole body to be developed should be prefigured within it. Before the evolution of the living bodies there may have been an evolution of the smaller complex bodies which form the organism, a process in accordance with mechanical laws and preparatory to life.

It is not necessary to carry further the criticism of Vitalism in general, for in the following chapter I have dealt at length with the philosophy of Professor Bergson, who may well be considered the chief modern representative of that creed. What is said there of his biological theories may be applied to other forms of Vitalism with little or no alteration. I have not limited myself to an examination of *L'Évolution Créatrice*, for though that is the best known and the most interesting to the biologist it is incomplete without the two earlier works, and is not, in fact, the most important of the three for the metaphysician. Together they come nearer to forming a complete system of philosophy than anything which has appeared in recent years.

CHAPTER IX

THE PHILOSOPHY OF BERGSON

A. *Essai sur les données immédiates de la conscience.*

In the first chapter, devoted to "the intensity of the states of consciousness," Bergson denies that there can be degrees of intensity, and endeavours to account for our belief that such degrees exist. His main argument is that sensations cannot possess more or less intensity as material objects possess more or less extension, because they cannot be superimposed on one another; one sensation cannot include another as a higher number includes a lower, or a larger space a smaller, and for this reason one cannot exceed another in intensity. But there seems to be some confusion here between spaces and bodies. One material body cannot really include another, for no two bodies can occupy the same space; it would follow, then, from the theory we are examining that we could not apply to them the terms "larger" or "smaller." But if we can, why should we not apply these terms also to degrees of intensity? These may exist together, as it were side by side, for we can hear two sounds, a louder and a fainter, at the same time, and this makes possible a comparison of their intensities. The intensity of one sensation may include that of another, as the magnitude of one body may include the magnitude of another, though the sensations and bodies themselves are mutually exclusive.

Bergson proceeds to deal with four classes of states of consciousness, the feelings or emotions, the sense of effort, the *sensations affectives*, *i.e.*, pleasure and pain, and the *sensations représentatives*, reflecting the external world. He argues in turn against any real quantitative difference in these, as regards their intensity. In the first case the growth of an emotion—a desire, for instance—is explained as meaning this, that it spreads more widely over the soul and colours a greater number of our thoughts and feelings. This he calls, unexpectedly enough, a change of quality, not of quantity. Yet he is obliged to use in every sentence words which can have no meaning except as applied to quantity, *i.e.*, " depth " and " number." In dealing, however, with another emotion, joy, he seems to account for its intensities in a different way. " In its lowest degree it is like an orientation of our states of consciousness in the direction of the future. Then, as though this attraction lessened their weight, our ideas and sensations succeed one another with greater rapidity ; our movements do not cost us the same effort. Finally, in the case of intense joy, our perceptions and our memories acquire an indefinable quality, comparable to a warmth or a light ; a quality so new that at certain moments, when we reflect on our feelings, our very being appears strange to us " (*nous éprouvons comme un étonnement d'être*). This too he interprets as a purely qualitative difference. But in that case we should merely consider the three phases as three different kinds of joy without having any ground for calling one " lower " and another " higher," two terms which were originally borrowed from an analogy with space and quantity. The fact that we do so call them suggests that there must be a quantitative difference in their intensity.

If we use any comparative terms of our sensations and feelings it is obvious that we are introducing the notion of quantity, whether intensive or extensive. Without that notion we cannot speak of any state of consciousness as " higher," for instance, or " deeper," as " more pleasant " or " more painful "; there would be mere variety without degree. But we must admit the existence of degrees in some form or other. If we do not admit degrees of intensity we must take it that all terms implying comparison imply degrees of extension, and we shall be attributing to the mind if not a spatial form, at least a form analogous to that of the spatial world. It seems to me that we must in any case suppose it to be spatial, for, as I said in Chapter III, sensations different in quality could not be brought together as they are except by proximity in space.

The reduction of intensity to extension, whether justified or not, is by no means favourable to Bergson's philosophy, but in dealing with the second and third of the forms of consciousness mentioned above he applies it without hesitation. In considering the nature of effort and what we suppose to be its greater and smaller intensities he gives the instance of a man gradually closing and clenching his fist, and declares that the appearance of a gradual increase of intensity in the resultant feeling is really due to an increase of extension, *i.e.*, to the spreading of the sensation over a wider area of the body, from the fist up through the arms. The feeling in the hand, the starting-point, remains the same. This explanation as it stands is not satisfactory, for while we are quite aware of this gradual extension of area there seems no doubt that we also feel an increase in the strength of the sensation in the hand. However, we must grant that this also might be caused by an increase of extension, *i.e.*, by the greater depth to which the sensation penetrates in the hand itself. In another instance, that of a man raising heavier and heavier weights in turn, Bergson admits that the sensation felt in the arm changes, but this he declares to be a change of quality, *i.e.*, a change from a feeling of heaviness to fatigue, and from fatigue to pain. But there must be an element of quantity in these changes; it is not to be supposed that the feeling of heaviness in the arm " remains constant " for some time, and then abruptly passes over into fatigue, or that fatigue abruptly passes over into pain. What reason could there be for this sudden transition? The change of quality must at least be prepared by an increase in the quantity of heaviness and pain respectively.

In pleasure and pain, too, Bergson supposes the only differences of quantity to depend on the smaller or larger area of the body affected. But he holds that these *sensations affectives* express not so much the molecular disturbances produced in the organism as the reaction that would automatically follow. Nature does nothing in vain, and the use of these sensations is to inform us of the future, not of the past or present; concerning these last, information would be useless. We are informed of the coming reaction in the body in order that we may choose whether we will resist it or give it free course. But is this the only possible interpretation of pleasure and pain? It has often been suggested that the purpose of pain is to warn us of something that already exists, *i.e.*, the disturbed state of the organism, in order that this may be remedied, and this seems quite as good a reason as that given by Bergson. Besides, it is not true that pleasure and pain, as he seems to suggest, are only produced where we are free to resist the reaction following the excitation received; they occur also where the excitation is followed immediately by reflex action, so that we have no time for resistance. Bergson, however, offers us another argument for believing that these sensations express the reaction and not the disturbance or excitation itself. A difference in the extent of the molecular movements arising in the organism is found to be accompanied by a difference in the feeling. But consciousness, he says, cannot measure for us the vibration produced by the shock from without; this can only enter consciousness in the form of a pleasure or pain, not as a movement. On the other hand, it can measure " the automatic movements that tend to follow the shock received." Yet his only argument for this is that it must be so, and that for the reason just mentioned, *i.e.*, that the feeling would be useless unless it acquainted us with the movements about to follow. In any case the molecular movements that are past or present can surely enter consciousness just as well as those that are on the point of coming.

In considering the *sensations représentatives*, those that reflect the outer world, the chief instance given is that of a light placed at a certain distance from the eyes; and the question is whether the difference in the sensation produced by a change in the distance is one of quantity. Bergson argues at some length that in spite of the attempts made to measure this difference it is not really quantitative; the various sensations of light produced at various distances differ in quality alone. Yet it seems obvious that if the cause differs in quantity—the change in the position of the light being measurable—the effect must be so too. According to Bergson there is a series of qualitative changes in the sensation of light as the light is brought nearer, or as we approach it; a series of abrupt changes, not one continuous change corresponding to the continuous movement of the light towards us. That is to say, the light may come nearer by a few inches without any change in the sensation, but after it has moved a further inch forward the sensation suddenly assumes a different quality. The variations in the effect, the consciousness of the light, will thus in no way correspond to the variations in the cause, the proximity of the light: the former will be abrupt and qualitative, the latter continuous and quantitative. But it is impossible to accept such a theory as this. The change in the sensation from one quality to another must at any rate be prepared by an increase or diminution of the former quality; otherwise our states of consciousness would form a mere chaos of various qualities without any law governing the relations of these to one another.

This objection applies to all Bergson's arguments in this chapter. To say that qualities have no degrees, no quantity, is to reduce them to a chaos; they cannot in that case pass into one another, for there can be no gradual change where there are no degrees, but one must simply take the place of another, without any connection or continuity between the two. There can be no order without quantity, so that there could be no reason why any sense-quality, on a given increase of the excitation, should be succeeded by this other rather than that. And to deny that there is anything in quality corresponding to quantity is to set up an irreconcilable dualism in the world, resembling that supposed to exist between matter and mind: for the effect, the sensation, will be unable to measure properly the cause, the external object. If, on the other hand, we admit degrees of intensity, we can imagine that all qualities form a rising scale, and that the transition from one to the other is effected when the intensity of the former passes above or below a certain point.

The last part of the chapter is devoted to a criticism of the psycho-physical theories which attempt to establish a quantitative relation, *i.e.*, a relation of greater or less intensity, between states of consciousness. This criticism is based on the view already mentioned, that it is impossible to speak of greater and smaller quantities unless the latter are included and seen in the former. This, of course, would make it impossible to compare the sizes of any two bodies, for no body can occupy part of the space already occupied by another. It would be impossible, also, to compare the velocities of two moving objects at different times through different spaces. But as we can and do compare these sizes and velocities there seems no reason why we should not be able to recognize a quantitative difference in the qualities of our sensations. The general belief is that we are able to do so; and this belief cannot arise from a confusion of physical cause and psychical effect, for it is from the greater or less intensity of the sensation that we judge the strength of its cause, not *vice versâ*. Nor can our estimate of the difference in intensity of one sensation from another, or our belief that two sensations are equally different from a third, depend on a remembrance or calculation of the number of possible *nuances* between the qualities compared, as Bergson suggests. We are quite unconscious of any such elaborate process when we thus estimate the difference or assert the equality of differences. Besides, the very word *nuance* implies a degree of intensity.

The object of the second chapter is to prove that time or duration is of a very different character from space, though the same terms have been freely applied to both. The parts of space are all alike and external to one another, whereas the parts of duration are different and do not lie outside one another but interpenetrate. To quote the author's own definition, "Pure duration may well be a succession of qualitative changes which intermix and interpenetrate, without precise outlines, without any tendency to keep themselves exterior to one another, without any affinity to number." This serves also for a description of our states of consciousness; one flows into another that succeeds it without any border-line of time to distinguish the two, whereas things in space have their boundaries clearly fixed.

The first part of the chapter is devoted to the idea of number, which according to the author is derived not from time but from space. Even when we count things successively in time, in order that these things may appear to us in the form of a number, the ones already counted must be retained in the mind and be set side by side in an ideal space; if at each moment we think of one, and of one only, we shall never have the idea of number, however many moments we may count. The idea of any number is a mental image of many objects at once; and whatever exists all at once must be spatial in character, not temporal. Number, therefore, can only belong to things in space, not to the states of consciousness succeeding one another in time.

But besides number, we are told, there is another form of multiplicity, and this the states of consciousness can possess. If a man hears the sound of a bell and counts them he retains in his mind at every moment the sounds already heard, and so they all exist there side by side at once, as objects exist in space. But without counting them he may simply receive the impression they make on him as a sort of tune, and then the idea with which he is left is that of a confused multiplicity, not a distinct number. This is the multiplicity that belongs to states of consciousness.

But if this impression of a confused multiplicity comes at the end of the series of sounds it must surely be spatial in character just as much as the idea of number, for it exists all at once. The only difference is that it is like a part of space, a picture, in which the colours have run together, not like one in which the outlines are distinct. A series of states of consciousness may be like this, but they would not for that reason be any less like the visible, composite things in space, which are by no means always clearly outlined and distinguished. If, on the other hand, the impression is not merely the final result of the sounds, but accompanies them, and is thus spread over some time, the series of conscious states may for all that resemble a number of objects lying side by side. The successive sensations form an organic whole and the impression is not one of definite quantity, *i.e.*, of number, but qualitative; but so too is the effect of a landscape. The scene before us, spatial though it is, may give us an indistinct idea of multiplicity and a sensation of pleasure, that is to say, of quality; for the parts of a landscape may harmonize as well as the parts of a tune.

The idea of a confused multiplicity is expanded later on in the chapter, when " pure duration " is defined, and here too we find the successive states of consciousness compared to the notes of music. " Pure duration is the form taken by the succession of states of consciousness when the self just gives itself up to living, when it refrains from drawing a dividing line between the present state and the preceding. For this it does not need to be wholly absorbed in the sensation or idea which is passing, for then it would, in fact, cease to experience duration. It does not need, either, to forget the preceding states ; it is enough that while recalling these it does not set them by the side of the present state, like one point by the side of another, but organizes them with it, as happens when we recall the notes of a tune blended together. May we not say that if these notes form a successive series we yet perceive them one in another, and that the whole may be compared with a living being, the parts of which, though distinct, interpenetrate as a result of the closeness of their union ? "

Here a further comparison is introduced, the parts of " pure duration," the successive states of consciousness, being likened to the parts of a living body. But this is to compare them with things in space, things which co-operate with one another but yet lie side by side and are distinct. If they are distinct they must be separate and cannot interpenetrate in any other sense than that in which Chinese boxes do so. One cannot really occupy the same space as another, however deeply it may be imbedded in that other ; in other words, each must be external to all the rest. And this is equally true of the parts of the living body and of the parts of pure duration.

In the course of his argument Bergson maintains that even to attribute order to the states of consciousness is to reduce time to space ; pure duration can have no order, and " if we establish an order in the succession, then succession becomes simultaneity and is projected into space." But how can there be succession without order? It seems almost a contradiction in terms to speak of the one as possible without the other, but we are left without any explanation of this paradox.

Another instance given to illustrate the meaning of " pure duration " is the sensation produced by the swinging of a pendulum. If I retain the memory of the movement just passed, together with the image of the present movement, I must either set the two side by side in my mind, and then they will be merely like two points on a line, not successive at all, or else " I shall perceive them one in the other, interpenetrating and organizing themselves together like the notes of a tune, in such a way as to form an indistinct or qualitative multiplicity, with no resemblance to number ; I shall obtain thus the image of pure duration, but I shall have also entirely freed myself from the idea of a homogenous medium, or of a measurable quantity." But if the ideas of the two movements do not provide us with a true image of succession when they are set side by side in the mind, can they give us a better image when they "interpenetrate and organize themselves together " ? In either case they both exist at the same time, the one as a memory, the other as a present sensation ; and since they are simultaneous the image they form together must in either case be spatial in character, however close an organism they form. And if nothing spatial can give us a true idea of succession they cannot give us such an idea when they interpenetrate any more than when they are merely set side by side.

This will be clearer if we consider the impression produced by the notes of a tune. The previous notes remain in the memory, and are therefore simultaneous with the present note ; otherwise the perception of the harmony would be impossible. They are like the strokes of the painter's brush, meaningless taken separately, but contributing to form a picture ; and like the parts of a picture they must all exist at once in the mind. But they must exist distinct in the memory and exterior to one another ; otherwise they would be like the mixture of colours on a painter's palette, not like a picture, and we should have the idea, not of a harmony, but of a confused noise.

The regular swing of a pendulum may make a man fall asleep, and this fact too is taken to prove the non-spatial and non-quantitative character of succession in time. Sleep, it is said, cannot be produced by the last sound alone, or by the last sound together with the memory of those that preceded. " We must therefore admit that the sounds were blended together and acted, not by their quantity as quantity, but by the effect of quality that their quantity produced—that is to say, by the rhythmic organization of all the sounds together." True, we may answer, it is not the memory of the previous sounds that produces sleep; yet each of these has had some effect on the mind, an effect which accumulates until sleep gradually follows. The movements of the brain grow slower by degrees with every sound, and this change is surely one of quantity not of quality. The argument quoted would only hold good if we passed in a moment from a state of complete wakefulness into a deep slumber. As it is, there is nothing qualitative in the effect of the sounds, any more than there is in the destruction of some object by repeated blows from a hammer; the final blow may appear to have done all or nearly all the work, and yet would have been useless without the others.

A little further on a contrast is drawn between events outside the mind and the series of states of consciousness; to the former belongs "mutual externality without succession," in the latter "succession without mutual externality." " But as the successive phases of our conscious life, which nevertheless interpenetrate, correspond each to a movement of the pendulum simultaneous with it, and as, on the other hand, these movements are clearly distinct, since one is no more when the other begins, we form the habit of drawing the same distinction between the successive moments of our conscious life; the movements of the pendulum decompose it into parts exterior to one another, and from this arises the false idea of a homogeneous duration within the mind, analogous to space, and such that its moments are identical in character and follow one another without mutual penetration." Each phase of consciousness has thus a particular event, a swing of the pendulum, corresponding and simultaneous with it; if so, it must begin and end at the same instant as the movement. The movements of consciousness must therefore form a series parallel to the movements of the pendulum, and be equally external to one another. In the mind, of course, the past movements remain in the form of memory, but these memories keep to the background and do not interfere with or "penetrate" our perception of the present movement. The objection may be raised that they still exist during the present movement and thus encroach upon the time it occupies, while outside the mind no past movements of the pendulum exist in any form during the time occupied by the present movement. Yet they might do so if a cinematograph film had been taken of them ; this would be quite a good equivalent in the outer world for memory in the inner. And just as the movements of the pendulum would not be made any the less external to one another by the existence of past movements on the film, so the phases of consciousness produced by, and corresponding to, the movements of the pendulum would not be less external to one another because the past phases existed in memory.

Proceeding to analyze movement in general, Bergson declares that though the successive positions of the moving body occupy space, movement "regarded as a passage from one point to another is a mental synthesis, a process within the soul, and therefore unextended." This is obscure, for it seems to make time wholly subjective, in which case how can there be "successive positions" in space ? On the other hand, if time is not subjective, why should not movement exist independently of the mind, in space *plus* time ? It is not necessary for the indivisibility of the movement that it should be regarded as the work of a "qualitative synthesis" in our consciousness ; the space it traverses in the outer world and the time it occupies may be just as undivided as any act of our consciousness can be. We do not see a series of positions but one continuous change, just as the space traversed is continuous and not composed of parts. "One may very well divide a thing," says Bergson, "but not an act." But a simple thing can no more be divided than a simple act. Consequently space itself is only divided as far down as the simple things, *i.e.*, the ultimate parts of matter, and the intervals between them. Or if it is regarded as divided by the movements of bodies, the parts of it thus formed are the whole spaces traversed in each movement, not fractions of these spaces, if the movements are uniform throughout.

In order that we may have an idea of motion it is necessary for us to retain the impressions left on the mind by the previous positions of the moving body, or rather by its continuous change of position in the past. Bergson argues that the synthesis of these impressions, which creates the idea of motion, is not effected by arranging them mentally in a line, but is " qualitative, a gradual organization of our successive sensations together, a unity similar to that of a phrase of music." " A rapid movement made by anyone with his eyes shut will appear to his consciousness under the form of a purely qualitative sensation, as long as he does not think of the space traversed." But can we call this purely qualitative sensation a sensation of movement? Without any accompanying idea of space it will be nothing but a blind feeling, an agitation of consciousness similar to a sudden shock. To have a perception of movement we must mentally range along a line the impressions received previously from the moving body. The velocity of the movement is judged by the length of the line and the difference in intensity between the first of these impressions and the last, the present sensation. There is no need of any " new synthesis to connect the positions together," for all those positions, or rather the whole past change of position, exists in the mind at once, at the present moment.

" In dealing with time and movement science eliminates at the outset the essential, qualitative element—eliminates duration from time and mobility from movement." It deals only " with space and with simultaneities." " We note the precise instant when the movement begins—that is to say, the simultaneity of a change in the outside world with one of our states of consciousness; we note the instant when the movement ends—that is to say, another simultaneity; finally, we measure the space traversed, the only thing that is in fact measurable." But science and common sense alike recognize the existence of duration well enough by recognizing that the different positions of the moving body do not exist simultaneously in space, that the line along which they extend is not only one of space but of time. In fact, however, we should speak not of a series of simultaneities but of two parallel lengths of time, in the moving body and in consciousness; two or more simultaneous " points " of time are impossible, for there are no points either of time or of space. As for measuring duration, surely we are measuring it always by experiencing events; when we have seen two movements, one of which begins with the other but lasts longer, merely by seeing them we have measured and compared them. How else do we measure two objects, except by seeing one put side by side with the other, or a third put side by side with each in turn? To say that science never really deals with duration but with simultaneities, *i.e.*, those of the beginning and end of a movement with two states of our consciousness, is as strange as it would be to say that it never deals with space, but only with the two points at the beginning and end of a line. It is true that it may never attempt to define duration or movement, but does it ever attempt to define space? It takes the meaning of both as already known.

We may remark too that what Bergson says about a change in the speed of all the movements in the universe would be equally true if applied to a change in the extent of all bodies and the distances between them. If these latter were twice or three times as large as they were, " there would be nothing to modify in our formulas, or in the numbers we employ in these," any more than there would be if all movements were twice as fast as they are. And supposing all the movements were faster, would there be any " indefinable and in a way qualitative perception of the change," as Bergson says? I do not see why there should be, for of course our consciousness itself would be moving twice as fast, so that everything would be the same to it as before. In any case the whole supposition is really unintelligible, for speed is purely relative, and in the supposed case, where all movements were changed, where would be the common standard in relation to which their speeds before and after would be different? Suppositions of this kind, which are often made by Relativists, as, for instance, by Poincaré, seem either futile or fatal to their theory. They suppose a change in the size of all bodies or in the speed of all movements. If, then, they take the change to be real, though incapable of being perceived, they are supposing size and motion to be absolute. But if they mean that the change is not real, they are supposing nothing at all, and their argument has no point.

" There is in space neither duration nor even succession,

in the sense in which consciousness takes these words; each of the so-called successive states of the external world exists alone, and their multiplicity is only real for a consciousness that can in the first place preserve them, and then set them side by side as external to one another." Each of them exists alone, *i.e.*, in its own time and not in another's, but why should this prevent their multiplicity from being real, even apart from our consciousness? Each of the bodies in space exists alone, in so far as it exists in its own space, but this does not prevent them from having "multiplicity." The successive states of the external world exist alone in a sense, but they also exist as members of a whole, and form a line continuous in extent, though different in different parts as regards quality. Whether they are really successive is another question.

But the expression "states of the external world" is an inexact one, for the course of the world cannot be divided like this; we could only use the term properly if all the elements always changed their states at the same time, so that there was no overlapping but each state of each element lasted just as long as the simultaneous states of all the others. As this is not so, we cannot speak of the states of the world as external to one another; this is only true of the states of an individual element. The stages in the history of large parts of the world overlap those of other parts, so that the course of the world as a whole possesses exactly that character of indistinct multiplicity which Bergson attributes only to our consciousness. Some of these stages, again, contain in a fainter or a more developed form things that are also found at earlier periods; these survivals affect the other contents of the later stage as memories affect present thoughts. Here too the external world resembles our consciousness, so that there is no ground for attributing "duration" to the latter which would not justify the attribution of it to the former.

It is impossible to accept the distinction drawn between two kinds of multiplicity, one quantitative, *i.e.*, number, and the other qualitative. This latter kind is said to belong to the states of consciousness; it contains number only *en puissance*, and we must not even speak of the qualities in our consciousness as "several," since we should in that case be treating them as external to one another. If that is so, ought we to speak of "qualities" at all? How can we use the plural if we may not use the word "several" or "many"? And does not "multiplicity" imply "many," and therefore a quantitative distinction between the qualities? In reality the two multiplicities are only two attitudes of the mind towards the same thing. We do not always count the qualities presented to us in sensation, nor attend closely to the exact boundaries between them, or to the numerous shades by which one may seem to melt into another. So far as our attention is concerned the patches of colour we see often form for us an indefinite multiplicity. But the definite number of different qualities always exists in the sensation, and though we may not trouble to count it, the fact that we could do so proves that the multiplicity is numerical. To count them may be difficult, for they may shade off into one another so as to be indistinguishable; yet on looking carefully we should be able to distinguish the different stages by which they passed into one another, narrow and numerous though these stages may be. If ever we could not, this would only prove that there were sometimes in sensation distinctions too small to affect our thought. All this is true not only of sensation but of the deeper states of consciousness. A memory may come to us confusedly at first, but the fact that we can make its elements distinct to our reflective mind shows that they must already be distinct in our subconsciousness, which is the material upon which our reflection works in memory, as in attention it works upon sensation. There is no ground for supposing that in reflection or attention we introduce a distinctness which is not already present, though unnoticed, in the memory or sensation as it first appears.

It is true that numbers may have an emotional effect, and "each number in ordinary use" may have "its emotional equivalent." But we must not confuse the number and its effect on our feelings, and call the latter a "qualitative multiplicity." The term "qualitative" can be applied only to the effect, the emotion, while the "multiplicity" belongs only to the number. The emotion may increase, so that it must possess a quantitative as well as a qualitative character, but its quantity is an extent or intensity, not a "multiplicity."

In the instance given by Bergson a little farther on, the effect on the mind produced by the four successive sounds from the clock is not qualitative, any more than the degree of speed attained by a moving body struck four times and made faster each time, or of four blows upon the same object. Even when the sensations are fused together the result is a quantity, not a quality; it is an increase each time in the extent or intensity of consciousness. But for a time at any rate the sensations still remain distinct in the memory, through the traces they have left in the brain. After the sounds have ceased we can often tell the number, if there are only a few of them, though we did not count them or even attend to them while they were continuing; and this would be impossible unless the sensations remained distinct in the memory.

All that is said in the last pages of the chapter about the feelings might be said equally well about external "material" things. The more complex these are, the more individuality each of them possesses, and this is especially true of living bodies. In applying general terms to any particular thing we ignore its differentiæ, just as we do in applying them to any of our states of consciousness, to our feelings and ideas. But the possession of individual characteristics does not make "material" things any the less spatial and external to one another, or prevent our feelings from being distinct and spread out along a length of time.

The dividing of our conscious life or of "duration" into distinct parts, as described by Bergson, would be impossible if it meant anything else but the turning of our attention to distinctions already existing. If that life or duration had no number or extent, no mutually exclusive parts, we should never be able to represent it to ourselves as having any, and it would give us no occasion for so representing it. The idea of a homogeneous time is a "symbolical image of real duration"; how could it be so if there were no resemblance, no parallelism, between the two? That there is such a parallelism Bergson himself admits, for he speaks of our sensations as caused by the movements of outer objects, and of our emotions and ideas as "contemporaneous" with our sensations. Each sensation, that is to say, corresponds to a state of some part of the outer world; but there could be no such correspondence if the states of the outer world were distinct and our sensations were not. And if our sensations are distinct, the deeper forms of consciousness must be so too, since they are contemporaneous with these. Out of a merely qualitative multiplicity we could never form the image of our inner life which we actually do form, nor could we "project it into a homogeneous medium" similar to space.

At the end of the chapter we are not left with any clear idea what is meant by "duration," except the purely negative idea that it must not be considered like a line in space. Yet every word we use of time is derived from space, so that even in attempting to define duration Bergson is compelled to use spatial terms. Are we to say that duration has length? If so, then it resembles a line of space. Has it any order? We can only think of order by analogy with space. The terms "before" and "after" are derived from the same analogy, and so are the terms "past" and "present." Where, then, are we to suppose that duration differs from space? Apparently in this, that the parts of it interpenetrate, whereas things in space are altogether external to one another. But the idea of "interpenetration" itself involves the idea of space, and the states of consciousness only interpenetrate in the same sense as do things in space. The velocity of one motion is conveyed into another, yet these motions themselves remain distinct enough.

It may be true that it is impossible to fix exactly where one sensation or thought begins and another ends, but it is also impossible to limit exactly the visible things in space. We cannot fix the outline of these things, the precise atom at which they end, for that outline is always changing and any limit we might decide on would be purely arbitrary. But this is because the larger bodies are composed of innumerable elements, and it is only the ultimate particles of matter that remain absolutely external to one another. And the same arguments that lead us to adopt the atomic theory must lead us to believe that our sensations and thoughts are made up of innumerable elements and movements of these elements, each of which is distinguishable from the others, though the whole complex sensation or thought may have no clear border-line, either in extent of time or of area, to distinguish it from the rest. For though the mind is one, like space, it must also be manifold, like the spatial world. There must be an element of consciousness and a movement of consciousness corresponding to every atom and every movement of every atom of the brain; and the former must be as definite as the latter are. Thus although we may not be able to tell where one sensation or thought ends and another begins, just as it is impossible with the things in space that we can see, this is simply because they are composed of the movements of many elements, movements which are distinct enough themselves, though too small for our apprehension.

The third chapter of the essay contains a defence of the doctrine of free will against the advocates of Determinism. The problem discussed is one of the most ancient in philosophy, and in none has there been so evident a failure on the part of each side to understand what the other side means. The supporters of free will, at any rate, have not made it clear what it is they are defending. The doctrine of Determinism is clear enough in itself, though not always clearly expressed; it is simply this, that the actions of every man are wholly determined by the conditions previously existing in his mind and in the world around him. To put it in another way, the state of the world at any time, including all human actions, could be deduced according to invariable laws from any previous state. But it is not so evident what is meant by free will. Even in this chapter it seems to be defined in two inconsistent ways; at one time an act is called " free " if it is uncaused, at another time we are told that " the act which bears the mark of our personality is free." This latter kind of freedom no Determinist would deny, for the definition admits that the actions of each man are determined by his character, in so far as they are not caused by external circumstances. But it is freedom from the law of cause and effect that is generally meant and defended in this chapter, as is shown by the arguments advanced.

Determinism in modern times is often based on physiology and on the mechanical theory of matter. The outer world, according to the most widely accepted doctrine, is composed of atoms obeying certain laws ; and even where the atomic theory is not accepted, the obedience of material things to law is regarded as established. But the brain is a " material " thing, and a close correspondence has been observed between states of consciousness and states of the brain ; if the correspondence is exact, then the states of consciousness, not less than those of the brain, must follow the rule of cause and effect. This parallelism between mind and brain extends beyond sensation into the deeper realms of consciousness, for a cerebral change may alter the character entirely. The knowledge of this has given rise to various theories, among which, in spite of Bergson's protest, we must rank those of Leibnitz and Spinoza. For undoubtedly it was the correspondence between the inner and outer worlds that suggested the doctrine of the " pre-established harmony," and the idea that consciousness and extension express the same thing in different ways. This latter is just one form of what is now called the doctrine of " psycho-physical parallelism," and a much more reasonable form than that which represents consciousness as an occasional effect or " epiphenomenon " of movements of the atoms in the brain. Why should consciousness arise only in the brain, and not everywhere else ? There is no such great difference between the brain and the rest of the material world as would account for the production of consciousness here and not there. Therefore, even if we admitted that consciousness could be " produced " by matter, we should come to the conclusion that it was universal, though reaching its most intense and most complex form in the human mind. It follows from this that we have no need to assume the existence of matter at all ; the world of consciousness forms a closed system and does not require as its cause another world running parallel to it. The origin of our sensations is always another consciousness outside ours, always, and not only when the object seen is a living body.

But the outer world, though shown to be conscious, must not be supposed to be free from laws, any more than when we called it " material." The movements of what appear to us as the planets are not any the less regular because those bodies, like the brains of all living beings, are really spheres of more or less intense consciousness; and the same may be said of the movements of the smallest bodies, of the atoms or electrons. In these cases we must accept Determinism, and it seems improbable that this should not apply also to the consciousness which is represented to others as the brain. For the elements of the brain are of the same kind as those found in other parts of the world, where the law of cause and effect is admitted to reign. Besides, when we consider the gradual evolution and the uniformity of the world we cannot think it possible that causation should exist here and not there; there would be no reason why it should exist anywhere if it were not universal.

This argument is not met by Bergson, who maintains the dualism of body and mind and is not willing to admit that the deeper forms of consciousness correspond to any atomic movements of the brain. That such a correspondence, or rather identity, is universal seems obvious from the fact that changes of character, as I said, can be effected by cerebral changes, and from the difficulty of supposing that the relation of mind and body—to use the language of Dualism—can be a casual relation, so that the one may exist here and there without the other. We cannot believe that certain states of consciousness, *i.e.*, sensations, have a series of an entirely different nature running parallel to them, *i.e.*, the movements of the atoms in the brain, and that other states have no such parallel series. For the Monist, of course, such a belief will have no meaning, and even the Dualist will find it impossible; for whether he supposes matter to create consciousness or consciousness to create matter, he cannot imagine that this creation is a matter of chance, as it would have to be if it took place on some occasions and not on others. For the difference between the forms of matter or consciousness, however great they might be, could only be differences between forms of matter or consciousness: they could not explain why one form of matter should not be content with its difference from others but should also possess the distinction of creating something wholly different from matter in general. The same is true of consciousness; it is inconceivable that any higher or lower kind of this, in addition to its own difference from others in quality, should also possess, as peculiar to itself, the property of creating, or being accompanied by, entities completely different from consciousness in general. Even the Dualist, therefore, will have to admit a universal parallel between the two natures in which he believes, mind and body. But in that case he will hardly think it worth while to remain a Dualist.

Another form of the argument for Determinism is taken from the doctrine of the "conservation of energy," according to which the sum of energy is neither diminished nor increased. All the movements in the world are determined by the movements of a preceding time, and no new force is ever introduced anywhere. This seems an obvious truth, for if a single movement of any atom were not determined by preceding movements in accordance with invariable laws, this would imply that an alternative to following the usual course of events was always open to every atom, and then the regularity of the world would be unintelligible. One cannot suppose that any moving element of matter, instead of following out the course it would naturally follow according to the laws of mechanics, may now and then take a course more advantageous to the whole to which it belongs. If that were so there would be no limit to the number of miracles in the world. It is equally absurd to imagine that consciousness could effect any such divergence from mechanical laws. The elements that form the brain were once part of the world that undoubtedly obeys those laws; can they begin suddenly to act in a different way when united in a more complex structure than that in which they previously existed? I use this materialistic language in order to make the argument clear to those who are not convinced that consciousness is universal. It would be truer to say that the elements of the universal consciousness follow the same laws when they form that part of it called the human mind as when they existed in a less complex form.

In answer to the argument from the conservation of energy, Bergson suggests that as, according to the most "radical form of Mechanism," molecular movements devoid of consciousness may create sensation, so a consciousness devoid of energy may create a movement. But the two suppositions are in fact equally unacceptable. The statement that molecular movements " create " sensation is simply an incorrect way of saying that sensations arise whenever certain movements occur. But this leads, as I have shown, to the doctrine of universal consciousness and to Monism. On the other hand, we cannot imagine consciousness intervening to divert, accelerate, or retard the elements of matter—to use dualistic language again—and giving a push to this one or that. We cannot imagine an atom drawn one way by its desire to obey the laws of mechanics, and another way by an energy from outside the world of mechanical laws. In fact there is no world but that of consciousness, and whatever laws we discover in matter must be transferred to that world.

The argument that the mind can never return to its previous state, as a moving body can return to its previous position, would not prove that the mind was exempt from mechanical laws, even if it were true. But in fact a state of the mind may be repeated, as much as the state of any " material " body. It is true that the repetition may not be exact in either case, for even the elements of such a body may be so numerous as to make it unlikely that they will ever exist in the same formation twice. But the laws of mechanics do not require any such exact repetition, but only that the difference in effects on any two occasions should correspond to the difference in the conditions. Again, the fact that the past leaves in the mind its traces in the form of memory does not prove anything against the doctrine that the sum of energy in the world is constant. These traces have their counterparts in the outer world, *e.g.* the geological strata on the outer crust of the earth ; and no one would ever use the existence of these strata to prove that the amount of energy in the world might increase.

The reasons given for believing that the present may sometimes be determined by the future, not by the past, are by no means convincing, and in any case could obviously not be regarded as arguments against Determinism. Anyone who maintains that the course of the world is a series of causes and effects must also maintain the possibility of taking this series the other way round. The effect is always proportionate to the cause, therefore the cause must always be proportionate to the effect, so that any law of nature might easily be taken in the reverse order to that in which we usually take it. The consideration of this should lead us, as I have pointed out already, to deny any distinction between " past " and " future." It leaves no reason, either, for regarding an event as determined by that which " precedes " it rather than by that which " follows." And if with Bergson we regard the " future " as determining the present, it must be equally possible to reverse this order; for the present, as effect, must be proportionate to the future, as cause; therefore the future is of course proportionate to the present and might be taken as an effect of it. All that is really necessary for Determinism, or for the laws of science, is that the event A on one side of the event B and the event C on the other side should both be proportionate to, and therefore deducible from, their common neighbour B. It makes no difference which of them we regard as coming " before " B or after it.

The case where two men, on resuming an interrupted conversation, find that they are thinking of the same new topic, though they have arrived at it by different trains of thought, might be explained as a simple coincidence, likely enough to occur to men with many interests in common. The explanation given by Bergson is not clear. " This common idea is derived from some unknown cause—perhaps from some physical influence—and, to justify its appearance, calls up a series of antecedents which explain it, which appear to be its cause, but nevertheless are really its effect." Does this unknown cause come into being at the beginning or end of the interruption of the two series of thoughts leading to the common idea? If it comes at the beginning it must determine the two series in the ordinary way, and there is no more to be said. On the other hand, we cannot suppose it to come at the end. Our thoughts, after following a series of cause and effect in one direction, cannot suddenly be met and continued by another stream of cause and effect flowing in the reverse direction. If such collisions could ever happen they might happen continually, so that our thoughts would continually be affected by the future, and we should have a memory of the time on both sides of the present. Besides, if the two " series of antecedents " really explain the common idea, why should they not actually be the causes of that idea? What better definition of a cause could you have than this, that it explains its effect?

Much of what Bergson says in opposition to the older psychologists who regarded motives as separate entities, identical in all men, might very well be accepted by the Determinists. All that is necessary for their view is that each state of the mind should be regarded as dependent on the state preceding, or on some external cause, or on both. They would be quite ready to admit that such motives or states of the mind as love or hatred assume a somewhat different form in different men—though all the forms of each must be identical in the main, for otherwise they would not be called by the same name of "love" or "hatred." They would admit, too, that our everyday actions are much less expressive of our personality than those called forth by a crisis. As I said before, if the only meaning of "free will" is that "the act which bears the mark of our personality is free," there must be very few who would not grant its existence in this sense. But we have to go farther and ask what is the origin of our personality. It must have an origin, and therefore all its elements and all the actions that proceed from it must be predetermined. For it cannot come out of nowhere with a character of its own; it must be partly inherited and partly qualified by external circumstances. While admitting that the character *se modifie* every day, Bergson declares that these modifications blend with it and are made its own. But that might be said of every effect in the world. When one moving body strikes another and increases its speed, the motion imparted by the first "blends with" the previous motion of the second body, which thus "makes it its own." Every force is qualified and appropriated by that on which it works, but is none the less said to determine it; external circumstances, therefore, may be said to determine the character in a greater or less degree. All that is not derived from these must be determined by the character of the parents. There can be no uncaused modifications; if there were such, there would be no reason why there should not be the most surprising changes in any personality at any time, whereas there have been only a few that have appeared unaccountable.

Even these few, therefore, must be supposed due to some physical cause, or to the rise of some element in the character that has remained in the background.

One of the definitions usually given of free will is that quoted by Bergson from J. S. Mill, who says that free will would imply the power of choosing a different course from that which one actually does choose. The idea is illustrated in this essay by a diagram, a curving line MO branching off at O into two straight lines OX, OY, representing the two alternatives presumed to be possible. It is admitted that if this diagram were a correct symbol the Determinists would be right, for it would have to be granted that the previous line of thought represented by MO induces the mind, when arrived at O, to choose the direction OX or OY. Otherwise the mind, on arriving at O, not being impelled in either direction, would hesitate between the two for ever. But according to Bergson this diagram does not represent the processes of the mind at all, for a spatial image cannot represent time; that is regarded as proved by the second chapter of the essay. The figure represents a thing and not a progress; it corresponds to the memory *en quelque sort figé* of the whole deliberation and of the final decision taken. But if our memory is wrong in representing time under a spatial form, how are we to trust any of our ideas about time? For almost every word we use in speaking about time shows that our ideas about it are based on an analogy with space, and that we can form no notion of it without the help of that analogy. Nearly all that is said of time in this essay is negative, and the " vague multiplicity " of " duration " is all that is left us.

A little farther on we are told that the line in the diagram may be taken as symbolizing time; not time passing, indeed, but time past. But what is meant here by time past, *le temps ecoulé*? Time never exists in a state of being past, though it is true we often talk as though it did. No time ever comes " before " or " after " another; each exists within its own limits and cannot be qualified or determined as " past " or " future " by another, any more than an extended thing is really " right " or " left " in space. Apparently " time past " must mean the image in our memory of the time on one side of the present, so that it is a mere repetition of the idea already expressed.

Like all the advocates of free will, Bergson appeals to the "infallible" instinct of the ego, which feels and declares itself free. But no man would deny that his actions were determined by motives. We feel, indeed, that the strength of the motives depends on our character, so that they are parts of ourselves, and that kind of freedom, as I have already said, every Determinist would admit. All that the ego "declares" is that its reactions to external events depend on its character. Its instinct tells us nothing as to the origin of that character, which cannot spring out of nowhere, but must be determined by heredity or other causes. To be told that his character was not the effect of any cause or causes would not give any satisfaction to any man; no one would thank philosophy for attributing to him that kind of free will.

Another form of Determinism criticized by Bergson is as follows: a superior intelligence, which knew all the antecedents of a certain action before it occurred, would be able to predict that action with absolute certainty. This was put by Huxley in a wider and more general way: if a superior intelligence, at a moment when our world existed only as a nebular mass, had known the properties and position of every atom, it would have been able to foretell the whole course of history down to the smallest detail. It is questionable whether this would be true of qualities, for if these depend on the velocity of bodies or some other quantitative element it is possible that some velocity which has existed since the nebular mass did not exist before it, and therefore its accompanying quality could not have been predicted, no similar instance ever having occurred before. But every other quality might have been, and every movement and relative position. However, to return to the limited form of the doctrine, we may accept for the sake of clearness the imaginary illustration of it given by Bergson. Of the proverbial pair, Peter and Paul, the former has to take an important decision and the other knows all the conditions under which he is to take it. Then Paul will be able to predict accurately the decisions which Peter will take. In answer to this, Bergson declares that there are only two ways in which one man can know the conditions under which another acts, the intensity of his states of consciousness or the strength of his different motives. He must either measure the intensity of those states by the result that follows, or else he must experience those states of consciousness himself. Peter can feel the strength of each of his own motives well enough, but he cannot assign to it a quantitative value and state this to Paul until he has compared each motive with the others and discovered the part which each takes in the final decision; that is to say, until he has acted. In this case, therefore, it will be impossible for Paul to predict the decision, since he cannot know the strength of the various motives which influence Peter until after the decision is taken. In the other case, in order to experience the states of consciousness through which Peter passes, he will have to be in exactly the same position as Peter, and since all the past affects the present consciousness, he will have to have lived through exactly the same life in every detail; that is to say, he will have to *be* Peter, and that right up to the last instant before the decision is taken. For up till then the conditions leading to the decision will be incomplete, and he will not have experienced all the states of consciousness of which the decision was the result. But then " there can no longer be any question of predicting but only of acting "; between the last state of consciousness and the action itself there is no time at which the prediction could be made.

The first part of the argument rests on the supposed inability of Peter to make clear to Paul the intensity of his various states of consciousness or the strength of his various motives. This, we are told, can only be measured by the result, by the part each plays in the final decision. Yet with material causes we can be aware of their force before we know their effect; we can know the rapidity of a movement before it is communicated to another body. The law of cause and effect would be an absurd tautology if we always measured the cause by the effect; it would merely affirm that a force which produces such and such a result is strong enough to produce that result. To give it any real meaning we have to measure cause and effect independently and observe that the same proportion is always maintained between the two in all the instances of the law. It is objected that we cannot so measure states of consciousness, independently of the result they produce. One may observe, by the way, that Bergson himself talks like a Determinist in speaking of "the part that they," the motives, "play in the final action," and of the action as being "explained" by a state of consciousness, for this could only mean that the law of cause and effect applies to the mind. However, to return to the objection, this is expressed as follows: "When I pass through a certain state of consciousness, I know the exact intensity of this state and its importance in relation to others; not that I measure or compare, but because the intensity of a deep feeling, for example, is nothing but this feeling itself." But how can we know the importance of one state in relation to another without comparing the two? Surely we can feel one motive, for instance, to be stronger than another, and that before the final action is carried out. If this is so, it implies that we can feel a quantitative relation between the two, for one quality cannot be stronger than another purely as a quality; strength or intensity is a quantity. This point was discussed in the first chapter of the *Essai*, and in examining the arguments there we saw that Bergson really admits some forms of consciousness to have a quantitative intensity, as, for instance, when a larger or smaller number of our thoughts or a wider area of the body is affected. Besides, if our motives had no quantity, how could they determine the movements of the parts of the body which carry out an action? These movements are purely quantitative and could not be directed by something of an entirely different nature.

It is true in a sense that the strength of motives as they determine the final decision cannot be known until the decision is taken; their final strength does not even exist till then, for the greater strength of one motive *is* the decision. We should amend the idea by saying that if Paul knows at one moment all the contents of Peter's mind, including its subconscious element and its environment, he will be able to predict its contents at another moment. This is obviously true from the fact that the better we know a man's character the better we can predict his decision at any time. It is evident that we can know the comparative strength of the emotions in a man, and which will prevail in a given instance, before his decision is taken and without experiencing those emotions in exactly the same form ourselves. We judge their strength in him from his actions at various times, which, as they are consistent, must express something permanent in him. Motives are only the forms which the various passions take in particular instances, and if the passions had no strength relatively to one another before they took the form of motives, we could never have the least idea how any man would act at any moment.

If states of consciousness, then, have a quantitative intensity, the only thing that prevents us from calculating them exactly is the want of instruments; there is no inherent impossibility in such a calculation. If one man knew at any moment all the elements in another man's brain—to speak materialistically—and all their movements, he would be able to predict the other's actions. The elements of the brain are of course in reality elements of consciousness, but so are all parts of the world, and it should be as possible to predict the movements in the brain as in anything else. Besides one might invent symbols to represent the exact intensity of every feeling, as symbols have been invented to represent the movements of the planets, and so calculate the result. Whether that will ever be possible for men or not, we may suppose a " superior intelligence " capable of doing so, with as much precision at least as science attains in calculating the movements of the planets.

That we can and do calculate the movements of these bodies beforehand is of course admitted by Bergson, but he endeavours to draw a distinction between " the future of the material universe " and " the future of a conscious being." If the material universe were to move twice as fast as it does, there would be no need for change in any of the equations used by astronomers to predict the movements of the heavenly bodies, " for in these equations the symbol t does not express a duration, but a relation between two durations, a certain number of units of time, or, in the last analysis, a certain number of simultaneities," that is, the simultaneities of positions of the bodies concerned either with one another or with a state of consciousness. Science does not trouble about the intervals between these simultaneities. But these intervals are important for consciousness; they form *la durée vécue*, the duration which consciousness perceives. "If, between sunrise and sunset, we had experienced less duration, consciousness would soon inform us of a diminution of our day." But to make the parallel with the movements of the stars complete, we must assume that one day reproduces precisely the same number of events, the same number of thoughts and feelings, as a previous day; the only thing altered must be the time each event, each thought and feeling, takes. I do not see how in that case we could notice any difference. Of course we often feel as though time were passing more quickly on one day than on another, but that is not due to any real shortening of time; a real shortening would produce no such feeling, for *ex hypothesi* we should do just as much work, feel as much or as little interested, and have exactly the same sense of fatigue.

It is objected that our states of consciousness are processes and not things, that they change without ceasing, and that " in consequence we cannot cut off from them a single moment without depriving them of some impression and so modifying their quality." But no proof is given of this assertion. It is quite possible that sensations do remain the same for a certain length of time, short though it be. At any rate, they may remain as much the same as the movement of a planet, for there must be changes in the speed of that movement according to the ever-changing attraction exerted by other bodies; and greater changes are continually occurring in the movements of the elements of which the planet is composed.

"In many cases," it is admitted, "we have the right to deal with real duration as with astronomical time. Thus, when we recall the past—that is to say, a series of accomplished facts—we shorten it without altering the nature of the event in which we are interested. The reason is that we are acquainted with the event already; on arriving at the term of the process which constitutes its very existence the psychologic fact becomes a thing which may be represented all at once." But in what sense can the psychologic fact be said to become a thing? Though it exists in the eternal " now," which includes the whole of time, and in this sense has an eternal existence, yet it is confined to the time during which it proceeds, and does not exist in any other form at any time on either side of it, the time we call " before it " or the time supposed to come " after " it. The " past " event therefore cannot exist at this moment, *i.e.*, at this part of the eternal " now," any more than a body a thousand miles away can exist in any sense here. It cannot, then, exist at this part of time as a " thing," in contrast to the " process " it is supposed to have been in its own time. Or is its existence as a thing simply its existence in memory? In that case the contrast between the conscious state or event while in progress and the memory of it is exactly paralleled by the contrast between the actual movement of a planet and the idea of it in the astronomer's mind. And since in memory we represent in a shorter form a process of consciousness belonging to the time on one side of the present, why should we not, in calculating them, shorten events of consciousness belonging to the other side, the " future," just as astronomers in order to calculate the movements of the planets abridge them in thought?

In its most general form Determinism is the doctrine that the facts of consciousness obey laws as much as the phenomena of Nature; that in the mind, as in the external world, the same cause always produces the same effect. In opposition to this, Bergson declares that no state of consciousness is ever the same as any previous state; " even the simplest psychological elements have a personality, a life of their own; they are always in process of becoming, and the same feeling, merely through being repeated, is a new feeling." " The same cause," therefore, can never exist among the states of consciousness, so that the law of causality, as just defined, cannot be applied to these. And to find any other definition of that law we shall have to return to the two forms of Determinism already criticized. We shall have to give it one of two meanings: " either that, the antecedents being given, the action that follows them might have been foretold, or else that, the action once accomplished, any other action appears impossible in the given circumstances." And both these alternatives have already been condemned as equally devoid of sense.

I have already tried to show that these definitions are not without a meaning. But one may also defend the application to consciousness of causality as first defined, the law that the same cause always produces the same effect; at any rate it may be defended with a little alteration. It is not necessary that the psychological state which is the cause on the second occasion should be exactly identical with that which was the cause before. Material bodies, too, so far as we know, are never in exactly the same conditions as before; for that to be possible, the whole world would have to be in the same state as on the previous occasion. But all that is necessary for the law is that on both occasions there should be the same proportion between cause and effect. To put it in another way, the effect in the second case must be identical with the effect in the first to the same degree as the cause on the second occasion is identical with the cause on the first. Where the cause is nearly the same, the effect must be nearly the same. If Bergson were right, we could never find a general formula covering a number of instances, because each of the instances would be different from any other.

The rest of the chapter is devoted to an analysis of that idea of causality according to which the effect in some form or other is contained within the cause, so that there is " in the present conditions a kind of preformation of the phenomenon to come." This existence of the effect in the cause may be of two kinds. The first consists in virtual identity. Science, ignoring the qualities of things, has done its best to reduce the laws of Nature to algebraical equations, in such a way that the effect, one side of the equation, may be regarded as almost identical with the cause, the other side—though never completely so, since the times at which the two exist are not the same. Spinoza, however, carried this so far that he supposed cause and effect, distinct in the world of phenomena, to be wholly identical in the Absolute, which is above time. The second kind of " preformation " is the previous existence of an action in the form of an idea. It is an imperfect kind, " since the future action of which we have a present idea is conceived as realizable but not as realized." Even at the last moment we may refrain from carrying out the idea. This kind of causality belongs to states of consciousness, but it has also been attributed to the external world. It has been supposed that what we call "material objects" may possess internal states similar to our own, in particular the sense of effort. This idea was first advanced in the Hylozoism of the ancients, but was only carried out to its logical conclusion in the monadology and "pre-established harmony" of Leibnitz, whose philosophy is founded on the second kind of causality, as Spinoza's on the first.

But the two kinds of causality have been so confused with each other, according to Bergson, that we attribute to the second the inevitability of the first, and suppose our states of consciousness to follow one another as mechanically as the phenomena of Nature. The scientists, however, have done their best to keep their ideas of these phenomena clear of any analogy with consciousness, and in spite of their use of the word "forces" do not really attribute to the external world anything like the sense of effort felt by the mind. On the other side we ought not to attribute to the mind, as we do, the same mechanical sequence which prevails in the external world.

In considering this argument it is to be observed, in the first place, that the second form of causality does not, as seems to be assumed, belong to the individual consciousness alone, but to that consciousness and the external world together. The cause, *i.e.*, the idea of the act, together with the sense of effort, belongs to the mind; the effect, the act itself, belongs to the external world. We do not find a preformation of one state of consciousness in the preceding state; not in any sense, at least, in which we do not find it among successive phenomena of Nature. And among these we may find, too, something like the preformation of an act in an idea; for instance, the projecting of a reflection by one body on another, a reflection which, like the act, may or may not be produced, according to circumstances. Such phenomena do not prove that the external world is ever free from mechanical laws. The second kind of causality, exemplified by them and by the pre-existence of acts in ideas, only applies to those complex groups of simple elements, the bodies we can see and our states of consciousness. The simple elements themselves are wholly governed by the first kind of causality, the only real kind. For where the sequence of cause and effect is not invariable, as with ideas and acts, it could only be regarded as a series of coincidences, unless we can find some wider law which will account both for the sequence itself and for the exceptions to its regularity. And that has always been done by supposing the objects concerned to consist of a number of small elements governed by laws that are not intermittent.

The difficulty that has been felt in the doctrine of free will, as generally defined by Bergson, is that it introduces into a world that obeys invariable laws another world that acts at haphazard, or at least does not maintain an unfailing regularity. If the carrying of an idea into action and so into the external world illustrates one kind of causality, a causality that has its exceptions, and if the external world is subject to another kind, to mechanical, unchanging laws, then there must often be occasions on which that world is distracted between obedience to its own laws and submission to the forces projected into it from the alien world of consciousness. Can anyone imagine a particle of matter, which has hitherto followed the laws of Nature, suddenly wrested aside from the course it would have taken and forced into another by an impulse from another sphere? This has always been the difficulty in any form of Dualism, and there is no way in which it can be surmounted; certainly none, if the two worlds of Dualism are supposed to obey different laws, or one of them to follow no laws at all, while often acting upon the other. The only possible course is to abandon Dualism and fuse the two worlds into one, everywhere conscious in a greater or less degree, and everywhere subject to the same laws.

When it is said that our moral being demands free will, all that is meant or should be meant is that our actions must not be regarded as wholly determined by external circumstances, as mere automatical reactions to impulses from without, but as dependent on the character. This, of course, will readily be conceded by every Determinist. At the same time it must be remembered that the character itself has to some extent been formed by external circumstances in the past. And so far as it has not been formed by these it must be due to heredity, for unless we assume the pre-existence of the individual we must believe it to be derived from somewhere. As for the question whether a man can ever change his character, that is obviously absurd, for each man *is* his character; he does not stand outside it, so that he could shape it better or worse.

What the Determinist maintains, and Bergson denies, is that every state of the mind is determined by the previous state and by influences from without. This causation of ideas is not inconsistent with free will as common sense understands that term. Common sense, it is true, believes that sudden changes of character are possible, but not that these changes are uncaused. If there could be any state of the mind that did not depend on the preceding state and on surrounding conditions, why should we not every day meet with complete reversals of character? For if the smallest modification of character can arise *ex nihilo*, why not the greatest? And even if that were really possible, such abrupt changes of character would not in the least satisfy that moral sense which demands free will. It could not regard as an instance of liberty a sudden impulse that arose from nowhere. The only kind of free will, therefore, in which we can believe and for which we can be at all concerned is not that which Bergson defends in this essay, but that which every Determinist would admit to exist; not the spontaneity which may bring anything out of the void at any moment, but the dependence of our actions upon our character.

B. *Matière et Mémoire.*

In this essay Bergson begins by adopting the standpoint of "common sense" or what has been called "naïve Realism." The world, he assumes, is an assemblage of "images . . . perceived when I open my senses, unperceived when I close them"; images which are neither the "representations" or "ideas" which are the only existences for the Idealist, nor the "things" supposed by the philosophical Realist to cause our sensations, but to be very different from them. They exist in themselves, independently of us, but at the same time they exist just as we see them. This return to common sense, *i.e.*, the primitive notions of common sense, does not seem any more promising than a return to the Ptolemaic system would be in astronomy, and leads to confusion when we come to the criticisms directed against both Realists and Idealists.

The first of these criticisms is aimed at those Realists who declare that certain movements in the brain produce in us our representation of the external world. Since the brain itself, from the standpoint of "common sense," is an image, this theory, we are told, implies that the representation of the whole universe is contained within that of the brain, the whole within the part, an evident absurdity. But the Realists thus criticized do not mean by the brain an image as defined above; the brain is something which causes that image in another man's mind, but in itself has only a limited resemblance to that image. Again, the "representation of the universe" does not mean for them that assemblage of images which for Bergson is the universe itself, but only a small picture, or small pictures, of a large part of it. Certainly if we saw the whole universe life-size and all at once, the sight of it could not exist in the brain, but there is no reason why a small copy of it should not exist there, as the picture or model of a room may exist within a small area of that room. Besides, our representation of the universe is by no means complete, and is not given to us altogether in one sensation but in a series.

It is true that the theory of the Realists is untenable in its usual form. There cannot be an unconscious matter which produces consciousness as an epiphenomenon in the void or by action upon a mind, nor can there be two worlds, one material and the other mental, running parallel. Only consciousness exists, and the "material" brain is nothing but a representation produced indirectly in one area of consciousness by another. It is indeed an image, but not in the sense defined by Bergson, for it does not exist except as a sensation in the mind of the beholder. The reality from which it is derived and which it represents is a certain sphere of consciousness existing over there, *i.e.*, the mind of the man to whom it is said to belong. And this, as I said, might contain a representation of large parts of the universe, like a picture, or in thought contain the whole of it, as a book may contain a description of the solar system. This seems obvious, but Bergson supposes such a representation in so small a space to be impossible, and from this draws the conclusion that the movements of the "brain," since they cannot produce the infinite variety of representations which every man has, are merely "movements destined to prepare and commence the reaction of the body to the action of external objects," *i.e.*, that they do not cause consciousness but begin action. The whole of the argument in *Matière et Mémoire* depends on that idea, but the weakness of this first link in the logical chain is evident.

There follows a discussion of the point at issue between the Realists and the Idealists, and the problem is defined thus:—
" How can the same images enter at once into two different systems, one in which every image varies for itself, just in proportion as it is affected by the real action of surrounding images, and another in which all the images vary for one only, according as they reflect the possible action of this particular image ? " The first system is " the world of science, in which every image, being only related to itself, preserves an absolute value " ; the second is " the world of consciousness, in which all the images are regulated upon a central image, our body, the variations of which they follow." This account of the external world and its relation to the body is a strange one, and seems to have been inspired by the conclusions which later on are drawn from it. In the first place, the images we see are not the same as the " images " with which science deals, but are only reflections of them at different angles and distances. The small picture of a house which sight presents to us is not the house itself nor any part of it, nor does the house itself vary according to the possible action of our bodies upon it. That is a matter to which I shall return later. Again, no one would have said that the picture of the world in our consciousness varies according as it reflects the possible action of our bodies upon that world, unless he were prepossessed by the idea that the use of consciousness is a purely practical one. It is more natural to say that the image in consciousness varies according to our position in space with relation to the object, or according to the action of the outer world upon the body. The position in space does, as a rule, determine how far we can act upon the object, but not always, for we may be near a thing without being able to act upon it

at all. We often have a large and clear image of things upon which we cannot act, and do not see things upon which we could act quite easily. We can see the stars, upon which we have no prospect of acting, but not the things close behind us, which we could quite easily move. Besides, to what time are our possibilities of action limited? Within a day we may act at a place hundreds of miles away; within a minute we may act at many places we cannot see at this instant. But if only the exact moment is meant at which we have the sight-sensation, then there is no possibility of action at all, for possibility implies the future.

When objects are enlarged for our sight by the microscope or telescope the enlarging is not due to any increase in our power of action upon the objects viewed. The telescope gives us no greater power of action upon the stars, and in the case of the microscope the increase in power follows and depends upon our larger and more exact perception of the object. It is not until we have seen the minute parts of this object through the microscope that we have any power of purposive action upon them. And if the power of action, without purpose, is enough to give us the perception, as when in acting upon a body as a whole we also affect, without considering it, the mutual relation of its parts, then we ought always to be able, even without the microscope, to perceive the most minute particles of every body.

Evidently one has every reason to prefer the ordinary view, that our sensations are determined by the present action of things upon us, not by our possible action upon them. The microscope and telescope serve as instruments for the first, but cannot be used as tools for the second. Bergson's theory disregards altogether the existence of light waves and sound waves as the media through which sensations are produced. Yet we can only see things, of course, when there is a light, though action upon them is possible without that.

Consciousness is explained as the singling out by a living being of those parts of the " images," *i.e.*, the external things, which interest it. It does not add anything to these images, which exist just as they are perceived by us but are much more besides, for they have innumerable other facets turned in all directions. Each is continuous with the rest of the universe, and affects, and is affected by, every other image, passing on the modifications it receives without the power to discriminate between them. But a living being can discriminate, selecting in the images what interests itself, distinguishing each from that which precedes and that which follows it, and disregarding its innumerable relations with all the others. And this discrimination is consciousness. The objects we call inanimate are like sheets of glass which pass on the rays of light they receive; a living being is like a mirror which holds up these rays, or rather it has the power to choose between them, holding up some and passing on others which do not interest it. This power exists in the living being owing to the complexity of the brain, which contains innumerable paths along any of which the reaction to a given excitation from without may pass. Thus a choice is possible, whereas inorganic bodies can only react in one way.

This account of consciousness assumes an essential difference between the brain and all other "material" bodies. Why should consciousness be supposed to exist only in connection with a brain and not elsewhere? The reason given is that the many different possibilities of reaction offered by the brain owing to its complex structure allow the living being to interest itself in certain parts of the external "image" and not in others. But in that case there might be a more limited consciousness attached to other bodies, corresponding to their more limited choice of reaction. Again, it is not clear what is meant by that "living being" which discriminates between the different parts of the images it perceives, singling out those that interest it. It cannot be the brain as a multitude of atoms, for these do not distinguish between the forces that act upon them, any more than do the elements of other bodies. The atoms of the brain must transmit the totality of that which they receive as much as any others. And if you treat the brain as a whole, as a single complex structure, there is no complex structure in the world which transmits the whole impulse it sustains. If, on the other hand, it is an entity different from the rest of the world, an individual soul, that thus discriminates between the parts of the image, this theory involves all the difficulties which beset the doctrine of individual souls, difficulties which I have enumerated in another chapter. Besides, the soul must surely be conscious of the entire image before it can discriminate between its parts, so that such discrimination cannot itself be consciousness.

But the most important question is this: What and where is that image, the parts of which are thus singled out in consciousness? From most of the statements made about it the image meant appears to be what we should call the real thing, not an image of it in the brain; for it is declared that the brain cannot contain all the images we perceive, and in speaking of a particular instance, a luminous point P, the author tells us that "it is in P, and not elsewhere, that the image of P is formed and perceived." The conscious being, then, perceives the object where the object itself is; but the amount of its perception is limited by its possible action on the object, and that is determined by the more or less complex structure of the brain. This is the only way in which the brain is admitted to have anything to do with the perception. It seems, therefore, that in order to single out the parts of the object it is to perceive *there*, the mind must already be conscious of the brain *here* and the possibilities of action it affords. There would thus be two consciousnesses, and I do not see how the one here, at the brain, could affect the one there, at the object, and limit the extent of its perception. And the idea that the mind perceives directly the actual thing where the thing is, and not an image in the brain, is open to all the objections I have mentioned in an earlier chapter. For certainly the image we perceive of a large object at a distance is often not so large as the image of a smaller object near to us. Obviously, therefore, the image we see is not the same as the image in Bergson's sense, the real thing. It would be no satisfactory answer to say that we do see the real thing where it is, but that its size for us is proportionate to the interest we have in it, or to our "possible action" upon it. It cannot have two sizes, one for itself, the "real" size, and one for us. And for the reasons I have already given in criticizing Professor Alexander's theory, the size actually seen cannot be a part of the real size. In fact all the objections I have brought forward in Chapter II and in the Appendix to that chapter are valid against Bergson's theory, and need not be repeated here.

In defending his own theory Bergson criticizes the view opposed to it, that the images we have in consciousness exist in the brain. In such a case, he says, it is impossible to conceive how we come to externalize these images and regard them as independent of ourselves. But the explanation is really easy enough; I have already given it in answering the question how we come to believe in anything outside our own sensations. When the same image appears, vanishes, and after a space reappears, it is natural enough to conclude that it has continued to exist even while we did not perceive it, for it would be inconceivable that the same image, still more the same collection of images in one sensation, should a second time arise out of nothingness, since an infinite number of different images is possible, and chance could not produce such a resemblance between them as we actually experience.

If we thought that sensations were without extension, as Bergson supposes his opponents to do, it would be difficult to explain how we come to attribute extension to the objects we see. But obviously such an idea is not a necessary consequence of the doctrine that our sensations exist in the brain, and are only images of the real thing. On the contrary, if they were not extended but purely qualitative they could not be associated with any body, nor could sensations of different qualities be joined together as they are, nor could those of precisely the same quality in any two minds be distinguished or distinct from one another.

The theory of perception given in the first pages of *Matière et Mémoire* is modified later on by a description of the important part in perception ascribed to memory. Matter, the object of our sensations, in each of its movements passes through innumerable distinct moments of time, which are contracted by memory into one continuous perception occupying a certain "duration." Our experience presents us with a series of sensations so heterogeneous in quality that one cannot be deduced from another; but the movements of matter, an enormous number of which occurs during any one perception, are homogeneous and can be deduced from one another. Yet in spite of this difference between the two series, the sensations and the movements, the former are produced from the latter by the action of memory, which creates the variety of qualities in consciousness by means of the contraction mentioned above, fusing the innumerable movements into " a certain thickness of duration." And in the *Essai sur les données immédiates de la conscience* we have been told that " duration " is of a qualitative rather than a quantitative nature, so that the conversion of the instants in the movement of the object into a " duration " for consciousness is a change from quantity to quality. But what is meant by this contraction and conversion said to be effected by memory ? Does matter exist in two states, in itself and in our consciousness ? But to say this is to say that there are two parallel series of events, the movements of matter and our sensations, and you do not make the relation between them any clearer by saying that the latter are " contractions " of the former ; you might just as well say that the movements are expansions of the sensations. Since the multiplicity of movements, the world of science, always remains as before, it cannot be affected by contraction : all we can say is, not that it is contracted itself but that it has side by side with it another qualitative version of itself, in which each event, *i.e.*, each sensation, corresponds to a number of movements in the first series. But it is not explained how there come to be these two versions of the same fact. Besides, this theory contradicts the earlier statement that the world consists of " images " which exist just as we perceive them, and that the only thing consciousness does is to exclude those parts of the images which do not interest it, or do not come within the range of the body's action. It appears now that the world in itself exists in a very different form from that which it has for our consciousness ; so different that we certainly cannot be said to see it directly, but only a version of it quite unlike the original. Nor do I understand how we can be said to see the thing itself where it is, for the innumerable homogeneous movements and the fewer, qualitatively different sensations cannot well exist in the same place.

A little later on we find it repeated that matter " exists absolutely as it appears to exist," and that to prove this is the only means of refuting materialism. " We must restore to matter all the qualities denied it by materialists and spiritualists alike." But in that case how could there be any such contraction as that described, changing the homogeneous movements of matter into the variety of qualities perceived in sensation? The concession made to the scientific standpoint, from which the world appears as a number of homogeneous elements in motion, is here withdrawn. Quite rightly, it is true, for a world of homogeneous elements without qualities is impossible; without quality there can be no distinction, and the world would be no different from empty space.

To return to the part played by memory, we are told that in consciousness there are no instantaneous perceptions of reality corresponding to the instantaneous movements of matter, but that our memory carries over into one another an unlimited number of moments of time " in such a way as to grasp them in a relatively simple intuition." This produces the contraction already mentioned. But there seems no reason why the faculty which thus links together the moments and makes them continuous should be called " memory." We cannot in any case understand how a number of instants could be turned for consciousness into a continuous length of time, any more than we can conceive of a number of unextended points becoming one line. But supposing we could, it would not be memory that made the instants continuous, for memory could only mean the recollection of one instant at another, and this would leave them still distinct.

Yet memory is declared to be that which gives consciousness its subjective character, and is virtually identified with spirit, on the ground that " it contracts into a single intuition a multiplicity of moments "; that, and the variety of qualities thereby produced, are the distinctive marks of the spiritual as opposed to the material. And at the end of the first chapter we are promised an examination of memory which will help to answer two questions on the subject: first, whether the brain is an instrument of action or of representation; and, second, whether in pure perception we are " placed outside ourselves " and in direct contact with the object. In the first place, if it is found that memories can exist in the brain we shall conclude that our perceptions also can exist there; but if the one is proved impossible, so is the other. In the second place, if we find that memory and perception are essentially alike, then we may agree that in perception we do not come into direct contact with reality; if there is an essential difference between the two, then it is probably this direct contact which distinguishes perception from memory. I have already given my reasons for believing that the images we perceive do exist in the brain, *i.e.*, in that area of consciousness which appears as the brain, and that we do not perceive the real thing outside us but a copy. If those reasons are sound, it must already appear probable that the memory-images also exist in the brain, and that memory must be essentially like perception.

The following chapter begins with a distinction between two kinds of memory. When we read a passage in a book several times over, we at length acquire the power of repeating the words, and this power is called the " habit memory." The frequent reading of the passage creates in the brain a mechanism which will automatically reproduce it whenever we wish. But besides this power we have also the memory of each separate occasion on which we read the words, and this may be called the " pure memory." Every event leaves such an image, so that the whole of our past in every detail is there in the background, always ready to come to the fore and affect our action whenever a situation arises similar to one that has already occurred. This memory does not exist in the brain; so much we learn, but other points about it are left in considerable obscurity. As our consciousness, according to the theory already stated, adds nothing to the outer object or " image," but only singles out the parts of it that interest us, those upon which we can act, why should it be only these parts that remain? Why should not the whole of every past event, the whole of history, remain in the same way? And even supposing it is only our past perceptions that exist in this kind of memory, how can this long line of images, to which we continually return in memory, be distinguished from the past itself? The series of images is completely like the past in every detail, so that there seems to be nothing to prevent our identifying the two. Otherwise we shall have to assume that each event, before it passes away, creates a duplicate of itself which remains. In either case the direct action of the past, or of ghosts of the past, upon the present world appears unintelligible. The action of the past lies in the past, and there can be no further action on its part in the present, except indirectly. And as for images of past events, if they cannot exist in the brain, how can they affect our action through the brain? But this is a subject we shall meet with later on.

There is in fact no reason why both kinds of memory should not exist in the brain. Each perception might deposit an image of itself there, thus ensuring the possibility of the pure memory, and also make a path along the "efferent" nerves, which, through being frequently traversed, would form an easy passage for the habit-memory. The image, too, would be strengthened in its general form by repetition of the perception; the original imprint would remain distinct for a while, but then blend together with those following, the more quickly and completely the more they were like it. This would explain why constant repetition of an event makes it harder to distinguish the different occasions on which it occurred.

For many purposes it makes no difference, in explaining the phenomena of memory, whether we regard the "pure memories" as existing in the brain or as inhabiting a world of their own, except that with the former assumption it is much easier to understand how they affect the movements of the brain and consequently our action. Whatever is attributed to the transcendental images of the past could be attributed equally well to images stored up in the brain, and so we have every reason for accepting the more intelligible theory. Take, for instance, two of the instances of mental diseases cited by Bergson. In the first a woman with eyes closed could describe quite well the town where she lived, but when actually in the street and with her eyes open could recognize nothing. This might be explained by the assumption that the communication between the perception and the memory-images in the brain was broken, but not that between the memory-images and the organs of speech. In the other instance a man who could not recognize the streets of his own town nevertheless knew that they were streets; he could not recognize his own children, but recognized that they were children. This is easily enough explained by supposing that the images in the brain representing particular things and persons were destroyed, or else cut off from the perceptions, while those representing general ideas or classes of things remained intact and could be reached. I do not see how from either of these cases we could " conclude that not all recognition implies the intervention of an ancient image " in Bergson's sense.

Recognition itself is next described as of two kinds. The first is purely automatic, as when the sight of a street corner makes us turn down it without reflection, owing to our having constantly turned down it before. The feeling of recognition here is just the feeling of habit, and with either of the opposed theories of memory must depend on movements in the brain. But in the other kind the pure memories, the images of the past, are found to intervene. Our present perceptions always pass into incipient movements in the brain, and " if ancient images also choose to pass into these movements, they seize their opportunity to introduce themselves into our present perceptions and be taken up into these." This opportunity occurs whenever the present perception is similar to one that is past ; but Bergson's theory is that the images of the past are called into fresh activity not by the present perception itself but by the incipient movements in the brain following that perception. On this theory the excitation given to the brain in every perception " merely sets up in the body a certain attitude into which memories can insert themselves " (*viennent s'insérer*), and does nothing more. According to the view criticized in *Matière et Mémoire*, each excitation creates or revivifies a memory-image in the brain, and Bergson argues that on this assumption disorders of the memory caused by an injury to the brain can only be due to the destruction of the memories occupying the injured region. But it may be said at once that this is not the only way in which the theory which places memories in the brain can account for disorders of the memory. For, as I have explained, these might be due to a cutting of the communications between the sensory nerves and the memory-images left in the background of the brain by previous sensations. On the other theory, according to which the image of the past does not exist in the brain but is recalled by the incipient movements that are similar to itself or caused by a perception similar to itself, disorders of the memory, we are told, might be caused in two ways; the injury to the brain might "prevent the body from taking up the attitude appropriate for recalling the image," *i.e.*, the pure memory, or it might prevent this memory from "realizing itself" by action, from affecting the perceptions, or the action following them.

It may be noted here that the second theory with its alternatives would not by any means exclude the supposition that memories do exist in the brain, for the images stored in it might play precisely the same part as any images outside it. On being aroused by the perception, they might be conceived as reacting upon it; or they might be supposed to possess a spontaneous activity which would make them "insert themselves" into a perception or the following action. Such an assumption, as I said, is much easier to understand than the idea of an action upon the brain accomplished by entities of an altogether different kind.

The account given of attention is somewhat complicated. The perception, or rather the incipient movements which follow it, is said to call up similar images from the memory, and these in turn affect the perception, filling it up in greater detail. Memory exists entire in many different circles; the one farthest back is the "pure memory," representing past events in every particular, while the others, consisting of what appear to be called indifferently *souvenirs-images* or *images-souvenirs*, are more or less condensed and generalized versions of this. Those which are most generalized and least precise in form can most readily affect every perception; but the longer our attention lasts, the farther we go back towards those circles nearest the pure memory, those which contain past events in greater detail; and from them more and more particulars are sent to fill up the picture of perception.

But in so far as attention concerns our perception of objects, and not our thoughts upon them, memory does not seem to play so large a part in it as would appear from the foregoing account. Attention implies first such an adaptation of the sense-organs, effected by a movement we can actually feel, as makes some of the images perceived clearer and fuller in detail, and secondly the readiness of the mind to admit these particular images into its deeper recesses, its susceptibility to these and exclusion of others. Just as the organs of sight admit certain of the vibrations continually radiated from all the bodies around, so the inner organs of the mind admit some of the sensations and not others. It is true that the memory of the same or a similar object seen before may lead us to search for certain details not yet observed in the image before us, or for other phenomena which were observed to attend it on the former occasion. On such occasions attention does indeed involve a circuit such as that described, from the perception to the memory and back to the perception again. But this is not essential to attention, which rather creates memories than is created by them; creates them, that is to say, by leaving deeper and more distinct traces of the object upon the brain. If in reading we do not observe every letter in turn but merely mark a few *traits charactéristiques* which suggest all the rest of the words or sentences, this does not mean that these salient points are perceived first, that they then awaken the memories, and that the memories then affect the perception, for this last remains as before. The points actually seen call up in the memory the rest of the word or phrase usually associated with them, so that for thought it is the same as though we had actually noted the whole, and we think that we have done so. But as the rest of the details are only called up in the memory, not in sight, and the idea that we have seen the whole is only an idea, I do not see how the memory here can be said to affect the perception.

Returning to his explanation of the disorders of the memory Bergson takes first those which he supposes to be caused by an injury to " the mechanisms which carry on the impulse received " in sensation " into a movement automatically performed," as, for instance, when we hear a word or whole sentence there follows within us an automatical movement " marking its principal articulations." He endeavours to prove this theory and refute the usual explanation as follows. When we hear two men speaking in a foreign language we hear only a confused mass of sound, whereas the men themselves can distinguish consonants, vowels, syllables, and whole words. The usual explanation is that for the men themselves, but not for us, the impressions of sound join and are reinforced by the auditive memories, formed by often hearing the same sounds before. This supposition is condemned by Bergson on the ground that we may imagine the sounds as loud as we like, so that the loudness would be an equivalent for any reinforcement that might be received from the memory, and yet it would not be any clearer to a man who did not understand the language. And unless the sound has already been distinguished into syllables and words, how can it join the auditive memories?

To this we may reply that the sounds are always distinct in the sensation—we hear in every detail exactly what is heard by the two foreigners—but in the man who understands the language the sound of each of the words awakes an auditive memory which keeps it distinct for some time, whereas in the man who does not understand it there is nothing to keep them distinct; each sound leaves a trace in the brain, but those following blur the traces of those that came first, so that in the end there is only a confused echo left in the brain. An essential difference between the two is that at the end of the sentence the one can remember the words while the other cannot, and this is due to the fact that in the one, as I said, each sound awakes a memory and is kept alive and distinct in it, whereas in the other it only leaves a trace in the brain which is immediately obscured by the following sounds. You cannot suppose that the sounds are not distinguished into syllables and words in the sensation itself, for then we should be unable to tell articulate speech which we could not understand from the noise made by animals; on hearing two foreigners whom we could not see we should not know that it was a human sound at all. And Bergson's own theory would be as impossible as the one he attacks. According to him, in learning a new language we organize more and more distinctly the automatic movements in us following the sound heard, so that on hearing each word we can reproduce it more and more exactly " under the form of incipient muscular sensations," *i.e.*, the feeling of the automatic movements aforesaid. But this would not make any more distinct the original aural sensations preceding these automatic movements and the feeling of them; so that unless these were already distinct a word would not produce one such movement rather than another. A confused noise could not be carried along this line rather than that of the mechanism formed for that purpose, however highly organised it might be, and therefore it could not be recognised. In a confused mass of sensation nothing could be distinguished. But if the sounds *are* distinct in the sensation, then there is no reason why each should not join an appropriate auditive memory in the way Bergson declares to be impossible.

Another objection brought against the idea of auditive memories existing in the brain is that there must be any number of memories, and not one memory only, of each word, since we hear the same word pronounced in very different tones and degrees of loudness. " Are all these memories heaped up in the brain, or if the brain chooses, which will it prefer ? Admitting it has its reasons for choosing one ; how will this same word, pronounced by a new person, join a memory from which it differs ? " But there must be some common element in all the different pronunciations of the word, for otherwise we could never recognize it in its different forms ; and this common element might be enough to send each repetition of it along the right path to join the one auditive memory formed by previous repetitions of the word. The voices of many different singers, uttering together the same words in different tones and degrees of loudness, blend together and produce in us one vibration in the ear, one distinct sensation of the word uttered. This must be due to the common element in them ; why, then, should not different pronunciations of the same word at different times produce in us one auditive memory ? The vibrations in the brain, on the different occasions when they arise, may die down to the same level of intensity ; or the vibrations may be the same, while the degree of loudness depends on the area over which they are spread.

It is on Bergson's own theory that the blending together of different memories of one word is difficult to understand, for we are told that the " pure memories " remain distinct. If so, I do not see, either, how memory would help us to form concepts ; for the different sensations we had of the same thing would never fuse together. In place of thought, therefore, we should have the long line of memory-images, each in its own place. Again, the objection concerning the auditive memories in the brain, if it were sound, would apply with equal force to the *schème moteur*, the organism created by the incipient movements following on sensations. For if the different sensations produced by hearing the same word differently pronounced could not join the same memory in the same brain, they certainly could not be followed by the same incipient movement in the *schème moteur*. Bergson recognizes that the criticism he advances against the opposed theory might be turned against his own, and tries to forestall it by saying that the automatic movements following the sensations are regulated by "a certain rudimentary intellectual operation," which apparently selects the common element in the different repetitions of the same word and always repeats it over again in the same way. But this is to introduce a *deus ex machina* whose presence really explains nothing. I can understand how a sensation, which is itself represented by certain vibrations in the brain, can be followed by similar vibrations in the *schème moteur*. But I do not see how certain differentiæ of the sensation, the tone or degree of loudness, can be held up, as it were, in an intellect which does not exist in the brain, while only the element it shares with similar sensations, *i.e.*, former pronunciations of the same word, is allowed to pass on into an incipient movement in the schema aforesaid. To say this is to say that parts of the cause of the sensation, *i.e.*, its differentiæ, its tone and loudness on this particular occasion, are not carried on into the effect, the following movement, but disappear altogether. And to attribute this to an "intellectual operation" is to explain nothing at all; it is simply to say, without giving any reason why it is so, that the differences in tone and loudness do disappear, so that the repetitions of the same word may be followed by the same movement in the scheme.

The third argument advanced by Bergson against the theory opposed to his own is as follows. When the memory of words is lost gradually, the words always disappear from the mind in a regular order; first proper nouns, then common nouns, and lastly the verbs. If memories were stored in the cells of the brain, why should the disease attack the particular cells holding the different kinds of words always in this order and no other? This, we may answer, might be due to the fact that the different classes of words are more or less firmly established in the brain according to the frequency of their use and the number of times we meet with the objects they indicate, or else according to the intellectual effort to fix them in the brain. A particular man is less often met with than Man, and it is only in the case of the latter, the common noun, that the intellectual effort of abstraction from differences of generalization is needed. This effort is still greater with verbs, since these denote an action, not a thing, and therefore they are more permanent. Some such explanation of the order of disappearance is possible.

But the reason given by Bergson himself could not account for that order. According to him the memories are recalled " by a kind of mental attitude, itself inserted into an attitude of the body," and " the verbs, the essence of which is to express imitable actions, are just the words which an effort of the body will allow us to recover when the function of language comes near to escaping us." On the other hand, the proper nouns will disappear from memory first because they are furthest removed from " those impersonal actions which our bodies can outline." But even if we suppose that the verbs could be recalled by an effort or attitude of the body, a movement to imitate a certain action, it is hard to understand how there could be any difference between the nouns, for neither the proper nor the common nouns, but only the verbs, could be recalled by the movement of the body, and so there would be no reason why one class should disappear later than the other. And even supposing this account of the recalling of the words were correct, it would be easier to suppose that the action of the body recalls memories if these are stored in the brain, than if they exist in a different sphere. The disease might weaken in intensity the memories of all three classes of words alike, but the verbs might still be recalled by the movements in the body which are the beginning of the actions they denote.

" The pure memories (*souvenirs*) called up from the background of the mind (*mémoire*) develop into memory-images more and more capable of inserting themselves into the schema of incipient movements" (*le schème moteur*). But if these pure memories are not spatial they could not stand in any relation to the *schème moteur*, for that is admitted to exist in the brain. They could not be attached to one brain rather than another, and there could be nothing to make them develop into memory-images and enter into action, unless you suppose that they are all struggling to do so all the time, and that only that one succeeds which happens to fit. The account given of the connection between these shadowy "pure memories" and the brain continually suggests the satire of Lucretius on the entry of souls into bodies. It is ludicrous, he says, to imagine that whenever a new body is born the souls stand waiting to enter into it and struggle violently

Inter se quae prima potissimaque insinuentur.[1]

But there seems no reason why the pure memories in their transcendental sphere should ever come down to earth, *i.e.*, the brain, even in the borrowed form of memory-images. They cannot know the movements going on in the brain, unless they are endowed with perception—an impossible idea. The whole conception seems to me sheer mythology, though its very vagueness renders it difficult to attack.

The argument next brought forward against the idea that memories exist in the brain is that perception and memory, on that theory, must occupy two distinct spaces, since loss of memory does not imply loss of hearing, for instance, and that this separation is inconsistent with the gradual transition from memory to perception. "We see that a memory, as it grows clearer and more intense, tends to become a perception, but there is no precise moment at which a radical transformation takes place, and therefore no one can say that the memory is transferred from the sphere of memory-images (*des éléments imaginatifs*) to the sphere of sense." But this supposed transition from memory to perception might be simply the heightening of memory in its own sphere to an intensity approaching that of sensation—no memory ever equals it—or the intensified image in the sphere of memory might gradually spread to that of sensation and create a

[1] Lucretius, *De Rerum Natura*, Bk. III. l. 780.

similar image there. Either supposition is at least as intelligible as the statement that "the auditive image remembered stirs the same elements in the nerves as did the first perception, and thus the memory is gradually transformed into perception." For the auditive image must be at least as distinct from the nerves as the sphere of memory in the brain from that of perception, and if its action on the nerves, which is said to produce sensation, could be gradual, so might be the action of the sphere of memory in the brain on the sphere of sensation.

At the beginning of the next chapter, which treats *De la survivance des images*, Bergson criticizes those psychologists who suppose memory to be a faint sensation, so that there is only a difference of degree between a present pain and the remembrance of one that is past. If it were so, he argues, the lessening of a great pain would be the same thing as the memory of it. But there must be very few psychologists who believe that a difference of intensity alone distinguishes memory and sensation. Such a belief is not a necessary consequence of the theory that both these forms of consciousness exist in the brain. The intensity undoubtedly does contribute to the distinction, and it must be observed that a memory is much fainter than any sensation of pain, for instance, can become as long as the nerves are affected by the cause of pain. But there must also be a difference of areas in the brain, the sphere of sensation being nearest the afferent nerves and that of remembrance in the background. The chief distinction, however, is the thought that accompanies and dates and places a memory. This latter does not cohere with the vivid image of our surroundings, and since these alone can change and act upon us we naturally infer that, as we cannot be in two places at once, the remembered scene is not real now, but only the scene present to our sensations.

But memory is not distinguished from sensation by being a direct perception of the past. We can raise in our minds images of our own invention, but of a type exactly similar to those of memory; for instance, after calling before his mind the room where he was a little while ago a man can form himself at will a picture of an imaginary room just like a memory-image. The difference lies in the fact that he has formed it at will and is aware of this. In their general character the pictures of imagination and memory are alike, and this proves that in memory we do not directly see the past itself, as Bergson and others have supposed. It proves this just as effectually as the sensation of things that have no objective existence, things seen by anyone in an abnormal state, proves that we do not see directly the " real things," the tree or house itself. Neither the past nor the things around us but only their images are the immediate objects of perception.

In the " pure memory," we are told, every detail of the past survives, though a past event only appears, as a memory-image, to our consciousness now and then. It remains, though usually outside our consciousness, just as the objects of our sensations, the things themselves, remain even when they are no longer perceived. But, if that is so, can the " pure memory " properly be called " memory " at all? What else is it but the past itself? The events are still there, in the background, just as the objects we have perceived are still there outside us, and there is no more reason for limiting these permanent events to those which we have experienced than for limiting the world of things to those which have at some time been, or are now, objects of perception. All events must persist, even those which occurred before the origin of life on earth. As we have already seen, Bergson himself allows no essential difference between the unperceived things and the things present to us in sensation; all are " images," and consciousness adds nothing but only excludes. There is no reason, then, why one class of images should continue to exist rather than another. Evidently Bergson does not accept the theory that consciousness takes a duplicate or photograph, so to speak, of every event in its experience, and that it is this duplicate which remains and is preserved to us in memory. Such a theory would resemble too much the one he is attacking, for even if we did not suppose these duplicates to be stored in the brain, we must suppose them to exist and be seen by memory in the present time. And if images stored in the brain, because they exist in the present, cannot be recognized as images of the past or distinguished from sensations, how could this be possible with these duplicates? Besides, the question where the past survives has more force than Bergson admits.

Suppose, as you very well may, that a sensation experienced by A is precisely similar to one experienced by B, how could the duplicates of the two sensations be distinguished from one another, how could they be two, unless they were separated in space? The original sensations exist in space and are thus separated; the copies of them must be so too, and therefore each must have a distinguishing place and possess extension. The idea that they exist in the brain would then be an obvious, even inevitable, deduction.

But if it is the past itself, and not a copy of it, that survives and appears to us in memory, there is no reason why we should suppose that only the events of which we have been conscious are permanent. The whole of the past must remain, though in the background of the present, and it should be possible for an event of which we were not conscious when it occurred to enter our memories now. For though our consciousness excluded it before, that exclusion cannot prevent it from continuing to exist or from affecting our action whenever a similar event is experienced. Whether we were conscious or unconscious of an incident in the past cannot make any difference to the possibility of our perceiving it and being influenced by it in the present. Besides, it has been shown in an earlier chapter that consciousness is universal. And even if only that part of the past could enter memory which had been perceived by a human mind, is there anything to prevent A from remembering an event perceived in the past only by B? If that which we have before us in memory is the past itself, and not an image of it preserved in the brain, there seems to be nothing that can now distinguish this part of the past as belonging to A's experience, and that to B's. The continuity or personal consciousness is interrupted by sleep; is there anything that can decide what stream of former sensations a man shall remember when he wakes, or limit him to any one stream, if the "pure memories" are independent of the body? When he falls asleep his memories must be left in the air, so to speak. If their only link with the body is their likeness to present sensations, why should not the past experience of one man have an influence on the actions of another man who meets with a similar experience?

We are given in this chapter a fuller explanation of a subject already outlined in the account of attention, *i.e.*, the different circles or strata in which memory exists, from the " pure memory," complete in every detail, down to the most generalized versions of the past which approach nearest to our perception. These circles are represented as constituting together an inverted cone with its point fixed in the present. The " pure memory," as containing every detail of the past, is the widest of the circles and forms the base of the cone; the point is the " memory of the body," *i.e.*, the *schème moteur*, or stereotyped system of reactions to sensation, gradually organized in the brain by habit. This latter alone is always spatial and material, though any part of another circle may become so whenever its likeness to a present perception enables it to affect the reaction which follows that perception. It is through doing so that such a part, *i.e.*, some more or less detailed version of a past event, enters our consciousness: for as consciousness only exists for the sake of action it excludes all memories that have no bearing upon present circumstances.

On this theory memory might be described as a fifth dimension to the three of space and the one of time. It cannot be identified with the time-dimension, though the " pure memory " alone must be identical with one part of that dimension, the past. The cone is formed of many different versions of the whole of the one-dimensional past, like many more photographs of the same scene stuck one above the other, the lowest being the smallest and showing the least detail; and since the whole cone does not exist in space, but only the point or lowest circle, it may well be called a separate dimension. But it is hard to believe in the existence of these numerous planes of memory, each containing the whole past in a more or less detailed form. That the past continues to exist might be readily admitted, but not that it produces a number of different versions of itself. Besides, this theory does not allow for the influence of time upon the memory. Many scenes and events in the distant past that resemble the present and might usefully affect our reaction to it are not remembered; for instance, we often find that we have forgotten the topography of a place when we return to it after many years. Yet on Bergson's theory we ought to recall it as easily as a place visited yesterday, for both scenes with all their details exist on the same plane, in the "pure memory," and the interval of past time between them and the present should make no difference.

It is not true that we only remember past events which have a bearing upon present action, those which from their resemblance to the present can affect or "insert themselves into" our reactions to our sensations. Bergson himself admits that there are many men who live only too much among memories which have nothing to do with their surroundings to-day. To enter consciousness, therefore, these memories need not act upon the *schème moteur* and so become for the time materialized; their recall does not concern our action, and so is independent of the material world, if Bergson's theory is to be taken as true. It follows that no injury to the brain and its system of reactions should prevent us from becoming conscious of such recollections. But as loss of memory does follow such injuries, it follows that the brain must do more for memory than supply an organism through which it may affect our actions. Besides, the injuries to the brain which cause loss of memory would not prevent those "incipient movements" or reactions, which are alleged to call the memories into consciousness, from following our consciousness as before; if such reactions did not continue a man would not be able, according to Bergson's theory, to remember even the things he had seen or heard after he had received the shock which had obliterated all his previous experiences. A repetition of one of those experiences must still be followed by an appropriate reaction, the body must still take up the attitude adapted to recall the similar occurrence in the past, and so the memory of that occurrence, if it exists apart from the brain, should enter consciousness once more.

Again, what decides which version or "plane" of the past shall affect our present action and so enter consciousness? To take Bergson's instance, the hearing of a foreign word may make us think either of the language to which it belongs, or of a friend who pronounced it in a certain way. The latter recollection, as the more definite and individual, approaches closer to the "pure memory," the version which reproduces the past in greatest detail and distinctness. But are we to imagine a struggle at the doors of consciousness between the two candidates for recall? All we are told is that we place ourselves from time to time on a particular plane of memory, and that it is the events or scenes or ideas on that plane which come back to us. But this implies that we are already conscious of that plane and of all contained within it even before our recollections begin; for what else could be meant by our "placing ourselves" there? If you do not admit such a preliminary consciousness, the phrase is nothing but a bare assertion that certain recollections do occur and others do not. If you suggest that the recall of these particular scenes or ideas is due to their greater usefulness at the time, you will have to assume also that there is some kind of court to decide which has the best claim on that ground, and the decision must often be difficult. Against the doctrine of the association of ideas Bergson objects that every idea is more or less associated with every other by resemblance and by contiguity, and that there is no reason why one should be recalled by a particular experience rather than another. The objection might be turned against his own theory, for anyone who reflects a little must recognize that his memories upon their reappearance do not always pass the test of usefulness for present purposes, and that in any case the test is not precise enough to decide between their conflicting claims.

The lowest plane of memory, the point of the inverted cone formed by the different planes, is the *schème moteur*, the organized system of reactions in the brain, and this is material. This being admitted, it would seem that the other planes must also have the properties attributed to matter, in particular extension and mutual exclusion of parts. They cannot be "more or less" material or be materialized whenever they are required to act upon the present situation. There can be no degrees between extension and inextension, and therefore no gradual ascent from the *schème moteur* to the "pure memory." These two planes are intelligible, but not the others which are supposed to exist between them.

It is true that in the fourth chapter the existence of such degrees is asserted, and an attempt is made to explain how memory, though not existing in the brain, can affect our actions in the material world. The chapter opens with a discussion of the nature of motion, and some modifications would be needed here in view of recent developments. But the fact on which most emphasis is laid is the continuity of motion, the fact that the moving body cannot be regarded as occupying or lying between a series of points at a series of moments. Motion is one and undivided. On the other hand, it is admitted that space must be regarded as divided *ad infinitum*, an admission which does not seem consistent with such an idea of motion and is quite unjustified. For space can only be divided by differences of quality in its parts; a void, or a space all of one colour, would have no parts at all, and unless we assume that each finite space has an infinite number of qualities side by side—a strange hypothesis—we must admit a limit to its division.

The idea of Relativity is mentioned, but from the fact that we naturally take motion to be absolute the conclusion is drawn that there must be something in it besides a change of distances; that it must have a qualitative character. This may very well be true, though to be proved it requires a stronger argument than the belief of " common sense " that motion is absolute. Certainly the quality of every body may depend on its velocity. But in criticizing the idea that motion is purely quantitative Bergson goes to the other extreme; his theory would leave it with nothing quantitative at all. He does not admit the existence of atoms as "bearers" of motion, if one may use such a phrase; for him only motion exists, and not moving bodies. Yet it is obvious that for motion there must at least be a change of distance between certain extents of colour or some other quality, extents which for a while remain the same or only alter gradually. If outline and colour changed at random we should have no idea of motion, for how could we distinguish one movement from another? These relatively or absolutely permanent extents of quality may very well be called bodies; in fact, as I have maintained in an earlier chapter, it is impossible to give any other meaning to that term.

Our tendency to divide the world into absolutely distinct bodies is due, we are told, to the needs of action. First of all, in order that the individual consciousness may manifest itself in act, it requires " the formation of a distinct material zone corresponding to the living body"; then we have to make further distinctions in order that we may know what we have to seek and what to avoid. The continuity and fluidity of matter are so strongly emphasized by Bergson here that one is reminded of the "universal flux" of the world of Heraclitus. From his first description of it one would think that he denied the existence in reality of any distinctions corresponding to those made by our minds. If his account were true it would be hard to see how the necessity for action could lead us to form the idea of separate objects. Action cannot be helped by false ideas; in a world where "all things flow" we should never achieve anything if we regarded it as full of separate and permanent things. Later on it is admitted that objects different from one another do exist, but we are forbidden to consider them as absolutely separate, as having definite outlines. This will be readily granted as true of visible objects; among the first things we learn from philosophy are the facts that all visible bodies are continually losing particles and receiving others from their environment, and that every body in the world stands in some relation to every other. But it does not follow from this that the particles themselves, the ultimate elements of matter, have no absolutely distinct outlines.

It must be noted that the belief in permanent atoms did not arise, as Bergson declares, from the needs of practical life; it was first advanced by Leucippus and Democritus to explain certain purely speculative problems suggested by the Eleatic philosophy. As it was inconceivable that anything should come into being or cease to be, it was natural enough to regard the origin and destruction of visible objects as being merely the union and separation of many invisible particles. The hypothesis of the Greeks has been taken up again in modern times, but not on the ground that it is useful for human action.

"If there is one truth that science has placed beyond all dispute, it is that all the parts of matter act upon one another." From this Bergson infers that no limit can be fixed to the existence of the atom, and he proceeds to criticize the distinction commonly made between force and matter. He quotes Faraday's definition of the atom as a "centre of forces," and his suggestion that " every atom occupies the whole of the space over which gravitation extends," in other words, that " all the atoms penetrate one another." To support his own statement that matter and motion are the same thing he mentions Lord Kelvin's theory of " vortex atoms," which are nothing but circular motions in the ether, defined as a " perfect, continuous, homogeneous, and incompressible fluid." But as regards the first point, if every atom occupied the whole of space, what distinction could there be between them and how could one attract or repel another? Whenever we try to form some idea of an atom we have to picture it to ourselves as a certain clearly outlined area of colour or of some other " secondary " quality; for a world without such qualities would be a void in which there could not even be any parts of space, for there would be nothing to distinguish this area from that. One atom, then, must distinguish itself from its environment, and so occupy a certain space, by means of its quality; in fact it is this quality itself, extended over a certain area. The notion that it exerts a force upon all others is due to that individualism which takes the atoms for essentially independent beings, only accidentally united by " forces." But the very fact that they exist in the same space and stand in relations to one another shows that they are primarily parts of one and the same existence and have only a secondary independence. Gravitation is not the forcing of A by B towards the place which B occupies, but the mutual drawing together of all the atoms in accordance with the law of their common nature. But though their independence, their distinctness from one another, must be taken as something secondary, this does not mean that it is not real, that they melt into one another and have no clear outlines. The world is not a picture in which all the colours have run into one another.

As for the " vortex atoms," it is impossible that there should be any motion in anything that is perfectly homogeneous, for there can be none without some distinctions of quality. But if the atom has some quality to mark it off from the surrounding ether, it cannot be called simply a motion. Besides, as I have pointed out in the chapter on Relativity, there can be no rotation of a homogeneous body, for its rotation would involve no change whatever; everything would remain exactly the same as though it were at rest. Being homogeneous the atom can have no parts, and so we could not say that now this side was nearer to a given point and now that, there being nothing to distinguish one side from the other.

Such theories as these are due to that exclusion of the "secondary" qualities from the study of Nature which has been so strictly observed in science from the time of Descartes. The atoms have only been allowed extension, which is quantity, motion, and various forces. But none of these have any meaning without the "secondary" qualities. Bergson is undoubtedly right in condemning that Dualism which divides the world into matter without qualities, and sensations without extension. But that is no logical reason for rejecting the atomic theory, which is not bound up with that Dualism, nor for the strange identification of matter and motion. He admits the existence of movements too small to be seen, the trillions of vibrations in the ether which precede our colour sensations; but in conceding this one must also concede the existence of something that vibrates, something that can be distinguished from its environment. In a perfectly homogeneous medium, as in a world of one colour, there could be no vibrations, for everything in it would remain the same, just as though it were at rest. Or rather, there could only be one thing, one homogeneous mass. The electrons which by revolving round the positive nucleus of the atom produce these vibrations cannot be mere movements; each must be a definite area of some quality like colour or sound. The fact that in order to produce our sensations of colour they need not be coloured themselves does not entitle us to suppose them devoid of any quality; if they were, all of them together would in no way be different from a void in which nothing could happen.

The difference between spirit and matter Bergson explains as a difference of rhythm or tension. The vibrations of ether or air are too numerous to be counted one by one in our consciousness, which has a duration of its own, not divisible far enough to distinguish them. It therefore combines them into one sensation, as the separate beats on a drum, if they follow one another quick enough, combine to produce one continuous sound. Many different durations or " rhythms of duration " are possible ; the loosest and farthest divided is that of the material world in its most mechanical forms, with its trillions of imperceptible movements. No rhythm, however, is so fragmentary as to realize the supposed infinite division of time and space into moments and points ; these are only ideals, abstractions formed by imagining the subdivision of the world continued *ad infinitum*. The faculty that combines the numerous material movements into one sensation is the memory, which carries each excitation received on into the next, thus performing a different function from that of recalling distant events and bringing them to bear upon our present action.

But this theory of different durations does not help us much to understand how spirit and matter act upon one another ; it is only another and not much more intelligible form of the old Dualism. Are we to suppose that a sensation exists as a number of vibrations and at the same time has a different existence as one event in consciousness ? Such phrases as " contracting the multiplicity " of movements seem to imply that it does exist twice, for everything that is contracted must exist in a loose and again in a more compact state. We might accept for the moment the theory that the many vibrations are followed or accompanied by a simple phase of consciousness. But when we come to the action of the spiritual upon the material world we cannot understand how a thought or memory, if it is undivided and unextended, can affect the numerous, minute movements in space. Has a memory also two forms of existence, as a number of movements and as one mental event ? To say that would be to admit what Bergson throughout the book tries to disprove, that memories exist in the brain, or are at least accompanied by movements in the brain. Just as some vibrations in the brain correspond to a sensation, so there would be others that corresponded to a memory. But if memory exists only as a simple event without division into parts or extension in space, how can it determine the direction or velocity of those minute phenomena in the material world which together form our bodies and so our action ?

If we admit that not only all sensations but all forms of consciousness, all memories and thoughts as well, possess extension and include numerous elements too minute to arrest our attention, we can understand how they act upon the rest of the world, which is also conscious to a greater or less degree. But we cannot explain such action by assuming first that memories and thoughts are not extended, and then declaring, in order to bridge the gulf between them and the rest of the world, that there are degrees between extension and inextension. These seem to me as inconceivable as degrees between existence and non-existence. Apparently they are to be taken as identical with the different stages between the unity and compactness of the highest states of mind and the multiplicity of movements in the material world; they depend on the different " rhythms of duration." The more divided a thing is, the more it is extended, and the supreme example of extension would be the infinitely divided space, supposing that it existed. This is a curious theory, for surely the number of parts into which an object is divided has nothing to do with its extension; a continuous, homogeneous area, an area that has no distinctions within it, and therefore no parts, is not less spatial than one that is discrete and heterogeneous. What is stranger still, that space which Bergson regards as only an abstraction, as a mental construction, he describes as both homogeneous and infinitely divided. But the homogeneous, which has no differences in it, can have no divisions. It is not necessary to regard space as divided into an infinite number of points, or as having any parts at all, other than the bodies and the areas between them, for in these alone are there any differences of quality. Its subdivision is limited by the number of these distinctions.

From the *Essai sur les données immédiates de la conscience* one would infer that by degrees of extension were meant degrees of freedom from interpenetration. But obviously the existence of space is implied in the idea of interpenetration not less than in that of mutual exclusion. Besides, if that were the meaning, it would follow that the pure memory must be regarded as the most spatial of all the different planes, for in it the events of the past appear most distinct and in greatest detail. It is in the lowest planes that there is most fusion, so that these should be farthest removed from the material world, where mutual exclusion prevails.

There can be no degrees of extension, then, and the numerous metaphors employed by Bergson are no answer to the main question, how the non-spatial and simple memories can influence the minute movements of the spatial world. If memories do not exist in the brain, what determines the precise point at which they begin to act there? One cannot be satisfied with a vague statement that they " insert themselves into " the reactions which follow our sensations. Every reaction consists of millions of atomic movements, all very much alike; which of these in particular does the memory affect, and what precise alteration does it make in each of them? Where exactly does it enter the efferent nerves? This is the problem with which every Dualist is faced, just as the Materialist for his part may be asked where exactly matter begins to produce consciousness. Descartes, the founder of modern dualism, supposed the pineal gland to be the seat of the soul; he did not put to himself the question what precise area of this gland, what number of atoms in it, the soul chose to occupy.

If all the elements of the world are more or less conscious, the individual mind may be a number of these possessing a higher consciousness than those around them, united not only as parts of one and the same existence, which is universal, but also as being conscious in that particular degree. But the number of them need not always remain the same, and any element may enter or leave it by rising to or falling below the required level of intensity. All the elements of the mind must possess extension, and be subject to the same laws as those of the rest of the world, if they are to act upon it. But if memories and thoughts are different in kind from the body and its environment, on what principle can they influence these? The path of an atom can be predicted from mechanical laws; are we to imagine some atoms as being suddenly turned aside from their natural course by entities which stand in no spatial relation to them? Their action upon one another depends upon the distance between them and their comparative velocities. But if we accept the dualistic theory we can find no common measure between memories and movements by which their interaction can be calculated. For that theory there can be nothing to decide whether or how far a memory shall be able to turn an atom from the course it would have followed had it been governed solely by the laws of its own world. If other atoms are impelling it in one direction and a thought or recollection urging it in another, which force will prove the stronger?

Bergson's form of Dualism, in fact, is open to all the criticisms which have been directed against the division of reality into a number of individual souls and an unconscious material world. At what moment in time did memories begin to exist and affect the course of events? If the answer is that they began with the origin of life, this only raises the question at what moment life began. Can we suppose that at one instant a certain mass of matter was inanimate and at the next was alive? That after obeying mechanical laws it suddenly began to act on teleological principles? The main difference between living and inanimate bodies, we are told, is that the latter can only respond in one way to any excitation, whereas the former have many courses open to them and can choose from these. But has a living body many possible courses before it in any sense in which an inanimate body has not? A ball when struck has apparently many paths along which it might travel, all the paths of air, but it is not free to take any one of these it pleases; the direction it actually takes is determined by its own previous movement and that of the bat or other object by which it has been struck. So it might appear that a living body could react along any particular nerves among a vast number; but in fact its reaction is determined by the impulse received and the existing structure of those parts of the brain through which it passes. If memory affected the result in this case, why should it not also help to determine the course of the ball after it has been struck?

Just as it would be impossible to select any moment in the history of the spatial world as appropriate for the entrance of memory, if memory is non-spatial, so it would be impossible to find any such moment in the history of the individual organism. And as I have pointed out before, if memories have no existence in space, it is hard to see how their action can be limited to any particular body. Surely they might be called up by the occurrence of similar situations in any part of the world. The limitation of the power of each man's thought, will, and memory to a definite, continuous area in space seems to me to prove that every form of the mind's existence must be spatial. In order to bridge over the gulf between "matter" and "spirit" Bergson admits that all our sensations have extension, and anyone who admits that should have no great difficulty in believing it an attribute of all modes of consciousness. But against that belief the whole of *Matière et Mémoire* is directed, and so after all we are left to a form of Dualism which does not escape any of the old difficulties except those which concern sensation.

C. *L'Évolution Créatrice.*

The opening pages of Bergson's crowning work recall the main theme of his *Essai*. They emphasize the importance of "duration," as distinguished from "spatialized" time, in life and consciousness and deny our right to divide these into a series of separate states. Change in them is continuous, and though it is admitted that many of their phases seem to be disconnected from those that precede and those that follow, and attract our attention most, yet " each one of them is borne upon the fluid mass of our whole psychological existence." They are not to be called " distinct elements," for " they pass over into one another in an endless stream." This seems inconsistent, for if they are " borne upon " the stream they must be distinct from it. It may be remarked, besides, that a continuous change without abrupt transitions is not so far removed from permanence as a change with such transitions. It implies that the rate of the process remains the same, and also that there is one permanent quality within which it takes place. For instance, the gradual slackening of a movement, which is a continuous change, implies a uniformity in the rate of slackening and the permanence of the property of motion within the moving body; whereas the change from any velocity, however small, to rest cannot be called continuous in quality, though it is so in time.

As in his earlier work, the author insists that no state of consciousness can be repeated, for the memory of the earlier occurrence, if nothing else, would differentiate that which came later. If so, we must suppose that every event in past consciousness influences the present, or at least influences a similar event in the present. But is this true in any other sense than that in which it is true of the inanimate world? It may be said of any chair or table that everything which has happened to it in the past affects it now more or less; if its condition at any particular moment had been different, its condition now would not be what it is. If it has been taken to a different part of the room and then put back again, it is not now as it would have been if it had remained in the same place all the while, for the movement must at least have disarranged the molecules of which it is composed, and so have produced some alteration, we may say, in its character. On the other hand, it does not seem altogether impossible that the whole course of the world, including all states of consciousness, might be, as some have imagined, repeated over and over again. Certainly there seems no reason why the same state of consciousness should not occur twice in different men, if not in one man.

It is not correct to say that "the present state of an inanimate body depends exclusively on what passed in the preceding moment," and that such a body is thus distinguished from a living organism, whose present state is declared to depend on the whole of its past. When motion is transferred from one body to another, the movements following the contact do not depend on the state of the bodies at the moment of contact, for then they could not be moving at all. One should not, in fact, speak of a "moment" of contact, for such unextended points of time do not exist. Even if they were conceivable, it is obvious that there could be no direction or velocity of a moving body at any moment A, since A has no length; and therefore it is impossible that the state of the body at B should depend on its state at A. Its later movement, covering a length of time, depends on its movement during the whole of a preceding length of time, for its direction and velocity cannot be defined without reference to the whole.

Duration, therefore, does not affect consciousness more than the inanimate world, and if events in the former can be predicted, it should be possible also to predict events in the mind, in spite of their greater complexity. Bergson admits that when once a new form of life, a new state of any living being, has been produced it can be explained by the elements discovered in it by analysis. But surely the possibility of explanation after the event implies that we might have foreseen what was to come, if we had known all the facts. Explanation implies the bringing of a particular event under a general law; what is absolutely unique cannot be explained afterwards any more than it can be foretold. A number of bodies joined in one system at various distances from one another might be new in this sense, that no equal number had ever stood at exactly the same distances from one another before. Yet the forces they will exert upon one another can be calculated, for though the distances may be new, the proportion of force to distance follows a law as old as the world. If the proportion too were changed prediction would certainly become impossible, but so would explanation; all that we could do then would be to note that the state B of the system followed the state A. If life is continually adding something new to the world in that sense, it is true enough that no intelligence could have foretold the present from the past, as Huxley supposed possible. But then it must be equally true that we cannot infer the past from the present. Suppose that later events stand in no regular proportion to the earlier, and you will not be able to prove any event in the history of the earth. Admit that contingency plays a part in the course of the world, and you will not be able to limit that part. You cannot limit it to some elements of the universe, for then the obedience of others to fixed laws becomes itself a matter of contingency; they must enjoy no less liberty to act independently, and all that can be said is that they happen not to use it.

The belief in final causes is criticized by Bergson on the same grounds as the mechanistic philosophy; it supposes that the whole history of the world is given from the beginning. It supposes not merely that all history might have existed beforehand, as a prediction, in a supernatural intelligence, but that it actually did so exist, as a design. It leaves no place for the introduction of anything new at any time, for every detail must have been present in the mind of God before the beginning of time; it can only pass from idea into reality. One might perhaps assume that only the general outline was foreordained, but then it becomes hard to define exactly how much of history was so arranged from the beginning, and how much has been due to an afterthought of the Creator, if that is conceivable, or to the free action of the beings created. This objection, however, is not mentioned by Bergson. He observes that the doctrine of final causes, if applied to the universe or even to the living world as a whole, cannot be sustained in view of the fact that the different species make war upon one another, and Nature is very far from presenting a scene of universal harmony.

On the other hand, if the doctrine is regarded as true of the individual organism alone, we have to define what we mean by an individual in the living world. But an exact definition is impossible. The different cells of one body are in a sense individuals, and some of them often carry their independence so far as to attack the rest of the organism. Again, the whole body is not so far isolated that it can be supposed to have a vital principle of its own. It is only an offshoot from the parent stock, a link in a long chain reaching back to its remotest ancestors. Thus it is united in a sense with the whole of the animate world. The theory of final causes, then, cannot be accepted without modification in either of its usual forms. For the idea of an original design followed by the whole universe or by each organism separately, we must substitute that of an " original impulse (*élan*) of life," which secures that the " diverse tendencies " of the different species " appear as complementary to one another," but does not prevent the species from coming into conflict. It is admitted that this view is vaguer than that of Finalism, and it is doubtful, I think, whether it escapes any of the difficulties which beset the latter.

Bergson accepts the general doctrine of the evolution of species from one another, but proceeds to criticize the different forms it has so far assumed on the ground that they fail to account for the wonderfully complex but harmonious structure of parts of the body, or for the fact that the same structure may be found on two quite different lines of evolution. They cannot explain, for instance, the co-ordination of the various elements that form the eye, the sclerotic, the cornea, the retina, etc., or why the same essential parts are found in the eye of the Pecten as in our own, although the Molluscs must have branched off from the Vertebrates long before the organ of sight attained its present complexity. He examines in turn three schools of thought on the variation of species. The first two agree in holding that the variations are purely accidental, but one, including Darwin himself, believes that they arise by slow degrees, the other that a new species comes into being suddenly, several new elements appearing in the body or in a particular organ all at once. To the first he objects that if a slight change is made in one part of the organ without complementary changes elsewhere, while not hindering the function of the whole it will not help it either, so that there is no reason why such an alteration should be preserved by natural selection. But those who believe that several changes arise abruptly, all dovetailing into one another and contributing to the effectiveness of the whole, may well be asked whether chance could produce such a harmony between the different new parts. It would be still more wonderful that the same phenomenon should occur on two lines of evolution so far apart as the Molluscs and the Vertebrates. The law of correlation no doubt produces several changes together, but does not explain why these should be complementary; in fact, so far as is known, such changes are always defects, losses, rather than improvements.

The third theory supposes that the variations are directed by the influence of surrounding conditions. In the eye light acts as an instrument of selection, permitting only those changes in the organ of sight which are useful. This would explain the similarity between the eyes of the Molluscs and the Vertebrates; light may be supposed to have produced the same reactions in both. To this Bergson replies that the action of light cannot explain the structure of so complex an organ, still less the continuity of its relations with the rest of the body. It can no more have produced the eye than it can make a camera. It is true that changes in an organism often follow a change in the surrounding conditions; the same chrysalis, according to the temperature around it, will produce either of two kinds of butterfly, and the organism of the *Artemia salina* varies according to the amount of salt in the water where it lives. But these variations can only be said to be caused by external conditions in the same sense as the playing of a tune by a gramophone is caused by the releasing of a spring. Here the cause does not explain the effect; the nature of the tune played does not depend on the spring, nor is the nature of the transformations of the *Artemia salina* explained by the saltness of the water. So, too, light could at most be only the " occasional cause " of that complex organism, the eye. Another objection made by Bergson against all three theories is that the same part of the eye, the retina, is produced by different means in the Molluscs and the Vertebrates, and that the crystalline, which originally comes from the ectoderm, is in some cases restored by the iris; by the upper part if intact, but if not, by the inner. It is as though Nature were determined to produce the particular form of the eye by any means available, and this is inconsistent with the mechanistic theory.

After dismissing the three newer forms of evolution Bergson comes to the older, Lamarckian form, which derives every variation from " an effort of the living being to adapt itself to the conditions under which it has to live." If we suppose that this effort is only " the mechanical exercise of certain organs, mechanically caused by the pressure of external circumstances," then we are only returning to the last of the three hypotheses already criticized. But if we grant that it implies consciousness and will, then we are nearer to a real explanation. Effort, however, does not create changes in the organism, though it may tend to establish any new element once it is there. Besides, even supposing that the effort of any individual body could create such variations, we cannot assume that it could transmit them to its descendants. If Weismann is right, this would be impossible; assuming that the germinal cells are independent of the rest of the body, we cannot believe acquired characteristics to be transmissible. And even if this theory is not wholly true, the facts so far known would lead us to conclude that a change in the body can only affect the germ in a general way. Therefore the modifications in the offspring need not take the same form as in the parent; a departure from type may be inherited, but the departure need not be in the same direction. No one could believe that such a limited heredity could produce and stabilize from the efforts of individuals such an enormous number of variations, all tending in the same direction, as must have been necessary to bring our organ of sight to its present perfection.

For the individual effort of the Lamarckian theory Bergson substitutes an " original impulse of life," common to all the forms of life, and causing all its permanent variations. The common possession of this impulse, we are to believe, explains the similarity of the structure of the eye on different lines of evolution. Sight is a part of this impulse, but we must not suppose that its organ, as it appears to us, existed in all its complexity from the beginning as an idea. That complexity does not belong to sight itself, which is simple; it exists only for the intellect, which divides the simple act into innumerable elements, as one might try to copy a picture by using a large number of small coloured squares. The picture as painted by the artist is " a simple act projected upon the canvas," but as imitated in mosaic it appears as a work made up of numerous elements skilfully combined together. To the intellect sight appears as such a mosaic, but the innumerable distinct elements we suppose combined together to form the organ of sight do not exist in reality. So, too, we may divide a movement into an infinite number of points along a curve, or into smaller curves; but the movement is a simple act, though the intellect imagines it as broken up into so many separate parts.

The reasoning here is very difficult to follow. At first Bergson appears to deny that the intellect has any justification for believing in an organ of sight composed of sclerotic, cornea, retina, etc., with their great variety of parts. But even if sight is like the picture painted by the artist, that does not prove it to be simple, for no picture is so. The only absolutely simple thing in painting is the plain stretch of white canvas. The forms and colours afterwards imposed upon it are manifold, and even the act of painting, though in a sense one, may with as good a reason be called a series of acts. If we keep to the analogy, the mosaic work of the intellect has to follow definite forms and colours in the original, and its picture of the organ of sight is not one of its own construction. Supposing that there are no distinct elements in the reality before it, we can see no reason why it should form the same picture of that organ in the Molluscs and the Vertebrates. As for the other analogy, the different parts of the eye cannot be compared with the points or parts into which we divide a movement. If that movement is really one, and not a series of zigzags, every part of it, when we imagine it as divided, is exactly like every other, which is by no means true of sight as it appears to the intellect, as the eye. The movement, as given in sensation, suggests no particular form of division, but the organ of sight appears to the intellect with a definite structure which the intellect has to accept.

A little farther on Bergson seems to admit that the structure of the eye is not a construction of the intellect but has a real existence. He represents it, indeed, as rather limiting, "canalizing," sight than as making it possible. It confines sight to those objects upon which one can act. But is this "canal" to be supposed really as simple as sight itself? It cannot be so if it is to distinguish between those objects upon which one can act and those which are beyond the range of action. The intellect, therefore, has some ground in reality for making its divisions. This account of the matter, however, appears inconsistent with another analogy employed by Bergson. The eye is compared to a heap of iron filings into which a hand and part of the arm have been thrust. The impression made there is not due to a mechanical or intentional arrangement of the filings among themselves, as might be supposed if the hand and arm remained invisible. It expresses rather the resistance offered by them to the intruder, the limitation to its movement. But certainly it does outline the form of the hand and arm, and if the eye is comparable with this impression, and sight with the hand, the form of the eye must be moulded by the sight, instead of limiting it to the possibilities of action. But if sight has a definite form which accounts for all the intricacies of its organ, and if it is a part of the "original impulse of life," we must suppose that the form existed from the beginning and so adopt the finalistic theory, which regards the structure of the eye as the realization of a design in the mind of God. Even if the eye only serves as a canal, or series of canals, we have to ask why the canals take the same form in such different species, and a mere reference to the " impulse of life " does not help us at all.

" The materiality of the organ " of sight " is composed of a more or less considerable number of elements co-ordinated together." This evidently implies that the numerous elements are not merely divisions made by the intellect in a thing essentially simple, for matter, according to Bergson, has an existence apart from the intellect, even apart from consciousness. " The order between them," the elements, " is necessarily complete and perfect. It could not be partial, for the process which produces it has no parts." But if the process, or vital impulse, has no parts, how can it account for the many and varied parts of the organ ? The development of the eye cannot have been like a movement in a straight line or in a single curve ; it has rather been like one movement branching out into many, each producing a different part ; and no " original impulse " can explain the intricate course it has taken.

This " impulse of life " is altogether too indefinite a thing to determine the form any organ shall take. It is said to produce order between the different elements of the eye, but what makes it choose one form of order rather than another ? If, having no parts, it has no order in itself, how can it cause order in anything else ? As a cause it is quite useless ; to attribute the structure of the eye to it is simply to say that in fact the eye does take that particular form. And if it is not bound by mechanical laws, why did it not produce the eye in all its perfection at once ? It is true that mankind has only by degrees perfected its instruments, the printing-press, for example. But the vital impulse cannot be conceived as standing apart and distinct, like the human mind, from its instruments, as considering how to improve them, having happy ideas now and then, and proceeding to carry them out. Besides, the progress in human inventions depends on the progress in our knowledge of the material world, and there can be no analogy here between the human mind and *l'élan vital*. And the nature of the mind, as well as its action on the outer world, is itself a problem, the solution of which would dispense with the need for further argument on the nature of life. Suppose that the mind does not exist in the spatial world, is free from the mechanical laws which govern at least the greater part of that world, and yet directs some of the events there; you will not be likely then to advocate a mechanistic explanation of life. But if you hold that the mind is governed by those laws, you obviously cannot derive from the method in which it invents and perfects its instruments an argument to prove that the organs of the living body may have been created in a non-mechanical way by an " impulse of life."

The relation between the vital principle and the inanimate world is as difficult to understand in this theory as in every other form of vitalism. Why does the impulse limit itself to particular areas, instead of animating the whole universe, or, if it is a limited force, why does it not form one large body instead of many small ones? Its reason for individualizing itself is by no means apparent; "contact with matter" cannot have divided it, as Bergson suggests, for if it had, living bodies would be no larger than the smallest particles of matter. Its range is continually growing, for the number of living creatures increases; how does it pass from atom to atom, assimilating greater quantities of inanimate matter? Evidently, as these come under its direction, they must be imagined as abandoning the mechanical laws they have hitherto followed and beginning to work for the good of the whole organism to which they now belong; and I must confess that this passes my imagination, for one cannot suppose them to receive notice that they are now subject to a different rule. The picture presented to us later on in the book, of an upward movement of life and a descent of matter, suggests to my mind a tug-of-war in different parts of the world between vital impulse and mechanical forces; unfortunately the latter alone can be mathematically calculated, and the struggle between these definite and indefinite quantities is as inconceivable as a comparison between the weight of a lump of sugar and that of a general quality like colour or genius.

Bergson never asserts that there is a creation of energy in the world, but points out that there are different forms of energy. It must be remembered, however, that the change from one form to another can be calculated, for there is a mathematical equivalence between them. Such a transformation cannot be compared with the passing of energy from the mechanical to the vital, if there is no similar equivalence between the two. From what we read in the second chapter life is not to be regarded as creating energy but as storing it up, especially in the muscles, and releasing it at the right moments. But if the storing and releasing involve a departure from the mathematical laws of inanimate matter, this is the same thing as the creation of energy. The materials of living bodies are the same as those found in the inorganic, and if energy in them is drawn out of the course it would have followed elsewhere, to a power-house in the muscles or to a particular nerve, this is no less a miracle than the departure of the earth from its orbit, or a sudden increase in its speed. A change from the normal direction implies a creation of energy just as much as would an acceleration not imparted by some other body. In spite of the network of nerves to and from the brain, the path along which the energy is released must be as rigidly determined by its preceding movement and the conditions around it as the path of a ball through the air; or else its course is governed by no principle but the good of the whole body, in which case it is hard to see why energy ever follows any other principle anywhere in the body, why disease or death ever occurs.

The second chapter deals with the main lines of evolution, and particularly with the differences between instinct and intelligence. The general directions of the movements of life are not determined, according to Bergson, by external circumstances, as the mechanistic theory holds, nor do they follow a pre-arranged plan, for then life would show a greater harmony the further it advanced. But in fact its manifestations, though complementary, are antagonistic to one another, and the disharmony between them increases. Why this is so is not explained; one would have expected that if life can effect a closer co-operation between the different organs of one body, it should have been able to effect it between the different species, especially as we have seen that every body is in a sense one with the whole animate world. It is not sufficiently explained, either, why the vital impulse has in many directions exhausted itself, and many species, instead of progressing, "mark time," or even turn back. It is true that the vital impulse is declared to be finite. There is, then, only a fixed quantity of it in the world at any time, and the natural inference would be that a smaller or greater amount of it flows along each line of evolution. This is too mathematical, too mechanistic a view to be admitted into Bergson's philosophy, yet no other would account for the failure of life in many directions. One cannot understand how so indefinite a thing as the "impulse of life" can be finite; to say that it is so is not to explain anything, but merely to repeat that in fact life is brought to a halt along some lines of evolution.

"There is hardly any manifestation of life which does not contain, in a rudimentary, latent, or virtual state, the essential characteristics of most of the other manifestations. . . . The group will not be defined by the possession of certain characteristics, but by its tendency to accentuate them." Generally speaking, plants derive their sustenance from inorganic matter, animals from organic, *i.e.*, from the plants themselves, or from other animals; generally speaking, again, plants are fixed to one spot and unconscious, animals can move from place to place and are conscious. The chief function of the former is to store up the energy derived from the sun, of the latter to use it. For life may be defined as being essentially an effort "to impose upon the necessity of physical forces the greatest possible amount of indetermination," and to do this it accumulates energy in the plants, which is taken over by the animals and released through the nerves and muscles in the direction chosen. From this definition of life it would follow that the amount of indetermination possible is limited, but how is such a limitation conceivable? If one event in the world is not determined by preceding circumstances, this implies the possibility for every event of being similarly undetermined. We must suppose that life has at its disposal a definite amount of power to counteract the physical forces, of energy to direct the course of the energy it has stored up. But this power cannot exist in the void, ready to be turned on when needed; it must all be employed at all times, just as every form of energy is expressed either in the position of bodies at rest or else in the velocity of those in motion. The vital power cannot be expressed simply in making the movement of the molecules in the body indeterminate, for that would create chaos rather than an organism. The direction along which it sends them must be determined by something, presumably by the good of the whole. But who can imagine the movement of a molecule as being directed partly by physical forces and partly by consideration of the whole organism?

In the animal kingdom Bergson distinguishes two main lines of evolution, the Arthropods, culminating in the Hymenoptera, and the Vertebrates, culminating in Man. The former are characterized mainly by instinct, the latter by intelligence, though each class possesses in some degree the faculty prominent in the other. When they have reached their complete development " instinct is the faculty of using, and even of constructing, organic instruments; intelligence the faculty of making and using inorganic instruments." The instruments of the instinct form part of the body of the animal using them, and are highly specialized; those of the intelligence are separate from the body, and may be turned to many uses. We may add another distinction, that those of the former kind, being parts of the body, can each be used by one animal only, whereas the tool of human workmanship can be used by many men in turn.

Bergson attributes a greater amount of consciousness to the intelligence than to the instinct on the ground that in the former " the distance between representation and action," " the difference between potential and real activity," is greater, and it is on this difference that consciousness depends. Every living being has representations of all the actions possible to it at any moment, but while an action is being carried out, owing to its perfect similarity to the representation, it keeps this in check and so prevents consciousness from arising. An animal governed by instinct has but a narrow field of operations, and the only action possible to it is generally being carried out, so that the representation of it is checked. But where intelligence is the dominant faculty a much wider field is open to choice; many actions are possible, while only one, or none at all, is performed, and therefore consciousness of these possibilities is not prevented by their becoming realities.

This theory of consciousness implies that there can be unconscious representations, which seems meaningless if consciousness is taken in its widest sense, as including any sensation. It is not altogether the same theory as that in *Matière et Mémoire*; according to that we are conscious of all those objects upon which we can act, but nothing is said about the annulling of that consciousness when possible action becomes real. In this latter version consciousness appears to be identified with attention, for obviously it is not true that we do not feel our actions when we are carrying them out, though it is true of our habitual actions that we do not attend to them. It is to be noted that our action upon things is not wholly like the representation of them—certainly not in quality—so that it could not block consciousness, as it is supposed to do.

As a further distinction between instinct and intelligence Bergson adds that the former possesses an innate knowledge of things, the latter an innate knowledge of the relations between things. But can the former be said to have any knowledge at all? Is there anything else in it but the following of a certain sensation by an appropriate action automatically? No thought intervenes; even recognition implies a knowledge of relations, for it implies that the object in these surroundings is known to be the same, or of the same kind, as an object formerly met in other surroundings. In so far as an animal is capable of such recognition, it is intelligent. Again, there is no generalization in instinct; the sensation of a similar object is followed by a similar reaction, but there is no knowledge that the object is one of a certain class, no idea of a common quality. It is unreasonable to exalt the instinct and disparage the intelligence on the ground that the latter gives us merely a knowledge of relations, a formal knowledge, for without that no other is possible. The "material knowledge" attributed to instinct is nothing but sensation, upon which intelligence works, and before the intelligence has worked we cannot be said to know anything.

" We hold human intelligence to be relative to the necessities of action." In consequence " it has for its principal object the solid and inorganic," for it is upon this that we can work most easily; the fluid and the living escape from our hands, and cannot be shaped as we please. " It represents clearly to itself only the discontinuous," for we have to treat the object with which we are dealing at any time as clearly marked out and as one, and so come to regard the world as made up of distinct and separate parts. " It represents clearly to itself only the unmoving," for motion in itself does not interest us; we deal with moving objects, certainly, but all that is important for us is to know their present or future position. It is " characterized by an indefinite power of dividing according to any law and re-arranging in any system," for when we make any article needed the most important thing is the form, and in seeking the most convenient material " we endow, at least in imagination, every kind of matter with the form of the object " we intend to make. The making of such articles " demands that we should regard the present form of objects, even natural objects, as artificial and provisional, that our thought should efface from the object perceived, even though it be organic and living, the lines which mark on the outside its internal structure—in short, that we should regard its matter as indifferent to its form. The whole of matter must appear to our thought as an immense quantity of some fabric in which we can cut out what we please, to sew it together again as we please." From this fact is derived our idea of space, divisible *ad infinitum* and indifferent to form. " This space is primarily the schema of our possible action upon things."

Such are said to be some of the essential traits of human intelligence. As a general criticism it might be remarked that if we know and can distinguish the solid, the discontinuous, and the motionless, we must also know the opposite qualities, fluidity, continuity, and motion. Bergson would doubtless reply in each instance, as he does of continuity, that our idea of the opposite quality is only negative. But is a purely negative idea possible ? Can we know that water is not solid without having a positive idea of the quality that does belong to it ? We may be indifferent to that quality if it is not useful for our purposes, but for all that we know it. As for discontinuity in particular, to say that we have to treat the object with which we are dealing as clearly marked out and as one, is to leave it open whether that object is so in reality. But if it has no definite outlines and is not one, obviously it is not an object at all; it is not even a part of anything, for a part must have something to distinguish it from other parts. There would be no object for us to deal with, if the world were in a state of flux. As usual, Bergson seems to hesitate between the idea that there are no definite outlines in the world and the idea that there are such, but that we exaggerate their definiteness. With regard to movement, surely we have as clear an idea of this as of rest. We represent it to ourselves as one change of position occupying a definite time, not as a series of changes nor as a series of rests at many points in turn; we define rest as maintenance of position during a certain time. What else is there in either condition for us to learn? Besides, to know that a body is moving and what is its velocity is just as essential for our action as to know that it is at rest, so that if "human intelligence is relative to the necessities of action" we should have as clear a notion of the one state as of the other. Lastly, our idea of space does not seem to have been derived from dividing matter up as we please in imagination, but from the general concept of extension as belonging to all parts of matter alike, whatever their quality may be, and to the intervals between them.

If our ideas were created by the needs of action alone, it would be surprising that they should be so successful, for it is not necessary that the reality should be determined by our needs. However much we might want to find static and clearly outlined things, Nature is not obliged to satisfy our desires, which might be continually contradicted by facts. In truth it is reality that determines both our ideas and our acts, and the former of these do not depend upon the latter; rather the reverse. Bergson grants that intelligence is successful in dealing with inorganic matter, consequently that our ideas are correct here. But he maintains that it goes wrong when it applies to the realm of life and consciousness these same ideas, formed in our dealings with the inanimate, or others of a similar type. Yet they could never have been applied at all, if life and consciousness had provided the intelligence with no opportunity of doing so. We should not have formed names for the parts of the living body, if there had been no definite parts to make us distinguish them by name. Our sensations of inanimate objects must obviously be as clearly marked as those objects themselves. And the very fact that we have words for different states of consciousness which convey a meaning to other men shows that the intelligence here too is not unsuccessful. Its main justification, however, is the fact that inanimate matter, life, and the consciousness possessed by the living are not separate worlds, but act upon and pass into one another, which would not be possible if they were essentially different in nature. It might be replied that only those forms of consciousness which deal with inanimate matter can be described by the same ideas as that matter. But all kinds of it can affect inanimate objects, and it is only too evident that inanimate objects—for instance, a life-preserver—can affect the most exalted thought. Besides, consciousness more or less intense is universal, even in the inorganic realm, and since living beings are derived from that realm, it is natural to suppose that their consciousness is not different from it in character.

Bergson, however, assumes that life and the sensations and thoughts of the living are essentially different from inorganic matter, and from this infers that the intelligence is inadequate to grasp the former. Only if that assumption can be proved is the argument valid; the statement that the intelligence is concerned with action, and action with inorganic matter, would not prove anything even supposing it to be true. But some of his followers at least have talked of " the relativity of the intelligence to the needs of action " as though that cast doubt on the claim of the intelligence to comprehend reality. And that relativity is not a fact; action, and consequently its needs also, are relative to our intelligence, for we cannot act until we know. Again, the fact that we find it far easier to understand and deal with the inorganic is no proof that our ideas are inadequate to express life and animal consciousness; our greater difficulty in dealing with these may be due to their greater complexity, the number and minuteness of the phenomena that must be investigated. The difference may be the same as that between a simple and a very elaborate calculation; it need not demand different kinds of knowledge.

But it is suggested that another kind of knowledge is possible, namely, intuition, defined as "instinct that has become disinterested, conscious of itself, capable of reflecting upon its object and of enlarging it indefinitely." The theory that instinct is a mechanism of reactions produced by natural selection is condemned on the same grounds as the similar theory of life. If the various elements of an instinct are produced gradually, one by one, natural selection could not have preserved them, for they are useless separately; on the other hand, chance could not have produced them all at one time, so well co-ordinated as they are. Nor can instinct be action originally prompted by intelligence and now become automatic through habit. It is not to be believed that those Hymenoptera, for instance, which paralyze their victims by striking successively at a number of nerve centres, conducted at first a series of experiments in order to discover the right points of attack. Between the assailant and the assailed there must be a certain " sympathy, in the etymological sense of the word, which informs the one from within, so to speak, of the other's vulnerability." Even in human life there is something corresponding to it, the sympathy or antipathy which is not due to reflection. In its more developed form, as intuition, it inspires the artist who " by a kind of sympathy places himself within the object" which he is portraying. He gains this inner knowledge only of the individual; but a more prolonged effort of intuition in the same direction would enable us to know life in general, though not so clearly as science knows its object, the inanimate.

It is questionable whether the idea of "sympathy," even in the etymological sense of the word, will help us to understand instinct. If the nervous system of the *Sphex*, to take Bergson's principal instance, were exactly like that of the caterpillar it paralyzes, it might feel in imagination, as it were, the wounds it is going to inflict and their effect. But as this is impossible, has the word " sympathy " here any meaning at all? From this account of instinct nothing seems to be left us but the bare statement that the *Sphex* does in fact paralyze its victim with the necessary wounds. To pass from instinct to intuition, the artist, of course, since he is living himself, may have a sympathy with the living subject of his picture;

he gains this from his own experience, for he has felt in some degree all the emotions of which life is capable. This theory of intuition as another kind of knowledge is simply equivalent, then, to saying that one can best know life by living. But in that way we do not know life, we only feel it. Merely by living we could not reduce its phenomena to order, and form general ideas of them which could be expressed in words; such intuitive knowledge, then, could not be communicated. Feeling could tell us nothing about the origin of life or about its relation to the non-living. And in fact the philosophy of *L'Évolution Créatrice*, of this new form of knowledge itself, is not derived from this new method of gaining knowledge but from the intelligence; all the concepts it uses to explain life are concepts of the intelligence just as much as those by which we explain the inanimate.

The success of the intelligence in dealing with inanimate matter is attributed to the presence of a similar tendency in both, a tendency towards decomposition. " The same movement which leads the mind to fix itself in intelligence, that is to say, in distinct concepts, leads matter to divide itself into objects quite external to one another." Are we to infer from this that matter once existed in one block, or in a few blocks, each of them devoid of parts and homogeneous throughout its whole extent? If they had parts, these must have been external to one another, for how could one be distinguished from another except by separation in space? The idea of interpenetration will not help us, for if A penetrates B, then that extent of A which entered B would be distinguished as a separate part from that which remained outside. If, then, the original forms of matter already contained parts external to one another, they were already divided. If not, had they any quantitative element at all? Extension, for Bergson, implies externality, so that he must mean us to take them as unextended. And differences of intensity he has reduced, in the *Essai*, to differences of extension or of kind. But can we conceive of matter as having been in its original form pure quality or qualities? If it consisted of a number of qualities, did each proceed to externalize itself from the rest? Then they must previously have been within one another, and the term " within " implies the idea of space as much as "external." And why did matter ever develop extension, and at what moment did it begin to do so? Such a cosmogony as this seems quite unintelligible.

The decomposition of matter is compared to a change of mental attitude in a man who listens to the reading of a poem. At first he may enter into the thoughts of the poet, "live over the simple state which he has sundered into phrases and words"; he may "follow his inspiration with a continuous movement which is, like the inspiration itself, an undivided act." But if he relaxes his attention the continuity breaks up for him into a succession of separate words, even of separate syllables and letters. So, we are to believe, the original simplicity and continuity of matter tends to be broken up into innumerable distinct elements. But surely the listener must have heard from the beginning the separate words and syllables of the poem. His sensation was not that of a flow of sound with no distinctions in it; if it had been it could not have conveyed any ideas to his mind and enabled him to follow the poet's inspiration. At first he hears the words separately and has thoughts and mental pictures besides, nor are these so " simple and undivided " as we are asked to believe. Afterwards he merely hears the words separately, without thinking of their meaning. Here, then, there is no decomposition like that attributed to matter; a simple state of feeling is not divided into many elements, perceptions of different words, for these perceptions existed at first, along with the feeling they caused.

"Matter is a relaxing of the unextended into extension, and consequently of liberty into necessity." But necessity does not seem to be an inevitable consequence of extension; a spatial world might have been a chaos governed by no law. Bergson, however, argues at some length against "the idea that there might have been no order at all, and that the mathematical order of things, being a conquest over disorder, possesses a positive reality." As is shown by the previous quotation, he admits that matter tends to obey mathematical laws, though he proceeds to condemn the mathematical form of physical laws as artificial, on the ground that "our measures are conventional, and, if one may use the expression, alien from the intentions of Nature." This is inconsistent, and the fact that our standards of measurement, our yards or metres, are conventional does not in the least affect the quantitative realities we express through them, such as the constant proportion between force and distance or the identity in speed of the light-waves and the waves used in wireless. But to return to his argument on the impossibility of a world without any order at all, he maintains that matter, being produced by an "interruption," *i.e.*, a breaking up of continuity, must have a tendency towards mathematical order. There is nothing so wonderful, he tells us, in this obedience to law as the scientists imagine; there is nothing positive in it, for it is due to a negation of life. There are two kinds of order, the vital and the mechanical, and everything must be subject to one or other of these; when we speak of finding disorder anywhere all that we mean is that we do not find the kind of order we desired or expected. Disorder, therefore, is impossible in matter, and as the movement of matter in general goes against the movement of life, dividing instead of uniting, it must come under the mechanical order, not the vital.

But, as I said, it does not seem necessary that inanimate matter should be bound by mechanical laws simply because it is not living. The idea of a chaos is not illogical. In some respects the world is chaotic; there is no general uniformity in the distances between bodies or in their velocities. Absolute mechanical order would only have obtained if all the bodies in the universe had been at the same distance from those next to them, and they had all moved with the same speed relatively to one in the centre. In so far as this is not the fact, there is what may be called mechanical or mathematical disorder in the world; but does this disorder indicate the presence of the other kind of order, that of life? Evidently this is not true. The great variety of spatial intervals between the stars does not impose upon us the belief that the universe is an organism. Here, then, there is neither vital nor mechanical order; consequently it does not seem inevitable that either of these orders should govern the proportion between force and distance, that this proportion should everywhere be the same, any more than the distances are so. Just as the distances vary enormously, so might the forces exerted by any two atoms upon another at the same distance, and their forces at different intervals might have been the same. The gravitational influence of a fixed star upon the earth might have been as great as that of the sun. What we have good reason to find wonderful is the order that controls the very disorder of the world, the fact that under infinitely varying conditions the same laws are followed.

For "vital order" Bergson also uses the expression "willed order," but that does not improve matters. The variety in the distances between bodies cannot be taken as evidence that a will has arranged them so. Even the theologians who believe that every star has been set in its place by God would not maintain that the wide differences in the intervals between the stars proved the universe to be the work of a will. It is argued that when we represent to ourselves a chaos " we begin by thinking of the physical universe as we know it, with effects and causes proportionate to one another; then, by a series of arbitrary decrees, we increase, diminish, and suppress in such a way as to obtain what we call disorder. In reality, we have substituted will for the mechanism of Nature; we have replaced the 'automatical order' by a number of elementary acts of will." And these elementary acts of will are all determined by a general will which takes care to avoid order in the picture it is forming. Therefore what we are representing to ourselves is not disorder; it is a willed order, as opposed to the automatical or mechanical. This is certainly a very strange way of reasoning. It comes to this, that because we will to have an idea of disorder, every reality corresponding to that idea must have been willed too, and so have a kind of order. An artist is governed by an intention in painting a picture of Chaos, and therefore Chaos itself must have been the result of an intention. I can discover nothing more in the argument than this. It is not even true that we form an idea of disorder in the way described; usually we merely call up, all at once, a picture of a number of scattered objects previously seen.

It does not follow, then, merely from the nature of matter as extended, as an inversion of the movement of life, that it **must** obey mechanical laws. The fact that it does obey them could not have been deduced from those definitions. And if the world of mechanical laws were simply an "inversion" of the living order, we should have to consider everything in Nature that is opposite to the mechanical order, everything that is not uniform, as a sign of life. That is impossible, and yet, we may note, it would be in accordance with Bergson's theory of knowledge. Intelligence, he declares, comprehends only the identical, the uniformity of the world, "the relation of the same to the same"; everything else is the object of intuition. But that object, he also tells us, is life, so that one must suppose that "non-identical" and "irregular" are to be regarded as synonyms for "vital."

In describing further the opposing tendencies of life and matter he speaks of reality as "a perpetual growth, a creation that continues without end." "The universe, beyond doubt, increases indefinitely through the addition of new worlds." This would suggest that a new planet may spring from the void at any moment. But later on we are forbidden to suppose that new "things" are created. "There are no things, there are only actions." What is an action, then, if it is not a change of the state or position of a thing? "Things are constituted by the instantaneous cut which the understanding makes, at a given moment, in a flux of this kind," *i.e.*, a flux of action. But we could make no cuts, if there were no distinctions in the flux, and if there are, then things exist in reality. The world, after all, is not a homogeneous, liquid mass. Bergson's words leave it doubtful whether he means us to believe that at any place in the universe we should ever see a new world appear from the void, not merely an accumulation of matter which had already existed in some other form. The terms "increase" and "addition" certainly suggest it, but the analogy he uses would indicate only a creation of form, not of matter. He compares reality to the making of a poem, which is a simple act of the mind, but as soon as it pauses "is scattered in words and letters which add themselves to all the letters that already existed in the world." But these letters only exist permanently in a book, and already existed before in the form of printers' ink. Nothing is added here to the sum of matter, nor to the sum of energy. The analogy is not a good one, for even if the emotion which leads to the making of a poem is simple, the making of the poem is not; there is far more in it than in the emotion, and it is not produced merely by the breaking up of the simple state which preceded it. And until it exists in words and sentences it does not exist as a poem at all.

The doctrine of the conservation of energy, if true, is a strong argument against Bergson's philosophy. But his ideas on it are as uncertain as his ideas on the creation of new worlds. It only indicates, he says, that something in the world is maintained at a constant quantity. "But there are energies of different kinds, and the measure of each of them has evidently been chosen in such a way as to justify the principle of the conservation of energy." That cannot be correct, for the measurements were chosen before the principle was discovered. And even if the assertion were true, would it be of any consequence, provided that we always used the same measure in each kind? We could only suppose that there had been an increase of energy if that of one particular kind had increased anywhere, or if, when it changed to another kind, the change were not in the same proportion as similar changes which had occurred before.

From the remarks on the " degradation " of energy and the resistance to this degradation offered by the vital impulse one would infer that life is to be regarded as directing, not creating, energy. The conversion of any form of energy into heat means its conversion into the irregular movement of molecules in all directions within the heated body. In order that it may be used again these movements must of themselves become a general movement in one direction, and that does not naturally happen. The molecules may indeed all be driven one way by an external force, but that is an addition of energy, of fresh energy, not the utilization of the energy already there. Energy converted into heat, then, is of no further service within the body where it exists, and all forms of it tend to become so degraded. Besides, heat tends to become uniform throughout the world; it passes from a hotter to a colder body until the temperature is the same in both, and when that state has been reached the reverse process does not occur. Heat does not pass from one body to another of the same temperature, so as to make the latter much the hotter of the two. It would seem, then, that the world must in the end be everywhere of the same temperature, a state in which no change would be possible.

If some power could turn in one direction the energy scattered at random in heat, this " degradation " would be arrested. It has been suggested, and not only by Bergson, that life is such a power. But the mere conversion of heat into some other form of energy would not necessarily be life; it might instead make the world chaotic. If such spontaneous deviations from the paths the molecules would normally have followed were possible anywhere, they would be possible everywhere, and there would be no limit to the number of miracles that might take place. They might just as easily occur in an inorganic as in a living body. If life is a storing up of energy and a releasing of it in a chosen direction, why should not all bodies possess this power? They all contain energy in the form of heat; why should not this become kinetic energy in a certain direction? To make choice possible there would be no need of a nervous system, for if the nerves along which the energy is released are chosen, not determined by previous movements, the direction in which an inanimate body is to discharge its energy might also be undetermined and so open to choice.

If life, then, had the power of diverting the movement of a molecule from the course along which mechanical laws would have sent it, no system of nerves would have been necessary. If it has not that power, the complexity of such a system, however great, will not alter the fact that the particular nerves along which energy is released at any time are determined by previous movements. If a ball is flung along a flat surface ending in a number of grooves, the groove it will enter is equally determined by its earlier motion on the flat surface, however many the grooves may be. The intricate system of nerves in the human body has not " broken the chain " of determinism. But the movements along them are controlled by the brain, or rather by that reality which appears as the brain, the human mind, and that this, in spite of its complexity, should obey mechanical laws is no degradation. It means nothing more than that the movements started by the mind depend on its structure. But to say more on this point would only be to repeat what has already been said in criticism of the *Essai*.

The last chapter of *L'Évolution Créatrice* does not require much comment, for the subjects with which it deals either have only a loose connection with the main body of Bergson's philosophy or have already been discussed in the earlier works. The statement that thought is "cinematographic" is simply another expression of the idea that thought substitutes for the continuous flow of reality a series of distinct pictures. In reply it must be repeated that the picture of the world as a stream of events without outlines or distinctions is an obvious misrepresentation; in such a world the intelligence would have no ground or motive for making its "cuts," its distinctions, here rather than there, and consequently would not make any. Besides, the intelligence recognizes the existence of the continuous as well as that of the discrete. It does not suppose a moving body to make a series of halts separated by intervals of time, or a movement to consist of a series of positions, as the film of a cinematograph contains a series of pictures. It can quite readily believe each movement to be a single event without any division.

To conclude, the main defect of *L'Évolution Créatrice*, as of *Matière et Mémoire*, is its dualism, the attempt to prove the existence of two orders which govern the world without having anything in common. In this dual sovereignty there is nothing to decide which shall prevail at any particular place or time, or how far it shall prevail, for there is no common measure of their powers. In the earlier work we are not told how our actions can be governed both by an unextended memory and by the laws of matter; in the later we cannot discover any mode of accommodation between the vital and the mechanical order.

CHAPTER X

RELIGION

THERE is one complete metaphysical system which is usually ignored by metaphysicians, and that system is Christianity. Perhaps the reason why it is ignored is that we hear very little about it from the representatives of religion themselves. The teaching of Christianity nowadays has degenerated into the teaching of Christian ethics, and that applied only to private life; for the general opinion is that the Church, though she may associate with publicans and sinners, must draw the line at politics. But the Christian religion is not merely a system of ethics, not even of public and private ethics. And yet to-day we hear only too many sermons on the text, "Be good, sweet maid, and let who will be clever," a text even more popular with the sceptics than with the defenders of Christianity. It is the favourite motto to-day, not only in religion but in education, the chief object of which is asserted to be the development of character rather than of intellect, *i.e.*, the production of strong-minded men, uncorrupted by ideas.

But the Church ought not to be, and has only lately become, a mere society for the propagation of virtue. It has always professed to have a theology, *i.e.*, a philosophical explanation of the world, and if we cannot hope for a new *Doctor Angelicus*, we expect at least some attempt to interpret that theology in the light of modern knowledge. As it is, we have to be content with vague hints picked up here and there from the works on Christian apologetics, or from some of the metaphysicians, who occasionally recognize the existence of religion. But it would seem to be the duty of every man who offers us a philosophy to explain how much, if anything, he accepts of the Christian doctrines, and in what sense he does so. If he rejects them he should give his reasons, as he would in rejecting any other metaphysical theory. In any case he should not ignore a creed which has been much more widely accepted than any explanation of the world put forward by the professed metaphysicians.

Religion is essentially a correction of the elementary metaphysics of the average man, a correction made by introducing into such metaphysics other doctrines which are on the same level of thought and yet compensate in some degree for its errors. I have given some instances of this in my introductory chapter. Most men are confirmed individualists in their view of the world; just as the newspapers are mainly concerned with the unusual and not the normal events of life, so the attention of mankind is drawn towards the particular elements of things, towards that in which they differ from one another. The result is that the world appears to most of us as a chaos of things that happen to be there and have very little uniformity. Religion corrects this by introducing the universal and the eternal; at the same time, like art, it limits these in one sense to a particular place and time. For instance, the idea of Creation is an attempt to explain the unity of the world, to show why there is a cosmos and not a chaos; but the Creation is represented as occurring at a particular moment, not as an eternal event. The presence of God in the universe was at one time thought to be limited to a particular place, to a mountain or the sky, and even now the idea has not altogether died out. So, too, orthodox Christians believe that the union of God and man has occurred only once in history, that only one book is inspired, and that only supernatural acts are really divine.

It is not only religion that offers us a correction of elementary metaphysics, for science also introduces the universal and eternal by establishing the existence of laws valid at all times and places. Unfortunately it gives us no explanation of these, and does not attempt to rid us of the belief that the world is just a collection of self-existent things, a belief obviously contradicted by this uniformity. It differs from religion also in that it does not represent the universal under a particular shape, and therefore appeals less strongly to the average mind, which prefers a striking event to a general law and a person to a principle.

It must be admitted that religion in its traditional form is well suited to the man who is content with the popular metaphysics. To him the moving of his arm whenever he wills it must seem as great a miracle as the rising of the dead at a Divine command, for he cannot perceive any closer connection between the will and the following movement than between the command to the dead and its fulfilment. The relation between mind and body, or matter, is a mystery to him; he can see no reason why the influence of a certain will should be confined to a particular area. Again, he believes every person to be an absolutely distinct and separate entity, not one of the many existences of an infinite Being; therefore the survival of this entity with all its memories appears to him the only real form of immortality. And indeed if the personality were distinct and permanent in this life its survival might well appear certain, for its existence could not depend on the elements of the body, which are many and continually changing.

Besides, the only part of the universe about which the average man troubles himself is the earth; he only concerns himself with the other parts in so far as they affect this. And for him time is limited to the history of mankind, so far as he has learned it. He supposes, too, that time is a movement from past to future, and a movement logically implies not only a beginning and an end but a progress. The traditional theology ought therefore to suit him well enough, for it regards the earth as the centre of interest, if not the centre of the universe, and the history of mankind as the only important event; it declares the world to have had a beginning and to be moving towards an end and fulfilling a purpose. At the same time most men are more or less clearly aware that the universe is too large and its history too long for that theology, and they know that the doctrines of Christianity in their old form are rejected by the scientists.

It is a dreary picture that is left to us when we have cast off the old theology but retain the rest of our primitive metaphysical ideas, with nothing to counterbalance them, one-sided and inadequate as they are. If we no longer believe in the story of the Creation, but still hold the pluralistic theory, we must regard the world as a miscellaneous collection of self-existent beings, a number of fragments without any real unity. It will appear to us not as one great thing but as a multitude of small things. If we still believe in the essential distinctness of the human personality, but not in its permanent existence, the history of mankind must appear as a series of tragedies, each ending in death, which would always gain the final victory. For you have no right to speak of the immortality of the race if you do not believe the race to be one thing dwelling in all men, but only a number of separate beings. You have no right in that case to speak of its immortality, because you are not justified in using the singular word and speaking of " it " at all. The same is true of such phrases as " the progress of humanity," which is meaningless unless that which progresses is essentially one and the same thing throughout the ages. No man who retains the old idea of personality can properly console himself with such words as these.

Again, if a man still accepts the popular notion of time as a movement from past to future, but no longer believes it to involve a progress, or to move towards a " far-off divine event," then the history of the world must appear to him the worst of futilities, a veritable labour of the Danaids. In his view everything that is done must be cancelled by the following moment, for though the results may remain for a while, they are not the deed itself, and are often quite unexpected by the doer. The greatness of a deed consists in the moment of self-sacrifice, and not in the years during which other men enjoy its results. Besides, even the results disappear in time, and whether it be in a minute or in a thousand years makes little difference, in comparison with infinite time. And this may be applied not only to single acts but to the whole history of the human race. For all we know, this may come to an end through some sudden catastrophe or the gradual cooling of our planet, and be blotted out as though it had never been, with no memory or trace of it left. For, according to the usual view, though time is a movement from past to future, it involves no progress, no gain, since the past is continually cancelled; utterly cancelled, except for memory and a few other traces, all purely accidental to the nature of time, which can exist and has existed without them. This is the picture of the world with which we are left unless we revise our metaphysical ideas, and it is a dreary one, as I said; but its dreariness does not make it true.

It is unfortunate that so many have accepted the modern criticisms of the old theology without being aware that criticisms equally destructive might be brought against their old week-day notions as well, notions which are on the same plane as those already abandoned. Such are the ideas already mentioned, the pluralistic view of the world, and the belief in the absolute distinctness of personality, ideas which are generally taken for granted. It is supposed that we need not trouble about any criticism of these, for that would be to desert common sense for metaphysics, while, on the other hand, it is admitted that we must revise our opinions in theology. But we have to remember that at one time it was common sense to accept the doctrines of Christianity, and any doubt cast upon them was regarded as not less strange and unnatural than doubts cast upon the popular philosophy are now believed to be. We ought therefore to retain the old theology as well as the uncritical philosophy of the average man, since the two are intellectually on a level, agree very well together, and together make a much truer picture of the world than our week-day philosophy alone: or else we ought to revise both. In fact, a change in the one often makes necessary a change in the other. The disappearance of the old idea of Creation makes impossible the popular notion that the world consists of a number of independent things, since there is then nothing to account for the mutual resemblance of these things and their obedience to universal laws. And the disappearance of the popular notion of personality is fatal to the traditional form of some doctrines of religion.

To begin with the idea of God and his relation to the world, there must be very few now, even among the strictest members of the Church, who accept literally the story, or two stories, of Creation told in the first chapters of the Book of Genesis. But it would seem to be still the general view in the Church that the world, at least the matter of the world, was created at a certain time, or rather at the beginning of time, by the fiat of God. But we are nearly all believers in some form of evolution nowadays, and therefore most Christians would admit that the different forms of life were developed gradually during a period compared with which the length of human history so far is very short. At the same time they would say that this was no reason why the world should not be considered the work of God, who may have continually directed the course of its development, or else have appointed at the beginning the laws it was to follow.

It would, perhaps, be more correct to say that these two views are usually combined. It is supposed that a normal order of things, created at the beginning of time, does indeed exist, but that this may occasionally be modified by God in order to produce some change for the better. It has been suggested that the origin of life and of the human mind may be due to a Divine intervention in the working of the world, and that there may have been innumerable other instances, accounting for the seeming evidences of design in Nature. But this is to suggest that God often suspends his own laws, as though He could not from the beginning have created an order of things which would always of itself work for the best, without needing to be corrected.

It is impossible that an atom of "matter," in obedience to any will human or divine, should swerve from the course it would normally have followed. The belief that it could arises from the idea that the world is composed of two realms, the mental and the material, which at certain points interact. Thus the movement of an atom would generally be determined by its own previous movement and by the other bodies in its neighbourhood, but occasionally would be propelled by an influence from another world, the realm of mind, *i.e.*, by the will. Such an idea is evidently absurd, and the dualism on which it is based is indefensible, for consciousness is universal and we have no need of the hypothesis of a material world, unless by "material" you mean "outside the mind of a living being." But the fact that the whole world is conscious does not exempt it from obedience to law. The same laws by which we supposed the "material" atoms to be governed must govern the elements of consciousness, and there can be no other realm of being which could alter their working.

The mind of God is not outside the world, but it is the reality which appears to us as "matter" as well as all those beings which we regard as separate minds. It is the universal consciousness in so far as that is uniform and obedient to general laws. If we believed the mind of God to be separate from the world and capable of changing its normal course, we should have to suppose either that the regularity of the world corresponded and was due to the regularity in the workings of the Divine mind, and that any change in the former must be paralleled and produced by a change in the latter, a sudden impulse diverging from the usual course of the all-directing will; or else that the normal movements of the world were independent of God, and that only the abnormal, the miracles, were produced by his power. But if the first hypothesis were true there would be irregularities in the workings of the Divine mind parallel to those supposed to occur in the world, and the course of the one would be as incalculable as that of the other. Just as the human will, if it were free in the sense in which some suppose it to be so, might abruptly change from good to evil, or *vice versâ*, without any cause whatever, so it would be with the will of God. If this could ever depart from its normal working, even to produce a good result, there could be no certainty that it might not at some time change from good to evil and bring about a harmful instead of a beneficent miracle. If a single element of the world could at any moment swerve from the path it would regularly have followed, then the nature of God might also become different.

It may perhaps be suggested that before the Creation God planned the whole history of the world, including its divergences from the normal course, so that there would not be any change in his will when the time came for these divergences to occur. But then we must suppose Him to have planned beforehand every movement of every atom in the world, and surely the planning would take as long as the history of the world itself. Besides, how can the realization of a Divine idea differ from the idea itself, except as a quite unnecessary copy differs from the original? Before a man acts he has not in his mind a picture of his intended action that is complete in every detail; he has not a mental image of every atom of the body upon which he means to act, nor can he foresee the movements of every atom. No man can realize within himself exactly what he will bring to reality in the world outside him ; if he could, his mind would have to be as large as the world, or at least as that part of it upon which he acts, and to contain in anticipation the movements of every atom and the feelings of every person affected by his action. It is just because it cannot be so that the result often falls far short of his purpose, or even proves quite contrary to it. But an idea in the Divine mind must prefigure its realization in every respect and contain every detail of the result. For anything which did not previously exist in the mind of God could not be regarded as his work. The result therefore will only be a copy from the original in God, or rather it will be so much the same that it is hard to see how it could differ even to the extent to which a copy differs from the original. At any rate, even if the world could be different from that previously existing idea in the mind of God, it would only be a quite unnecessary duplicate.

On the other hand, if we believe that the regular course of things is independent of God, or that all things were originally so created by Him that they now follow a regular order of themselves ; if we ascribe to Him only certain interruptions in this order, interruptions made for the purpose of introducing something better—life, for instance, or some higher form of life ; then we must suppose that the world is often divided in its allegiance between its own laws, its own established system of causes and effects, and a sudden impulse from the will of God contrary to those laws. If so, one might expect it rather to follow its own nature than to be affected by a cause quite different from its own series of causes, an influence from a power outside it. And the moments of such intervention could only be chosen in a quite arbitrary manner. If the elements of matter for millions of years obeyed mechanical laws, what reason could there be for introducing life among them at this instant rather than that ? It could not be that the Supreme Being waited for a favourable occasion, for the interruption of mechanical laws, if ever possible, would always have been so. The idea of such miracles introduces an arbitrary element into the Divine nature, and when once you have done that you can set no limit to it. For in this case the will of God would not be continuously exercised, and one phase of it could not be determined by the phase of the preceding moment, as are the states of all things that follow a regular order. It would flash out into activity every now and then in an altogether incalculable way, so that there could be no certainty that it would always preserve the same character and always work for good. To put it shortly, if you can imagine miracles to be possible anywhere, you can—in fact you do—imagine them as occurring in the mind of God, so that nowhere could you expect to find any permanence and security.

If the universe, even when considered as conscious throughout and as obeying general laws, is regarded as different from the mind of God, then I do not see why it should not work miracles of itself, without Divine agency, if miracles were at all possible. Perhaps it will be said that life, for instance, could not be suddenly produced by the state of the world preceding its appearance, as one motion is caused by another, for there could be no similarity or proportion between the inorganic and the organic, as there must be between cause and effect; whereas there would be such a relation between the previously existing idea of life in the Divine mind and its consequent realization in the world. The transition from the inanimate to the living would be unnatural, but not the transition from the idea of life to its reality. But this only transfers the problem from the world to the mind of God. For if the idea of life arose suddenly, then its origin in the mind of God would be as inexplicable as the appearance of life itself in the world without Divine agency. But if we suppose that it always existed in God, though only brought into activity at a particular time in history, then we are faced with the difficulty already mentioned, that the realization of a Divine idea cannot differ essentially from the idea itself, and would therefore be an unnecessary duplicate.

This difficulty affects also the problem of evil, which has been such a stumbling-block to the theologians. If God is not the author of all the pain and sorrow in the world, then the course of events is only in part controlled by Him, and the orthodox form of Christianity must give way to Manichæanism. But if all power is his and He is the cause of every particular event — not only of the general laws that govern the universe—then He must have in his mind an idea of the pain which He brings into being. And this would imply that God Himself must be subject to pain, the idea of which is impossible without the feeling of it. Otherwise we should be driven to the conclusion that God had introduced into the world, or at least permitted to be introduced, by means of power derived from Him, a thing of which He had no adequate conception. Christianity does indeed admit that one of the Persons of the Trinity suffered, but only at a certain time in the history of the world, only after thousands of years of suffering among mankind. But if God causes every particular event He must have had an idea of every pain felt since the beginning of life; not the faint idea or memory which men have of pain when they are not feeling it, but an idea identical with the feeling itself. For if He did not suffer the pain Himself He would have no adequate idea of the events He brought to pass.

Christian theologians might admit that God was the cause of suffering, adding that it was caused for a good end. On the other hand, if they kept strictly to the old doctrine, they would say, with Milton, that it was brought into the world by sin, a doctrine difficult to maintain nowadays, when we know that there were many forms of life, and therefore of suffering, before Man came upon the scene. On any theory the suffering of animals is hard to understand, for one cannot pretend that it is for their moral improvement. And the assertion that human suffering is due to sin only leads to the question who or what was the cause of sin itself. If God were the cause not only of the general laws of the universe—which have nothing to do with morality, except in so far as all order is good—but could break through those laws at any particular time or place for the sake of some material or moral end, whom else could we regard as responsible for the existence of moral evil? If He could alter the normal course of events by a miracle, He could prevent a crime, and even the impulse to crime.

Perhaps it will be replied that He refrains from working miracles upon the human will in order to leave it free. But in that case He would leave it beyond his power to determine whether there should be more goodness or sin in the world; consequently the evil might overbalance the good, and if this were so would free will be worth the cost? Besides, the

Creator of all must have created each human mind with its character, whether good or evil. For if it were created without any character at all what could there be to determine its first actions in the direction of right or wrong? And if it came into existence without any tendency in either direction its decisions would be merely matters of chance, and there could be no consistency in any man's character. You cannot suppose that all human wills are created neutral between right and wrong, for then they would never act at all. Obviously they were not all created with a bias only to good, and we are therefore driven to the conclusion that if they were all brought into existence by special acts of God, not merely in accordance with the general laws of the universe, then God would be responsible for the existence of wickedness: a doctrine which might be approved by extreme Calvinists but not by Christians. The belief that wickedness was created because without it goodness would be impossible is as inconsiderate as the belief that the poor were created in order that the rich might be charitable. Mephistopheles certainly makes the world a livelier place, but there are some forms of evil which cannot be justified even by that excuse.

But if God is the Creator of, or rather identical with, the world only in so far as it is one and obeys universal laws, then He cannot be accounted responsible for particular events as such, *i.e.*, in their particular aspects, and therefore not for moral evil. Everything that happens is perfect in so far as it is an instance of some law, of the orderliness of Nature; even the earthquake or volcano that destroys thousands of lives is an instance of the laws of the cosmos and not of the anarchy of chaos. And as order is better than chaos, in its universal aspect even the earthquake or volcano is good. This applies even to morally evil actions, for the minds of men must be governed by general laws as much as are the processes of Nature. Such actions are good in so far as they are governed by those laws, just as strength, health, and intelligence are good things in themselves even when used for an evil purpose. It is in their particular aspects, regarded apart from the general law they obey, which on other occasions may produce good, that the earthquake and the crime are evil. These aspects are not due to God, who is only responsible for events in so far as they are identical and follow the same law. But if God could break through the normal course of things at any time and perform miracles on any particular occasion, then He would control each event in its particular as well as in its universal aspect. For if those general principles would on any occasion produce an evil result, He could suspend or change them; the decision whether they should be followed or not would at every moment belong to Him, and therefore the responsibility too, when the result is materially or morally evil. So that anyone who believes in miracles and special providences is attributing to God the origin of evil as well as of good, since both are made to depend upon the Divine choice. If God ever works miracles in order to produce some good or avert something harmful, why should He work one on this occasion rather than that? Why should He not always work them, so that the world might be perfect?

In order to avoid these difficulties some have supposed that the power of God is limited, and that Nature is partly independent of his control. This is not the orthodox doctrine of Christianity, but it has been accepted by some theologians and philosophers as an inevitable deduction from the imperfections of the world. It leads, however, to some special difficulties of its own. For since the whole universe cannot be regarded as subject to the action of this limited God, He must be conceived as controlling only a finite sphere, as do the supposed individual minds of men. Now if the Divine mind is unextended, as the human mind is wrongly believed to be, how could it be attached to any particular space, and why to this space rather than that? Could its power be limited to a certain area in such a way that it acts at this place just within the area but not at another place quite near which is just outside it. A similar argument is decisive against that Dualism which links together in every man two separate entities, an unextended mind and a body that has extension, for why should, or how could, the former be limited to any particular area? That the Divine mind should be unextended but finite is also impossible. It is inconceivable, too, that Nature, with laws of its own—for *ex hypothesi* it is partly independent—should occasionally be turned from its course by another power. What could decide on any particular occasion whether the laws of Nature or the will of God should prevail ? The old difficulty returns ; how can the movements of the atoms, which are normally determined by previous movements, be now and then determined by something of an altogether different nature, by an impulse from an unextended mind ? How can one imagine God as thinking that the atoms would be better in this order rather than in the one they would naturally take, and altering their positions by his will ? On the other hand, if the Divine mind has extension, it must, if finite, be a part of the universe and subject to the same laws as all extended things. And then why should we single out any part of the universe and call it Divine ?

It might seem, then, that the only God left to religion is the *Deus sive Natura* of Spinoza, the one Being of whom all men and all things are "modifications." But we must not identify all these modifications as different with God ; rather they are identical with God in so far as they are identical with one another. Just as one law may have an infinite number of instances, as the law of gravitation, for example, is the same for the many different distances between bodies, so God may exist in many different forms. But when we think of the general law, we mean by it the many instances in so far as they are the same, without regarding their differences ; and so, too, God means for us the universe in so far as it is one, in so far as its members are the same and obey the same laws. His nature is composed of all the common qualities that they have, or rather are, since the qualities are the things ; of universal qualities, as being, extension, power, and consciousness.

That this last exists everywhere I have argued elsewhere, and there is no need to repeat the arguments here. It is therefore an attribute of God, but only in so far as it is universal and everywhere the same, not in so far as it takes various forms ; just as the general laws of the world are his acts, in so far as they are general, apart from the difference of their results in particular instances. We have as much right to call the general consciousness a distinct Being as to apply that term to particular forms of consciousness, *e.g.* to men. But though consciousness exists everywhere thought does not, if we mean by thought the reflective kind of consciousness.

For since that which we call "matter" is everywhere only an image in the consciousness here, produced from and representing the consciousness there, wherever a more intricate structure appears, such as the brain, the reality must be a more complex kind of consciousness. Now what appears to us as the material universe does not approach in intricacy of structure the human brain or any living organism, and therefore the consciousness it represents cannot be like human thought; and since the meaning we give to the word "thought" is derived wholly from human minds, it might be said that it could not be called "thought" at all, and could only consist of elementary forms of sensation. But the universal consciousness is like thought, and different from our fragmentary sensations, in that it forms an orderly whole, proceeding in accordance with regular laws. Human thought attempts to introduce order and uniformity into the confused materials presented by our sensations, and out of these to create in the mind an image of the whole universe. But this would not be necessary for a consciousness which perceived, or rather was, the whole universe itself, and whose sensations were therefore not confused but governed by the laws of Nature, its own laws. Again, the human will attempts to introduce order and harmony into the individual feelings, by satisfying some personal desire, or into the whole world, as far as possible. This would be unnecessary for a consciousness whose feelings *were* the whole world, and therefore as orderly and harmonious as science declares the world to be. Not that the simple and fundamental laws which form the order of the universe do not often produce disorder in those complex structures, the living organisms, which form as it were *imperia in imperio*. But the universal consciousness cannot alter those general laws for the sake of avoiding disaster to the particular harmony contained within a small fraction of the whole; that would be to bring chaos into the macrocosm for the sake of avoiding it in the microcosm.

Up to this point, then, we mean by the name "God" the universal consciousness, in so far as it is uniform and follows universal laws. Such is the God of Brahmanism and of Spinoza, though the philosopher sometimes speaks as though the one Substance—which he too declares to be everywhere conscious—could be called God not only in so far as it is uniform, but also in its particular modes. Such a creed as that just stated ought not properly to be called Pantheism unless a further explanation is given; for we must not assert each thing to be God in respect of its particular characteristics, but only in the qualities that are common to it and to everything else. So for Brahmanism God is simply the common Being of all things that are, and none of the particular forms of existence belong to Him. As such He may be considered as giving existence to all things, and therefore as the Creator; and as One He may be considered as the author of the unity of the world. But this only gives us an elementary part of the Christian creed, a part which forms the bare outline of all religions. It is possible to justify much more of Christian and other theologies than this, though the justification will probably not be accepted by many while the metaphysics of the average mind remains what it is.

When we abolish Pluralism and regard the fundamental Being of the world as one and not many, we can consider as one existence any part of the world which has a certain uniformity of character, though it is usually taken to be a collection of distinct entities, as a wood has been called a "collective body of straight sticks." And when we believe the world to be everywhere conscious, we can attribute to every such part, even to those called "inanimate," a much greater resemblance to human existence. We can see more truth in the old mythologies than do those who regard them as poetical fictions, admirably adapted for perusal by the young. The ancient religions were not unreasonable when they deified types of character and gave, for instance, a personal name to the fighting spirit. Since Nature is one existence and is everywhere conscious, they were not far wrong when they attributed personality to every distinct part, to the sea and the sky, the trees and the harvest. They have at least as much of an individual nature as men; each of them has as much unity of character, and is conscious, though with a different degree of consciousness. The only mistake was to assimilate this last too much to the human mind, the only form of animate existence which the ancients could conceive. The mythological or poetic view of Nature has therefore as much literal truth as the scientific, or more, if the latter regards everything in the world as a mass of inanimate, colourless molecules.

The ancient religions had even more justification when they deified the general forms of human life, the habits and emotions that are found in all places on earth and in every age. The spirit of youth, for instance, is one and the same in all the young, as much as a man is one and the same on different days; and since we cannot believe a man's identity to rest on the permanence of a distinct substance or subject called the "self," but must ascribe it to the permanence of character, we can regard the spirit of youth, which is equally permanent and identical everywhere, as having an existence not less real and not less individual than that of a man. And the same may be said of every spirit that animates the world. The universal Being is the one God; but there is no reason why divinity should not be attributed to those forms of existence which, though not universal, are widespread and lasting; for they are much greater than those forms of existence which we call particular men. This explains the course taken by the Hindu religion, which is fundamentally Pantheistic and yet has more gods than any other; for while declaring that the Being of all things is one, it deifies many of the general forms in which the one Being exists, the forces of Nature, the modes of life, the emotions, and the constantly recurring types of human character. It was in the same way that the Stoics and the Neo-Platonists justified their support of the ancient mythology.

Sometimes it is the spirit of a nation that becomes the object of religion. Even at the present time it is usual enough to represent that spirit, with all the national characteristics, as a person, and certainly it is as individual as any member of a nation. Whatever may have been the origin of the idea of God in certain countries, the name in the end came to signify the spirit of the whole people, past and present. They would not, of course, consciously worship their common life as such, but the natural and not unjustified tendency to personify that common life would work upon the idea of God until this became in fact an image of the nation itself, one and indivisible throughout the ages. Such was especially the God of the Jews, and such to a less degree were Athena and Roma to their cities. Religion of this kind cannot be called false, for a nation is as much one and identical in all its members as a man is identical at different times and places. Besides the unity which belongs to it in that all its members are forms of the one universal Being, it has also the special unity of character which belongs to the individual man; and for memory it has its history, for habits its traditions. The great deeds and the laws or commandments of the people are rightly attributed to the God who inspired it, and it is for his honour that all its battles are fought.

It is interesting to notice that the only attempt made in recent times to found a new religion resembles a nation's worship of the Power that has inspired it throughout the ages. It is true that the theology of the Positivist substitutes Humanity, *le grand Être*, for a particular nation, but otherwise the idea is the same. Humanity is regarded not as a collection of countless millions of men, past, present, and future, but as Man, the one spirit existing and working in those millions. And certainly when we dispense, as does the Positivist, with the idea that a man is something else than a series of thoughts and feelings, that he is something, a substance or soul or *ego*, which " has " those thoughts and feelings, then there is no reason why we should not speak of Humanity as one Being, for the same, or mainly the same, forms of consciousness exist everywhere among men and have existed throughout the ages. Consciousness is the only reality, and that is one and immortal; parts of it do not " belong to " particular men, as though these were separate entities, but particular men are the one universal consciousness existing in certain forms at certain times and places. And even if we did suppose that there were many souls with separate consciousnesses, we should have to regard these souls as the many existences of one Being. The plural always implies an identity, one and the same thing repeated in many existences. And all the reasons given for believing in the oneness of the world of course apply equally well to the human race.

Unfortunately the Positivist, while rejecting the metaphysics of the philosophers, does not clear away the metaphysical notions of the "man in the street." The latter believes most firmly that every man is a primarily distinct being, which "has" certain qualities possessed by other men and "enters into" certain relations with others, but *is* an existence by itself. The qualities and relations are supposed to be merely secondary entities belonging to the man, so that if he shares them with other men that does not affect his essential difference from all others. The same view is taken of his thoughts and feelings; when one of these recurs in a "different" man we are not allowed to speak of it as the same thing existing again, for according to this philosophy they are not real things themselves but are the property of souls or minds, and the souls or minds are said to be different in the two cases. This is the general theory, and it is as metaphysical as anything taught by Plato or Spinoza. It holds firmly to the metaphysical category of substance and accident, or quality, as applied to a human being, and obviously implies belief in an individual soul as the substrate of each man's thoughts and feelings. While such ideas remain, belief in the oneness of Humanity is impossible, and Man will be regarded as a collection of essentially separate entities, only united by what is secondary, *i.e.*, by qualities and relations.

But the religion of Humanity is after all nothing new, for the Christian doctrines contain it in a more elaborate form. When these superseded Judaism they substituted the human race for the nation, not only as the worshipper but as the object of worship. For Christ is the ideal of the human character personified, as Jehovah is the ideal of the Jewish character, so that in worshipping Christ mankind is worshipping all that is good in itself. "All that is good" is a necessary limitation; the Positivists too do not propose to take Humanity with all its imperfections on its head as the object of their religion, but only the good spirit of the race. It is true that most Christians do not consciously worship Christ as the good spirit of mankind, but regard Him as a person who appeared on the earth only for a certain time. But the theologians constantly speak of the spirit of Christ as dwelling in men, though the common idea of personality prevents them from giving any definite meaning to the phrase.

As the first, or at any rate the first important manifestation of the Christian spirit, and that from which most others are derived, the Christ of Galilee of course occupies a position above all others. Attempts have been made to whittle down to nothing the history of his life as told in the Gospels, but it is obvious to anyone who has not lost the sense of proportion that only the greatest of characters could have produced so great an effect in the world. Whether all the sayings attributed to Him came from his lips or not, they were due to his inspiration and are therefore to be counted his. But the miracles we must exclude, or take them in an allegorical sense. This exclusion or allegorical interpretation may appear in the eyes of some to do away with the essential part of Christianity. But as regards the minor miracles, these must be held to be of less importance than the sayings of Christ, which affect not merely a few men but all Christians in all ages. The message must be of greater interest than the deeds by which it was believed to be confirmed. The greater miracles, on the other hand, especially the Resurrection, contain more important truths when given a spiritual meaning than when taken literally, or rather according to the popular metaphysical notions of such subjects as personality. For the contrast is not so much between spiritual and literal truth—there could, indeed, be no contrast between these—but between the truth in its pure form and the form it wears when contaminated by those popular notions just mentioned. The essential being of every man is really his character, his thoughts and feelings, which live again from one age to another; but according to popular ideas it is his body, or at least his body and memories together, on which his identity and personality depends. Hence the truth of Christ's survival leads to the doctrine of the Resurrection in its traditional form. The story of the Ascension partly corrects this, for it suggests that the particular body in which the spirit of Christ had up till then appeared was no longer necessary for the manifestation of that spirit on earth. Certainly the story is hard to interpret otherwise; for to take it in the traditional way is to return to the old notions of a Heaven in the sky, not so very far above the earth.

The life of Christ during the thirty-three years has indeed an eternal value, apart from its continuation in later ages. It is only according to a false idea of time, as I have shown, that the " past " is cancelled, except for its effects, by the present, for in reality the distinction between past and future is not absolute. Time should be regarded as a whole, of which no part cancels any other; there are no limits but purely arbitrary ones to the " now " or the " present," and " what is "=the whole history of the universe. What we call " past " is just as real and important as what we call " present." This being so, men ought to feel as great an interest in the events of two thousand or two million years ago as in any event of to-day with which they are not in direct contact. Only if the past is real are we justified in taking such a disinterested interest in history. On this theory of time the life of Christ is part of the eternal " now," and as the first important manifestation of the Christian spirit He may rightly be worshipped to-day not as a dead but as a living person, though distant from us by nineteen centuries, just as we may admire and reverence a person nineteen hundred miles away. It is true that such worship will not differ essentially from the honour paid to other great men, but only in so far as the character of Christ surpasses theirs and his work has produced a greater effect. But then the honour paid to those others will have much more substance and sincerity in it when we regard them not as belonging to a " past " that has been annihilated but merely as distant, relatively distant, from us in a time not successive but like space. For then they must be regarded in just the same way as men who live many miles from us, men who do not communicate with us except through acts and writings intended for all the world, or a great part of it, not for any one of us in particular.

It is worth noticing that the definition of time given above corresponds closely to the theologian's definition of eternity. It is a generally accepted doctrine with them that to the mind of God there is neither past nor future, but an eternal " now." It is only our minds that arbitrarily set limits to the " now," just as we do to the " here " : how arbitrary those limits are can be seen from the fact that we sometimes define the " now " as an unextended moment, *i.e.*, nothing at all, sometimes as this minute, sometimes as to-day, and sometimes as this generation, the Christian era, or the age of Man. The view of time I have maintained must have considerable importance for religion; it does not, like the traditional doctrine, place eternity after time, but shows it to be the reality of that which is usually taken for a successive series of events. And it makes each human life, in fact every event, eternally important, not through its consequences but in itself.

Taking the doctrines of Christianity in detail, we can interpret each of them in a way which is true but may make it seem unreal to the " man in the street," unless he recognizes that all his notions, not only those on religion, need to be similarly revised. To begin with the doctrine of the Trinity, this implies of course for the orthodox a belief in the eternal divinity not only of the Creator but of Christ and of the Holy Spirit. In the Bible the three Persons seem to be manifested in turn, and for most believers the actions of God the Son only began nineteen centuries ago, thousands of years after the Creation, and the Spirit only took up his work on earth after the Ascension. The ordinary Christian, when he reflects upon the subject, admits, as I said, the eternal existence of the Three, but regards their activity as successive, not simultaneous, as though the existence of each for a great part of time remained in the background, and did not affect the world. Besides, he draws no clear distinction between the presence of Christ in the human heart or in the Church and that of the Holy Spirit, and often virtually accepts the heresy of a sect of whom he has probably never heard, the Macedonians, who denied the Godhead of the third Person in the Trinity. The theologians, on the other hand, and some metaphysicians too, have endeavoured to give such an explanation of the orthodox doctrine as will ascribe to each of the Three an eternal activity as well as existence. The most famous, perhaps, is that contained in the words which Dante saw written over the gates of Hell: "The divine Power made me, the supreme Wisdom, and the primal Love." This description of the three Persons, which resembles that suggested by St Augustine, can hardly be distinguished from the heresy of Sabellius, who declared the Three to be merely attributes of one and the same Person. Many other instances of the threefold nature of existence have been put forward to illustrate the doctrine, and of the modern metaphysical interpretations the best known is that of Hegel, who finds that threefold nature in the universe as a whole and in all its particular forms and parts. For him the three Persons are God as existing in Himself, God as manifested in the world, and God as beholding Himself in the world, as reaching self-consciousness in Man. He identifies the Divine Spirit with the human. But the objection to any such interpretation is that it limits the third Person to a particular time and place, since the human mind has not existed from the beginning, nor does it exist everywhere. One might better take the doctrine of the Trinity to represent the Being of the world as one, as existing in particular forms, and as returning to unity again in the mutual action and interrelation of these forms. So Man exists as one entity in the universal form of his nature, as individualized in particular men, and as growing into an ever closer unity through the relations formed between men. The common element, the differentiation, and the coming together into an organized whole are found everywhere in the world, so that analogies to the universal Trinity enter into our everyday life. And it is essential to recognize all three principles, as it is essential not to forget the common humanity of mankind, the particular characteristics of individual men or nations, and the tendency to union.

The doctrine in its limited, historical sense may be explained in various ways. It may be taken as indicating three successive stages in the recognition of the nature of the Deity, who was first known as the universal Being, distinct from the particular forms in which it appears, then as manifested in particular forms, or rather in Christ, as representative of them all, and then as bringing all the separate existences into unity as the Spirit drawing men into one society, the Church. Again, it may be taken to describe the universal consciousness as such, then as distinguished into different minds, *i.e.*, men, of whom Christ was the first to be conscious of his identity with God, the universal consciousness, and then, in the Spirit, gathering the different minds into one mind. Or the first Person of the Trinity may be regarded as the Creator, *i.e.* that moving and living Power for good in the world which has brought it to its present state; the second as the founder of a new world, *i.e.* the Christian, which is yet but a continuation of the old; and the third as the inspirer of that new world, impelling it to new progressive movements. This last interpretation comes nearest to the orthodox form of the doctrine. The other two will probably be rejected as mere metaphysical subtleties. But a statement may be both subtle and metaphysical and yet true. Though none of these explanations is precisely what was meant by those who first taught the dogma and those who have since believed in it, they all give that meaning in another form, a form not corrupted by that insistence on the unique and the particular and that rigid but false idea of personality which make men limit eternal things to certain times and places and attribute reality to each individual man, or to a mind like the human, not to the spirit that lives in many men. It may be asked whether it is worth while to rationalize the traditional teaching of Christianity in this way, as many Greek philosophers allegorized the ancient mythology. But that allegorizing of the old legends did not draw men's attention to any truth that was new to them, whereas such interpretations of Christianity as those given above may bring men to regard the world from a different attitude and substitute truer notions for those of popular metaphysics.

To come to a second article of the Christian faith, the doctrine of the Creation, this also may be explained in an eternal and a temporal sense. It may be taken to represent the transition of Being from its universality into particular forms; not that the latter supersede the former, or that the word "transition" implies anything but a purely logical sequence, with no reference to time. The world, as distinct from God, is the differentiating as opposed to the common element in existence, the finite as opposed to the infinite, which it presupposes; for nothing can be defined or limited without reference to something beyond it, which is yet of the same kind and therefore one with it, and so on *ad infinitum*. The common element in existence is ignored by those who believe the world to be composed of many essentially distinct and self-subsistent entities; a belief which renders the order and uniformity of the world quite unintelligible. Others, who see that there is no reason why these entities should be at all like one another, or obey the same laws, if they were really independent and self-subsisting, have attributed their uniformity to their creation by the one God. And it is true that they may be said to derive their existence from God, for He is the common Being and all that is universal in them, all that which makes them one. The reason why they are uniform in nature and obey the same laws is that they are essentially one and the same being existing in many places.

On the other hand, if we speak of a Creation in time, we must identify God with all the history of the earth, with every motion, even the smallest, that has preserved life or led it on to new and higher forms, every turn for the better that has helped gradually to create the present state of things. According to the Persian religion the good and evil principles, Ormuzd and Ahriman, carry on their warfare in every part and every particle of the universe. And there is no reason why we should not thus consider the good in the world—not only the moral good—as one individual reality, just as much as we consider a man to be so. For it is a much wider and more lasting form of the one Being than any man, and is as much the same in character at different times and places. And as we have seen, it is chiefly sameness of character that makes a man one throughout his life. It is true that we cannot attribute to the principle of good a personality like the human, and that it only possesses will so far as it exists in beings endowed with will, and thought in so far as it exists in men. But it possesses consciousness, since that is universal, and it has everywhere the same unifying tendency which is the essence of thought. It is in actual fact that of which thought is an image and to which the will is a means; for it is that order and harmony in the world itself which thought seeks to establish in its ideas of the world and the will endeavours to produce in the actual world. And it has created and still maintains all the forms of life in the universe, for it is only by the good in them—not necessarily the moral good—that these exist.

According to the traditional account the Creation was almost immediately followed by the Fall, an event of which one hears very little nowadays, since the story told in the Book of Genesis is too naïve to be accepted even by the most simple-minded of believers. But Hegel has interpreted it in a way which may be heretical, but is certainly more in accordance with modern ideas than that of most theologians. As he explains it, "the fruit of that forbidden tree" is the knowledge of the distinction between moral good and evil; before that knowledge was gained men were innocent indeed, but only with the innocence of animals and young children, who cannot be accused of sin for the simple reason that for them moral laws do not exist. The only laws for them are the laws of Nature, which they obey as a matter of course. Man was the first living thing to become aware of the moral code, and hence rendered himself liable to the charge of sin when he transgressed; but with the knowledge he also became for the first time capable of virtue, so that the Fall was also an ascent in the scale of being. Others have given an explanation of the doctrine very similar to this. Man, they say, was the first being endowed with self-consciousness, and therefore aware of a distinction between himself and God; he was therefore the first to be able to set up his will consciously against the will of God, and therefore to sin. On the Pantheistic theory, of course, he could not be essentially distinct from God, but only as an *imperium in imperio*, a mind within the Mind, a particular form as distinct from the universal Being. His actions, good or bad, always obey the fundamental laws which govern the ultimate elements of the world, those which we call the laws of Nature. But the complex bodies formed of those elements do not, as complex bodies, observe such uniform laws with such unfailing regularity. And the more complex the organisms the less uniform they are, as wholes, in their action, though the ultimate parts of all of them always act in the same way. Men, as the most complex of organisms, seem to escape furthest in this way from the universal reign of law, and so to separate themselves from the unity of the world, *i.e.*, from God. They become conscious both of that unity and of their separation from it, but at the same time they recognize a new demand for harmony among themselves made by that principle of unity, a demand which they may or may not obey as they choose. But this freedom only applies to the moral law and to men as composite wholes; the parts which form those wholes, and which are eternal, not temporary, maintain the same order of things at all times and cannot depart from it.

That Christian Pantheist, the author of the *Theologia*

Germanica, also explains the Fall as the self-assertion of man against God. " It is said, it was because Adam ate the apple that he was lost, or fell. I say, it was because of his claiming something for his own, and because of his I, Mine, Me, and the like." [1] The whole book may be described as a commentary on this text. The original sin and the source of all sins is taken to be the belief of man that he has a being distinct from God. " For God is the Being of all that are, and the Life of all that live, and the Wisdom of all the wise " ; a saying which, as appears from the whole tone of the book, is not to be watered down into a statement that God is merely the cause of man's being. The account of the nature of sin given by this author is certainly the truest. For, as we have seen, if men were in reality essentially distinct selves, distinct from the one Being and from one another, then selfishness would be natural and rational and could not be considered a sin. The maxim " Each for himself " would be in accordance with the reality of things, and the only sin, if there could be sin at all, would be to act contrary to this golden rule.

" Original sin standeth not in the following of Adam (as the Pelagians do vainly talk) ; but it is the fault and corruption of the Nature of every man, that naturally is ingendered of the offspring of Adam." This is perhaps the most widely accepted of all the Thirty-nine Articles, for men who do not believe in Christ are ready enough to confess their belief in heredity. The only thing in the ninth Article to which they would raise any objection is the reference to Adam as the ancestor of all mankind. But there is a difficulty which was felt by the early theologians and should be felt by all who believe each man to be an essentially distinct being. Those who maintained, as did St Thomas Aquinas,[2] that the human soul was created directly by God, and not derived from the parents, had to explain how in that case sin, which is a corruption of the soul, not of the body, could be propagated from Adam to all his descendants. St Thomas Aquinas endeavours to surmount the difficulty by declaring that original sin is propagated in the same way as the nature of

[1] *Theologia Germanica*, tr. by S. Winkworth (Golden Treasury Series), ch. iii. p. 8.
[2] *Summa contra Gentiles*, ii. 86–7.

the human species, which is not directly derived from the parents, any more than is the human soul, but depends on the nature of the body, which is so derived.[1] But he seems in this way to make the nature of the soul and its corruption to depend on the body, and to imply that souls, though created by God, are created evil in order to go with the evil bodies. It is therefore the body which is primarily responsible for sin, since the soul *must* be in agreement with it; a supposition which could only be accepted by Materialists. Besides, it raises the question why God should continue to create souls to match the evil bodies.

These may seem to be useless speculations that have lost all meaning for modern thought. But in fact the difficulty just mentioned is a difficulty for all those who believe that each man is a fundamentally distinct entity, a belief which lies at the root of the popular philosophy. For it is impossible to explain on that theory how a man can inherit the virtues or vices of his ancestors. Only the body is derived from the parents, and by the body is meant a number of separate entities, molecules, possessing no consciousness. But it is recognized that there must be more in a man than this, for the "body," so understood, leaves unexplained both consciousness itself and its unity; that multitude of separate entities, even if they became endowed with consciousness at the birth of a man, would each have a separate feeling, and could not become one mind. Therefore, since the idea of separate personalities is still retained, individual souls are introduced to explain the oneness of each man. But if these souls have different characters of their own, it becomes difficult to account for heredity, the transmission of character, since they are not derived from the parents; whereas if they are all identical in nature, each being one simple entity that observes and unites in one consciousness the manifold and complex organism of the brain, then there must be not many souls but one only. For unless they are separated by intervals of space there cannot be a number of simple entities of the same character, since there would be nothing to distinguish them. And a soul cannot exist at a particular place, for then it would have to be of a certain shape and size, which is

[1] *Op. cit.*, iv. 52.

inconceivable. It could not, therefore, be distinguished from another in that or any way. The only possible theory is that there is one soul which unites the whole world and exists everywhere. "Soul" is then a name for the world as one, and "body" a name for the world as manifold; but no part of the world, we must remember, is unconscious. The existence of particular characters must be attributed to the "body," but their transmission is due to the "soul," without which nothing, no force or influence of any kind, could be transmitted from one thing to another.

The doctrines of the Incarnation and the Atonement have given rise to more theological speculation than any others that are distinctively Christian, and have often been discussed by the metaphysicians as well—for instance, by Kant and Hegel. Both these articles of faith can easily be adapted to Pantheism, especially the former, since Pantheism sees everywhere that union of the infinite and the finite which Christianity sees in Christ, but which even the most orthodox do not profess to understand. Similar objections to those raised against the doctrine of the Incarnation have been raised against the theories of all the metaphysicians who have tried to account for both the unity and the multiplicity of the world. So Plato and the scholastic Realists were criticized on the ground that it was impossible for the one "idea" or universal to exist in the many particulars, for colour in general to exist in many colours, and humanity to exist in many men. So in Spinoza's philosophy the existence of the many modes in the one substance was thought to be unintelligible. So perhaps some will find it hard to understand the relation between a general law and the particular instances. In every case the objection is due either to a confusion of categories, as when the idea of quantity is introduced into the relation between the universal quality and its particular forms, or else to the fallacious idea that the relation between the one and the many must be the same as that between any two of the latter.

To return to the doctrine of the Incarnation, this expresses the truth that God exists in every man, that in respect of the universal element in him, man is God. "For God is the Being of all that are, and the Life of all that live, and the

Wisdom of all the wise." Each man is the universal consciousness limiting itself to a particular form. I do not mean, of course, that the early Christians explained the doctrine to themselves in this metaphysical way, or applied it to every man. But it is by no means certain that Christ in calling Himself the Son of God regarded that title as belonging to Himself alone, not to other men, for it was often applied to men generally. And sonship implies much the same as that metaphysical relationship described above, for in some degree every son is his father over again; it comes as near as any non-metaphysical category to expressing the identity of God and man. It is true that according to the traditional creed Christ is the only man who is also God. But that is explained by the inveterate tendency of the human mind to limit the universal to one particular time or place or person. The reason which made the doctrine of the Incarnation so welcome to men in general from the earliest days of Christianity is fundamentally the same as that which makes it attractive to the philosopher, and we do not change its spirit when we give it a metaphysical meaning. Both for the simplest of Christians and for the most subtle of philosophers alike it involves a union of the Divine and human, a union much closer than that described in other religions. The Greeks, Romans, and Scandinavians told of the descent of gods to the earth and their appearance in human form; but the human form was only a disguise and the appearance momentary. As a rule those who " dwelt in the halls of Olympus " lived apart from men, a race of aristocrats spending their eternity in true Epicurean fashion. And as the pre-Christian religions, Judaism included, were affected more and more by philosophy, the Supreme Being became for them more and more remote from the world. But the Christian saw Him walking the earth again, taking upon Him not merely the human form but the human nature, and living a whole life subject to human conditions; not merely appearing for a moment, nor distinguished from the mass of mankind like the gods of Greece and Rome, but representative of the whole race. And in that Christianity comes nearer than the old religions to the philosophy which sees God in every man of every class. The infinite and the finite are no longer kept apart but exist together. That is the fundamental idea of Christian theology, which has caused it to exert so powerful an influence on the world; the belief that a heaven far off in space is the dwelling of God is merely taken over from the older religions, and has affected human thought very little as compared with the distinctively Christian doctrine.

The idea of the Incarnation, as I said, may be taken in a metaphysical sense to express the self-limitation of the universal Being in each particular man, or even in each existence. So the universal Humanity exists in each man, its general character united with the individual characteristics, and the union of the two natures often forces itself upon our attention. For we may regard a man as worthless individually, so that it would be a question whether anyone should trouble to save him if his life were in danger; yet, as human, he is worth so much that if he were the only man alive his life would be of more value than the earth and all other beings upon it.

As expressing the "self-limitation of the Absolute," to use Hegel's phraseology, the doctrine of the Incarnation resembles that of the Creation of the world, for this latter also may be taken to represent the entrance of the universal Being into particular forms. It was in fact interpreted by many theologians as a self-imposed limitation of the Divine Power. And it is an accepted though not often remembered point of theology that all things were created through the Son of God, which seems to indicate some connection between the Creation of the world and the Incarnation of the second Person of the Trinity.

On the ethical side the latter doctrine expresses the fact that human good is the same as that which governs the world, that the laws of morality are of the same kind as the universal laws of Nature. "Order is Heaven's first law," and the atoms do not act each on its own account but each in harmony with the rest, so that together they form a cosmos and not a chaos. Another passage from the *Theologia Germanica* deserves quotation here: " Ye must know that no creature is contrary to God, or hateful or grievous unto Him, in so far as it is, liveth, knoweth, hath power to do or to produce ought, for all this is not contrary to God. That an evil spirit or a man is, liveth, and the like, is altogether good and of God." Every form of life depends on the proper working of its organism, and this in itself is a good thing, even in the lowest of creatures or in the worst of men, though it is true that this good may be obtained at the cost of another. This natural good by which everything exists is of course universal and necessary. But there is another which belongs only to men and depends on their choice; for men, though every particle of which they are composed is bound by universal laws, have as wholes a certain independence, since they do not all or always act in the same way. This independence would lead to chaos in their relations with one another if it were not for the moral law, which establishes between them something like that unity and uniformity established by the natural law among the ultimate elements of the world. The moral order is just the appearance of the universal order among men as wholes—it already existed among the elements of which they are composed; and as the representative of the moral law, without discrimination of class or race, Christ may be called the Son of God, for his appearance on earth symbolized the entrance of the universal law which governs Nature into that particular and limited form which governs men as wholes and their mutual relations.

The doctrine of the Atonement has received the most various interpretations, and even in the earliest times it was taken in what may be called a metaphysical sense. The meaning we give to it will of course depend on the meaning we give to the Fall of man. Since that has been explained as the coming of man to consciousness of self and so to consciousness of his difference from God, in so far as he is different, so the reconciliation must consist in his recognition of his identity with God. And the recognition of this identity existed first in Christ. The idea that the death of Christ was necessary for the Atonement must be explained in the light of the Christian principle "Die to live," a principle of so wide an application that Hegel made it the basis of his philosophy. In recognizing his identity with God a man loses the idea that his individual life is something absolute; he knows that he is nothing separate but a form of the one, the universal Being. His understanding of this fact is for him the surrender and death, in his thought, of his individuality regarded as a thing existing in itself. And his physical death does away with his individuality, proving that it is not such a self-existent thing. His willingness to meet death, therefore, indicates how far he understands this truth, the unreality of his own existence except as a form of the Eternal. So the death of Christ represents the surrender of the individual personality, the consciousness that it is nothing in itself—for that is what its death implies—but is a form of the universal Being, and the consequent readiness to sacrifice it for the good of the whole. The Fall was an act of self-will, man regarding himself as a being entirely distinct from God and therefore not subject to his laws; the Atonement was an act of unselfishness by a man who regarded himself as one with God. To fall into sin is to consider oneself as a being essentially separate from the rest of the world, a separate centre of existence, and to act with an egotism in accordance with that belief; whereas moral goodness consists in acting as part of a whole, as one of the many members in which the same Life exists. Even where the metaphysical truth is not recognized in thought, such action is in accordance with the metaphysical truth of the oneness of the world.

The Atonement has always been recognized by the theologians as valid only for those who accept it. And the acceptance of it implies that a man no longer counts his life as his own and acts independently, but makes it a part of the life of Christ. There are many passages in the New Testament explaining the doctrine in this sense, passages which are usually taken for metaphors but are literal truths for the man who has a true idea of personality. Since the character is the person, everyone who changes in character becomes in fact a new man, and if he changes to the Christian character may be said to become Christ, who lives many lives. The idea contained in Baptism is like this; before that sacrament everyone is regarded as a separate individual whose life is distinct from all else, but through it he becomes in the eyes of all true Christians a member of the one life which is in them, the life of Christ in the Church. Considered merely as an individual he is apart from God, but when he renounces that exclusiveness and becomes a " member of Christ," his individuality now consisting only in his being a particular form of Christ's existence—for that is the meaning of the phrase just quoted—he no longer regards himself or is regarded as a being separate from God or justified in acting as such. Not that any man is ever distinct from God in his essential nature, in that which he has in common with all other men and things; but he may think himself so, and in so far as he differs from the rest, in so far as his existence is a particular one, he may act contrary to that principle of unity which may be called the law of God. But as all men in the roots of their being, common to all things, are one, so Christianity endeavours to make them one in their moral nature, by making them so many lives of Christ.

From the same standpoint we may interpret the Resurrection and the Ascension. The former must be taken as the reappearance of Christ in new lives, the latter as the withdrawal of the particular form in which He first appeared. A person is nothing but the thoughts and feelings which he is said to "have," and wherever these recur the person lives again. The Resurrection, then, may be called an actual fact, since the thoughts and feelings of Christ, which are Christ Himself, exist again in the lives of Christians. This is also expressed in the story of the descent of the Holy Spirit upon the disciples, and in the often repeated statement that the Church is the body of Christ. But theology from the earliest times has confused itself by giving its doctrines a double form, a cruder and a more spiritual interpretation. According to the former the body of Christ, transfigured after the Resurrection, exists in a vague region called Heaven, far apart from the world. But there is another body of Christ, namely, the Church, and in the Eucharist there is a third. The first two ideas at least are obviously inconsistent, and one must either explain the statement about the Church as a metaphor, as meaning only that Christ from his distant Heaven, his real dwelling, produces certain effects in his followers upon earth, or else the idea that there is a body of Christ other than the Church must be abandoned. From what has been said it is evident that the latter is the only rational course. Heaven is the Christian Church itself, that is to say, all in whom the Christian spirit lives.

The doctrine of the Ascension, as I said, may be, and has been, taken to express the transition of that spirit from the particular form in which it first appeared, from that life of Christ which marks the beginning of our era, to its wider existence in the lives of many men. But the particular form has of itself an eternal value and exists out of time, as time is usually but wrongly conceived. Past, present, and future are not real distinctions; events are no more successive than things in space, and if we are to define the term "now" we cannot stop short of the entire history of the universe. Even if we did suppose one-half of time to be past and the other future, we should have to believe that the past was eternal, for if it were non-existent it could not be distinguished from the non-existent future. No event, therefore, is ever cancelled; even on the ordinary theory of time all that happens when an event ceases to "go on" any longer is that its duration becomes fixed and is no longer indeterminate like that of the events "going on" now. And not only the duration but the character of every life becomes fixed at death, whereas the life now proceeding, *i.e.*, still lengthening its existence, may still change its nature. This withdrawal into an eternal sphere, the past—a withdrawal which is only apparent, since there is in reality no other sphere than the eternal—is symbolized by the Ascension of Christ to Heaven. It is the same with all men; their character, the place their life occupies in the world, is fixed at death, and becomes permanently part of the good and evil in it. Thus we can give a meaning to the words "Heaven" and "Hell," whether we take eternity to be the past alone, or the whole of time as it is in reality, not successive but like space. The true eternity does not follow time but is time itself rightly viewed.

The explanation just given of the Resurrection and the Ascension of Christ shows in what sense we can accept the belief in human immortality. If men were essentially separate individuals, if each of them were wholly mortal, and if the past were nothing except for its effects, we should have to look upon the history of the world as a series of tragedies, in each of which death had the last word. New lives would continually come into existence, but they would not be the same thing reappearing, since each is *ex hypothesi* essentially distinct from all the others. You cannot reply, if you are an Individualist, that though the lives are destroyed life survives, for according to you, life, as a universal, is a mere abstraction, to which nothing in reality corresponds. It is as a matter of fact impossible even to suppose the ideas of the Individualist to be absolutely true, for in speaking of "lives" we are calling each of them by the same name, and implying therefore that they are the same thing multiplied in space and time. But if as far as possible we take each by itself and make the assumptions mentioned above, we find that each conforms to the idea of a tragedy by ending in an absolute negative, a final failure, death. Even if the results of a few lives remain for a while, the results are not the life itself, and they too do not remain for ever. On the Individualist's theory the "Everlasting No" appears to be everywhere triumphant.

This is not a conclusion to be accepted with equanimity, and even if it were really supported by arguments that satisfied the intellect for the time, our general sense of what is rational and what is not would lead most of us to suspect that the arguments must somewhere be unsound—though we ought not to content ourselves with a suspicion. There are some, it is true, who denounce the "longing after immortality" as a weakness. But it is rather the lack of such a desire that, like a want of ambition, shows a real poverty of spirit. Every man ought to wish for both infinite and eternal life, which in fact he has, since he is one with the infinite and eternal Being. Deeper down than the opposition between moral good and evil is that between life and death, existence and non-existence, and to be content with finitude, or to desire death instead of life, is to be neutral in this ultimate conflict, or to take part with "the spirit that ever denies." There are many Puritans who hold the strange idea that it is a virtue not to wish for the good things of life, whereas it is a happily uncommon failing. But these ultra-stoical philosophers of whom I am speaking go even further, and think that one should be indifferent to life itself, or limit one's desire for it. They seem to believe that there is something meritorious in the absence of a desire for immortality; a belief even more absurd than that of the Puritan who thinks it virtuous to avoid pleasure, for the Puritan hopes to gain something better.

Incidentally it is worth while to observe that the old argument for immortality from the need of " a future state of rewards and punishments " was morally quite sound. One ought to wish that the universe should be just, and consequently that a good man who has been unfortunate in this life should be repaid for his good deeds in another. The idea that virtue is its own reward is quite unconvincing as long as the usual idea of individuality is maintained; no one would think he acted justly towards a man who had done him a service if he acted on that idea and left the repayment to virtue. Justice requires that the good deed and the reward should be the same in kind.

Schopenhauer maintained that since the essential being of all men, the immanent Will, was the same, any man who injured another was in reality injuring himself. " He who inflicts the pain, and he who feels it, are one." One might apply this principle of " eternal Justice," as he calls it, to the conferring of benefits as well, and declare that he who does good to " another " is doing good to himself. In a sense that would be true; but he would be doing good to himself not as this particular person, but in so far as he is the same " self " that exists in all men. One cannot go so far as Schopenhauer in ignoring human individuality; even if all men are forms of the one absolute Being, they are different forms, and life would lose all its interest and variety if it were not for that degree of separation which exists between them.

But to leave this digression, if you accept the idea that past and future are not distinctions in reality but only in our minds, that time is like space, or at least that the " past " is eternal, you are accepting the doctrine of immortality in one sense, since you are admitting that nothing in what we call the " past " is cancelled, any more than one part of space is cancelled by another. The history of the world is one event without any " before " or " after "; each part of time exists in itself, and none annihilates or supersedes another. Therefore no life can be swept into nothingness by time.

But there is another kind of immortality which I have already described at some length in an earlier chapter.

Every life is a phase of the one life, as each day is a phase of the individual life; death, therefore, is no more final than sleep. Even the individual as such may be said to be immortal, for not only is consciousness, the universal, everlasting, but the different forms of it as well; and wherever consciousness exists in the same form again, the same man exists again. Such phrases as "another Milton" or "a second Nelson" are quite literally true. A man of the same character or engaged in the same pursuit as one who lived a thousand years ago is the same man in a new life. Supposing a man who lived a thousand years ago had continued living up till now in the same way as one may live a hundred years, what would there be that was permanent in him, except his character and his occupation? One would not expect him to retain the same style of speech and dress, or even his memories of the tenth century; we do not remember much that happened to us thirty or forty years ago, and what we do remember gradually becomes alien from us. The only permanence is that of character and occupation. This conception of immortality just described closely resembles the idea of the transmigration of souls, while that described in the preceding paragraph approximates to the Christian doctrine, except that it identifies eternity with time as rightly viewed, instead of placing the one after the other.

Those Dualists who believe that a man "has" consciousness and is therefore an entity distinct from it, or, what comes to the same thing, divide consciousness into "subject" and "object," must also believe in human immortality. For when the body which is or causes the object of consciousness is destroyed at death, there is no reason why the subject should perish too, since *ex hypothesi* it is different from the object. If the latter can exist apart, as is assumed by the Dualists, it seems natural that the former should have the same privilege. Besides, if each mind is essentially distinct from every other, each must have a separate time of its own, for a common Time would imply that all are parts of one and the same Reality. And if it has a separate time it cannot be annihilated. Annihilation implies existence at one moment and non-existence at the next. But since time is only an attribute of the mind, there could not be a final moment of the mind's existence and then a later time at which it did not exist, for apart from the mind and its movement there could be no time at all. And since there could be no later time to limit it, the last thought of the mind could not be finite but would be everlasting. Nor would the Individualist have the right to say that the time of some other mind B continued after the time of A, and that A could thus cease to exist; for in order that the time of B should come "after" the time of A, it would be necessary that both should be parts of one Time, and this would imply that A and B themselves must be parts of one Reality to which that Time belongs. And to admit that would be fatal to the belief in essentially distinct minds.

In this way both Pantheism and Individualism must affirm the immortality of the human mind, and though the modes of immortality taught by the two philosophies are different, one is as genuine a mode as the other. But from what has been said already it is evident that it is the Pantheistic version which we must accept. It affirms an immortality just as real as does the doctrine of distinct souls, and is not subject to any of the difficulties which might be brought against that doctrine.

For Product Safety Concerns and Information please contact our EU representative GPSR@taylorandfrancis.com
Taylor & Francis Verlag GmbH, Kaufingerstraße 24, 80331 München, Germany